THE KITCHEN
BUILDER'S HANDBOOK

No. 1462
$21.95

THE KITCHEN
BUILDER'S HANDBOOK

BY CHARLES R. SELF

TAB BOOKS Inc.
BLUE RIDGE SUMMIT, PA. 17214

FIRST EDITION

FIRST PRINTING

Copyright © 1982 by TAB BOOKS Inc.

Printed in the United States of America

Library of Congress Cataloging in Publication Data

Self, Charles R.
    The kitchen builder's handbook.

    Includes index.
    1. Kitchens—Remodeling. 2. Kitchens.
I. Title.
TH4816.S44 1982   643'.3   82-5932
ISBN 0-8306-2462-7   AACR2
ISBN 0-8306-1462-1 (pbk.)

Front cover photograph: Paragon Wood Products, courtesy of Osborne Associates, New York, NY.

Contents

Introduction

A WELL-EQUIPPED KITCHEN IS ABOUT THE MOST expensive room in any house to construct. You can save some money by planning and doing the work yourself. Attention to details in planning any kitchen usually results in lower building costs, greater efficiency, and more enjoyment of the space when the work is completed.

The designing and building, or redesigning and remodeling, of kitchens involve many skills—carpentry, plumbing, and wiring. The building of cabinets can often be a complex job. The building of kitchen cabinetry is much easier, though, than constructing most furniture pieces.

I've tried to design this book so that you can decide what you need; then you can learn what to do about getting it and doing the work yourself. Many types of partially assembled and finished cabinets are available, and I've included cabinets from Yorktowne Cabinets and Sears, Roebuck and Company in this book. I've tried to cover the processes and tools needed for building cabinets.

Flooring is a decision you must make, so all I can do in this book is provide the basics for laying all types of flooring—from wood strip to ceramic tile—and let you take it from there. Vinyl foot-square tiles today cost

under a dollar per square foot, as do the roll-out types of resilient foam-padded floorings. Wood parquet tiles can easily cost as much as four dollars a square foot. Some ceramic tiles are priced at more than nine dollars a square foot. These prices do not include installation or, in the case of wood and ceramic flooring, adhesives or nails needed for the installation. Wood strip flooring can be found unfinished, tongue and groove; unfinished butt joint; finished in both joint styles; or partially finished.

Countertops are covered in this book. It is possible to refinish present countertops simply by adding a laminate of plastic, using contact cement and a router with a laminate trimmer on the edges. Also, you can remove the entire countertop and install new, prefabricated countertops. These preformed or prefabricated countertops run just under 10 dollars a linear foot, with a front to back measurement of about 25 inches, and a 2 to 4-inch backsplash with a drip ledge at the front.

Plumbing and wiring for the kitchen are examined. Kitchen wiring doesn't work well if set up like most other wiring circuits in the home. Fifteen-ampere lighting circuits are the most common. The kitchen still needs at least one 20-ampere circuit for small appliances. The refrigerator should be on a separate circuit. Other appliances, ranging from dishwashers to garbage disposal units, need similar planning.

Plumbing for most kitchens is a simple matter. There is only a need for a hot and cold water supply to the sink, plus a DWV (drain/waste/vent) pipe drain and a vent to the outside. When dishwashers, garbage disposals, and other appliances are added, the job becomes more complex.

Proper selection of kitchen appliances is important due to increased energy costs and there is a chapter on choosing small appliances for your kitchen.

Kitchen remodeling can be as simple as laying a new floor or adding molding to old cabinets, or as complex as removing partition walls, moving all appliances, and adding new cabinets, appliances, and fixtures. Kitchen construction or remodeling is basically a microcosm of housebuilding and should be treated as such. If done right, it adds many thousands of dollars to the value of a house. Good luck with your kitchen building or remodeling.

Chapter 1

Planning

THE VAGARIES OF KITCHEN PLANNING DO NOT begin and end with the selection of the correct appliances, countertops, and cabinets. Floor materials, wallcoverings, and lighting are important.

THINGS TO CONSIDER

There are many considerations when you are making a kitchen plan. Do you use cast-iron pots and pans? If so, ceramic countertops may not be a good idea. Ceramic tile is virtually indestructible under normal use. Dropping a cast-iron, 12-inch frying pan on the surface, though, will usually crack several tiles.

You may want to consider countertop and appliance height increases or reductions to accommodate very tall or short family members. It is wise to reduce the height of countertops, sinks, and stove so that a person in a wheelchair can make use of them (Fig. 1-1).

Consider door openings into the kitchen. If the back door opens directly into the kitchen, and you have a golfer in the family, don't use a foam-backed resilient flooring unless you can convince the golfer to change shoes outdoors.

Kitchens can be remodeled in steps. Don't install new countertops and flooring, then paint the walls and ceiling. Do the higher jobs first. If you plan to install new counters, plumbing, and wiring, don't install the counters before the wiring. Put in the plumbing before you install the new cabinets for the sink and any other water-using appliances.

If you are going to buy a new refrigerator, choose the model and get its measurements before you install cabinets around it. That will save problems if you buy a refrigerator much larger or smaller than your current model. Popular refrigerator sizes range from about 28 to 36 inches wide. Allow at least 6 inches of total side clearance for any refrigerator so that it can be readily moved for cleaning and repair. Cabinets over a refrigerator should not be closer than 6 inches to the refrigerator. You need air flow around any refrigerator; otherwise, the cooling coils will overheat.

DOODLING AND MEASURING

Before tackling kitchen building or remodeling jobs, obtain a yellow legal pad, a good pen, an architect's rule (a triangular-shaped rule), and some graph paper. Note the present room layout and rough measurements. Then it is doodling time. Try to cover all possibilities—assuming the windows and doors are

1

Fig. 1-1. Kitchens to be used by handicapped persons have lower controls and surface areas (courtesy General Electric).

to remain in their current locations, not to mention walls.

Careful measurement begins when the doodling ends (Fig. 1-2). When the final installation is begun, all measurements must be within ⅛ inch (Fig. 1-3). If a wall tapers out 2 inches, the plan should show the taper. You can fudge fittings to get around this, but it becomes important when figuring countertop fit against walls and when determining floor covering fits.

Transfer all these accurate figures to a rough on the legal pad. Make another transfer to get the final measurements of the room to a drawing on the graph paper. You don't have to be artistic, but you must be as accurate in showing dimensions as possible. Make all measurements at least twice. Rushing measurement will almost always slow the entire job. When cutting is

involved, an incorrect measurement invariably means a waste of material and a loss of time. All measurements must be shown to the nearest fraction of an inch. If a measurement along a wall where you plan to install cabinets is 108 3/16 inches, do not go to 108¼ inches. The resulting cabinet will be, at best, a force fit. Go to 108⅛ inches, if you can't use the exact number. You will probably have to order cabinets—assuming you don't want to make your own—at the 108-inch size.

When measuring for base or wall cabinets, if a wall tapers out and the corner is not square, use the measurement at the inner portion of the corner, or the smaller measurement. A cabinet cut to fit the wider portion of the wall can't be jammed back into the narrower portion. Any problems can be covered with base filler pieces. Countertops must be cut to fit the larger dimension first.

Detail the exact locations of all windows, doors, electrical outlets, baseboards, baseboard heights, and ceiling heights on wall elevations. You can thus determine the actual height needed for wall cabinets and how much space that height allows over the countertop. Detail all plumbing fixtures, if in place, and if not detail their exact places. Check local codes for vent pipe sizes. Find out the drain locations and on-center distances of all faucets so that hot and cold supply lines can be run, and DWV (drain/waste/vent) pipe can be located. With modern faucet design and plastic pipe, it is possible to make many changes without greatly disrupting the entire room. You can get plastic pipe connectors to work with copper pipe and tubing. Using sweat soldering is then often unnecessary, even when adding to an old copper system.

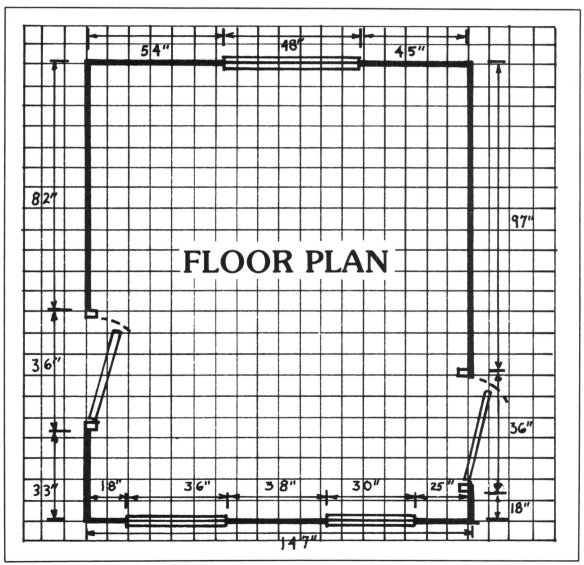

Fig. 1-2. Measure carefully (courtesy Yorktowne Cabinets).

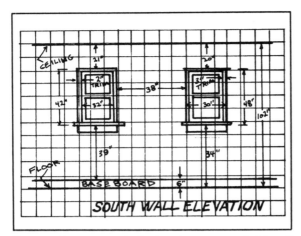

Fig. 1-3. Exact—to ⅛ inch—locations are needed for all outlets, appliance positions, fixtures, and so on when you make the final plans for cabinetry and overall kitchen design (courtesy Yorktowne Cabinets).

APPLIANCE AND CABINET LAYOUT

When all wall measurements and window, door, plumbing, and electrical supply locations are drawn on graph paper, you must consider appliance and cabinet layout. If the kitchen layout isn't well done, all the smaller detailing will be so much wasted time as far as the efficiency of the completed kitchen is concerned. Detail on your drawing any counters and appliances that will be left in place, and you're ready to begin locating your basic kitchen work triangle (Fig. 1-4).

The kitchen *work triangle* is formed by the stove or range, refrigerator, and kitchen sink. Sides of this triangle will ideally add up to no more than a total of 22 feet. A bit less is probably better, although cutting the size of the work triangle too much tends to shrink overall work space badly. No more than three steps from one appliance to the next are best. Two steps are better for most people, meaning each triangle leg needs to be from about 5 to 7 feet long.

Basically, there are four kitchen shapes. Three adapt the work triangle and one, the corridor kitchen, is seldom used these days (probably because unless the kitchen corridor back ends on a wall, there is little you can do to prevent traffic through the work triangle). The single wall kitchen is often seen in small apartments and suffers from a lack of efficiency and working ease. Refrigerator doors will not open all the way, and oven doors stop two-thirds of the way down (Fig. 1-5).

The most common kitchen designs today are L-shaped and U-shaped kitchens. Both offer good work

triangles and can be adapted to rooms considered too large to hold efficient work triangles simply by separating the various kitchen areas. Broken L and U-shapes are adaptations and can be good problem solvers when passageways and other spaces break into the work triangle. There is never enough kitchen space as far as countertop and cabinet space go. It may seem like too much, though, if pots and pans are stored too far from the stove, and the refrigerator is too far from the sink, with foods having to be carried a long distance for cleaning and other preparations.

A small, limited efficiency kitchen will generally have no less than 15 linear feet of wall space for cabinets and appliances. A medium efficiency kitchen needs 17½ linear feet. A kitchen with 20 linear feet of appliance and cabinet space is considered ample in size, though far from outsized. If a corner is to be occupied by a cabinet, allow 4 linear feet more for that. Any working space that is to be used by two people should have at least 4 feet between any facing base cabinets or appliances, and more if possible, to allow for adequate working space (Fig. 1-6).

The layout of doors and windows in any bare wall kitchen area will determine whether you use a corridor style, a U-shape, or L-shape, or one of the variations. You must determine the use of the rest of the space. Base cabinets are typically 36 inches high. Most have a countertop at that height, then a single drawer and a couple of fixed shelves inside the drawers. Pull-out or adjustable shelves are better. The depth of most base cabinets is 24 or 25 inches, including the lip on the countertop.

Wall cabinets are usually 30 inches high with three shelves that can be fixed or adjustable (adjustable is preferable). Wall cabinets are never placed lower than 15 inches above the countertop, so room is allowed for storage of small appliances such as toaster ovens, mixers, and blenders. Sometimes more space is allowed with smaller wall cabinets. Some appliances are higher than others, but even microwave ovens seldom need more than a foot or so of space. You will need about 4 feet of wall cabinet frontage to provide storage (if the units are 30 inches high) for dinnerware for 12 people. Naturally, any wall cabinets over appliances such as the refrigerator or range are tiny and not included in the frontage count.

Storage walls and specialized cabinets are used when you have greater space requirements than can be handled with just cabinets over, under, and around appliances. These are most often full-height units, rising from floor to ceiling with depths of 1 foot to 2 feet,

Fig. 1-4. A work triangle is needed (courtesy Yorktowne Cabinets).

depending on location and your needs. The Georgetowne line from Yorktowne Cabinets (P.O. Box 231, Red Lion, PA 17356) includes a full height broom closet, which comes with basically one fixed shelf but offers a three-shelf adjustable kit. A food storage unit is also full height (84 inches high and 12 or 24 inches deep) with a single fixed shelf. The lower section has a swing-out shelf unit and three adjustable half-depth shelves behind the swing-out unit. Shelf kits are available as additions.

Space between cabinets or cabinets and walls must be allowed for appliances. Get appliance sizes before adding holes. A refrigerator with no room to tilt and maneuver needs to be on wheels, and few are. A double bowl sink will need about 3 feet of countertop, but again it's better to measure the actual appliance first (or get the manufacturer's measurements). Dishwashers, too, vary in width, and some are meant to be built right into the counter front. The most general size seems to be 24 inches wide, but there are compact models and countertop style built-ins. Again, get the measurements before planning the hole.

Microwave ovens need some consideration, too. Several companies make microwave ovens mounted atop standard ranges. You must figure the correct spacing for those. Microwave ovens for built-in mounting are now easily found.

Countertop Space

Once the appliances are selected and measured,

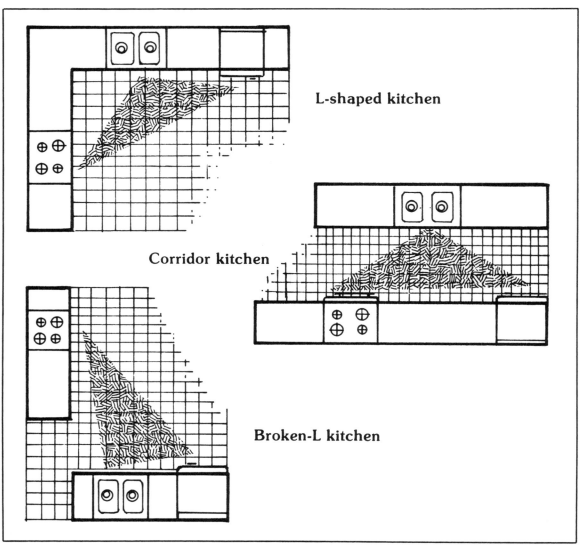

L-shaped kitchen

Corridor kitchen

Broken-L kitchen

Fig. 1-5. L, corridor, and broken-L kitchen layouts (courtesy Yorktowne Cabinets).

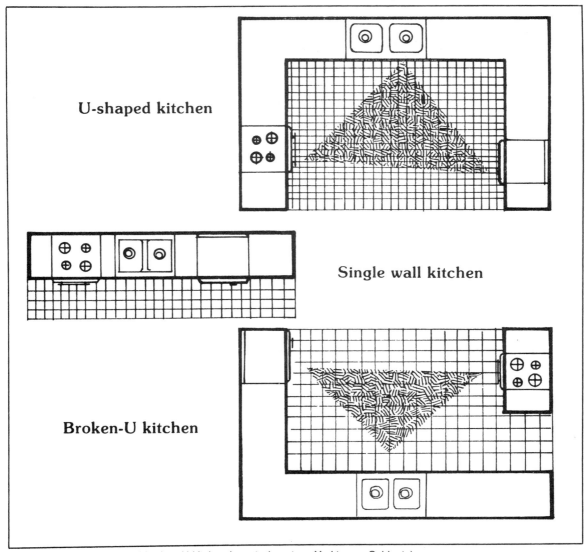

U-shaped kitchen

Single wall kitchen

Broken-U kitchen

Fig. 1-6. U, single wall, and broken-U kitchen layouts (courtesy Yorktowne Cabinets).

you need to determine the amount of space needed on each side of each appliance—useful countertop space, in other words. If you allow at least 15 inches of space on the latch side of the refrigerator door, you will be okay but 18 to 24 inches allow you room for larger bowls and containers. A 2-foot space on the right of the the sink is considered enough for stacking dishes before washing, but a 30-inch space is better. You need at least 18 inches of space to stack washed dishes for draining. With a dishwasher, you should almost never

need more than 2 feet. For food preparation, you should have an area of at least 3 feet. If you do much canning or bread baking, 4 feet or more may be desirable. Leave at least 18 inches on one side of the range or surface-mounted stove unit. Next to your oven, you need about 18 inches of space on which to sit items to be baked, broiled, or roasted.

Clearance Space

You need to take a look at the clearance spaces

behind or in front of appliances when the doors are opened, and someone might be working on them. If you open an oven door, and there is a total of 60 inches of clearance from the range front to any other cabinet, appliance, wall, or other obstruction, that is considered liberal. Another person can walk behind anyone opening the oven door without a lot of bumping. The minimum clearance is 4 feet. The same holds true for dishwashers and refrigerators. Clearance from a range top should also be 4 feet, and clearance from a countertop should be no less than 30 inches, with 40 inches much better. If a dining area is included in a kitchen, there should be a 26-inch clearance to any counter or other obstruction. A 3-foot clearance is far better and will allow one person to get up and leave the table without pushing things around and bothering other people seated at the table. If there is a passageway along one side of the table, allow at least a 30-inch minimum clearance from one side of the table, with 48 inches preferred.

Things to Avoid

Doors must not create conflicting actions. It is best not to have any doors opening into a kitchen. If the refrigerator must be backed to a passageway, then the refrigerator door can't be slammed shut when the pas-sageway door is opened. If such doors are unavoidable, make sure there is at least 1 square foot of glass area in the door to allow viewing into the kitchen. Make sure aisles are wide enough; Yorktowne Cabinets recommends at least 4 feet of aisle space. See that there is counter space near a built-in oven and that the oven is not installed too high in the wall. Don't install a countertop range unit and an in-the-wall oven against each other. Always follow the manufacturer's directions to prevent a fire hazard.

Don't locate a dishwasher just around the corner from the sink in a U or L-shaped kitchen. Be sure there is enough distance between the sink and the range that you won't be backing from the sink and bumping into pot or pan handles on the range or into open oven doors. Handles of utensils should always be turned to the inside area of the stove, so you do not hit them and tip possibly boiling materials onto yourself or the floor. Avoid planning useless corners. Such corners contribute nothing to the kitchen except as possible storage space for items like knives.

Kitchen Areas

The *storage area* is the refrigerator/freezer unit or units and should allow free flow into the cleaning area at the sink and dishwasher. The *preparation area* in-

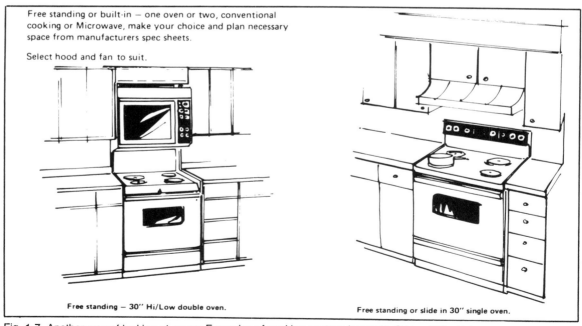

Free standing or built-in — one oven or two, conventional cooking or Microwave, make your choice and plan necessary space from manufacturers spec sheets.

Select hood and fan to suit.

Free standing — 30″ Hi/Low double oven.

Free standing or slide in 30″ single oven.

Fig. 1-7. Another way of looking at areas: Examples of cooking centers (courtesy General Electric).

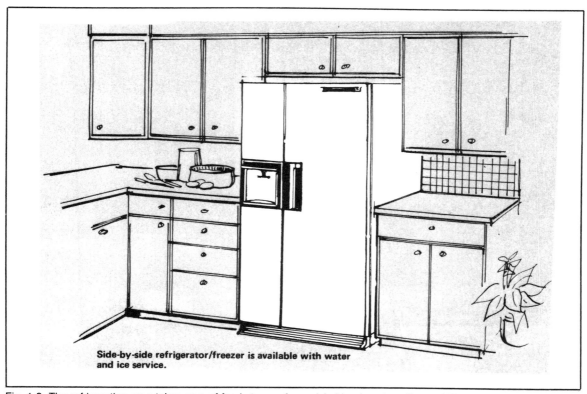

Side-by-side refrigerator/freezer is available with water and ice service.

Fig. 1-8. The refrigeration area takes care of food storage for perishables (courtesy General Electric).

cludes the range and oven and should allow a good two-way flow to and from the *cleaning area*. The *mixing area* will be next to the sink, and the *serving area* is between your *dining area* and the stove. If these seem to flow nicely, your planning is coming along well (Figs. 1-7 through 1-9).

CABINET UNITS

When the clearance and size planning is over, you can choose the units you need. Yorktowne units are coded to show if they are base or cabinet units, their width, and whether the door opens right or left. A base cabinet, 12 inches wide with a left opening door, is B12L. If the door opens to the right, the code is simply B12R. All the cabinets are 2 feet deep and 34½ inches high. Wall cabinets are coded in the same manner, with an 18-inch-wide cabinet classified as W18R or W18L. Wall cabinets vary in height. You may choose from 12, 17, 25, or 30-inch-high wall cabinets. A 30-inch-high cabinet is coded W18OR; the second figure denotes the height.

Cabinets are available in 3-inch-width gradations. Rooms don't always divide too well that way, so all companies make items known as *base fillers*. These fillers are usually 3 or 6 inches wide and are of the same height and finish as the rest of the cabinetry. They can be cut to exact widths and are used in the most inconspicuous areas of the base to fill in (or the wall, for wall fillers). Corner models are also available, with trimmable 3-inch sides. They are usually required to keep drawers from knocking pulls together and to allow easy opening of doors (Figs. 1-10 through 1-14).

The *lazy susan* units for turning corners make available a lot of space that is generally wasted. They do, though, tend to cost more than blind corner base cabinets. A Sears 45-degree lazy susan unit will cost about 40 percent more than a standard cabinet. Lazy susan units are also available for wall cabinets and add useful corner space there. The lazy susan unit in the corner will usually replace a two-door unit of comparable cost, though the lazy susan unit offers somewhat less storage space.

9

THE ECLECTIC

One wall is cabinets, one brick and one glass — a bit of this and that. Illuminated beam lighting is supplemented by the period fixtures. A small railing along the counter area provides an unusual touch with the practical feature of "fencing in" the countertop.

THE LONGVIEW

Corridor design lets this kitchen provide maximum storage area while using a budget amount of floor space. Judicious lighting compensates for the lack of windows.

THE ENCORE

Tucked in a corner, the Encore uses a minimum of space to good advantage. A multifold door can be used to shield the kitchen from the adjacent room.

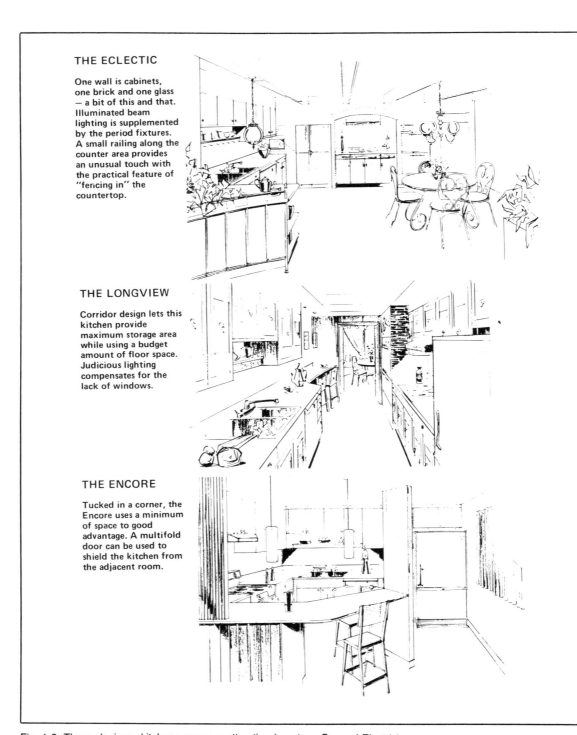

Fig. 1-9. These designer kitchens are very attractive (courtesy General Electric).

KITCHEN-IN-THE-ROUND

For the family that loves to cook and entertain, this circular arrangement puts it all together. There are 3 separate cooktops and two built-in wall ovens plus the free standing open grille at the hub.

THE GREENWICH VILLAGE

A distinctive kitchen with ample room for an eating area. The deep window sill over the sink could well be used for an herb garden or pass thru to a patio. To the right of the Refrigerator center is a handy laundry area.

THE VILLAGER

The traditional "U" shape is broken in this kitchen by the opening into the dining area. Note the view from the dining area is toward counter (not sink or range) area. This is good to keep in mind in your planning.

THE PATIO

The large expanse of glass lets the chef enjoy the patio and garden while cooking. The island bar doubles as an auxiliary work area.

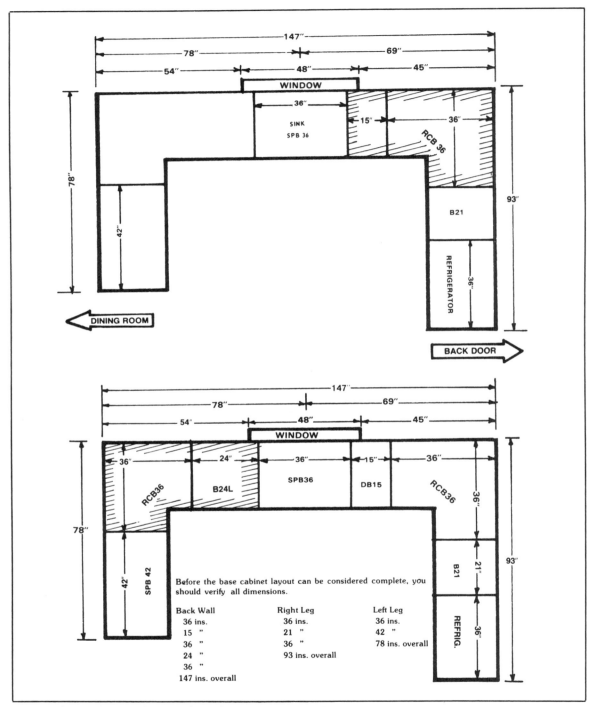

Fig. 1-10. Lay out base cabinets as shown (courtesy Yorktowne Cabinets).

Before the base cabinet layout can be considered complete, you should verify all dimensions.

Back Wall	Right Leg	Left Leg
36 ins.	36 ins.	36 ins.
15 "	21 "	42 "
36 "	36 "	78 ins. overall
24 "	93 ins. overall	
36 "		
147 ins. overall		

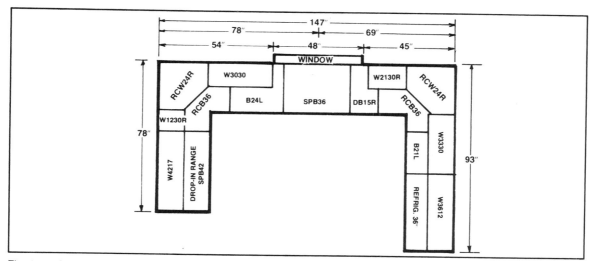

Fig. 1-11. Complete arrangement of wall cabinets (courtesy Yorktowne Cabinets).

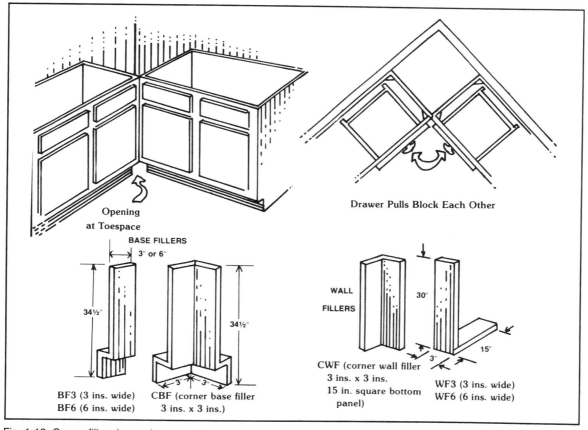

Fig. 1-12. Corner fillers in use (courtesy Yorktowne Cabinets).

13

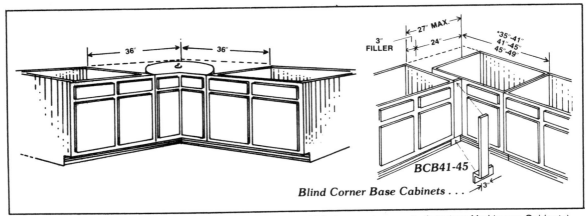

Blind Corner Base Cabinets . . .

Fig. 1-13. Corner problems can be solved by using revolving and blind corner base units (courtesy Yorktowne Cabinets).

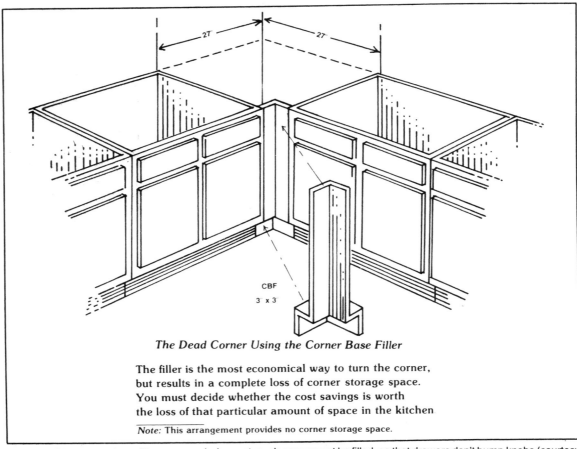

The Dead Corner Using the Corner Base Filler

The filler is the most economical way to turn the corner,
but results in a complete loss of corner storage space.
You must decide whether the cost savings is worth
the loss of that particular amount of space in the kitchen

Note: This arrangement provides no corner storage space.

Fig. 1-14. Other corner base fillers are used when not much space must be filled, so that drawers don't bump knobs (courtesy Yorktowne Cabinets).

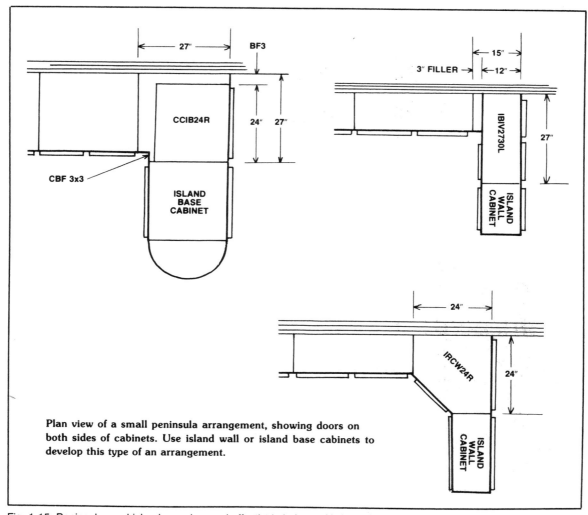

Fig. 1-15. Peninsulas and islands can be used effectively in larger kitchens (courtesy Yorktowne Cabinets).

Island base cabinets are made so that you have access from both sides (Fig. 1-15). Only a little ingenuity is needed to divert traffic away from the work triangle. Later in this book I will explain how to construct a movable island. I built this island because available counter space wasn't enough to allow the use of a food processor, even of the in-counter installation type made by NuTone Division of Scovill. The island was made with wheels, and the in-counter NuTone food processor was converted to make a semiportable unit. The cabinet of the island is large enough to hold glassware as well as the accessories

for the processor (ice crusher, juicer, various cutters, blender, can opener, shredder-slicer, meat grinder, mixer, and knife sharpener). This NuTone unit is not inexpensive, but it does many jobs well.

COUNTERTOPS

Countertops come next when the cabinets are installed. Usually Formica laminated plastic is a good choice and the easiest to install. Butcher block inserts can be used. These butcher block inserts are really only of semibutcher block construction, because the edge grain is used as a cutting surface, but they make very attractive countertops.

Ceramic tile is harder to install and more costly, but it is one of the most attractive countertop materials. The varied designs and sizes allow for flexibility in use. Ceramic tile is very durable.

FLOOR MATERIALS, WALLCOVERINGS, AND PAINTS

Washable carpeting may be used on a kitchen floor. Ceramic tile makes a durable kitchen floor. Vari-

Fig. 1-16. Wallcovering does much to improve a kitchen's appearance. This is Caprice by Benchmark (courtesy Benchmark).

Fig. 1-17. Keepsake wallcovering by Thomas Strahan (courtesy Thomas Strahan).

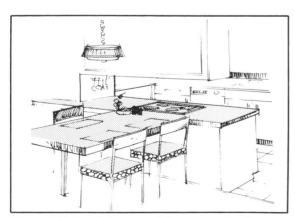

Fig. 1-18. Using a light over a dining area makes the space seem greater (courtesy General Electric).

ous forms of plastic flooring are available. Wood, when properly finished, makes an excellent kitchen floor.

Today's wallcoverings—paper is no longer even close to the proper word—are often prepasted and are easily installed. They are easily stripped from the walls if a change is desired. Wallcoverings may be vinyl-coated or even solid vinyl, and some even have reflective metallic designs (Figs. 1-16 and 1-17).

Paints for kitchen walls and ceilings are more durable than ever. Generally, at least a semigloss paint should be used for walls and ceilings because flat paints are seldom washable, which means grease buildup is going to occur until repainting time. Top quality semigloss paints should be durable for at least six years. Textured and sand paints should be avoided in kitchens, as they tend to trap grease.

17

Fig. 1-19. A light hung directly over the table helps to divide areas (courtesy General Electric).

LIGHTING

Many people simply put a central light in a kitchen and then add one in a range hood, but these lights are probably not enough. The American Home Lighting Institute (AHLI) suggests a large, shallow, diffusing fixture centered in the work area. Fixture size depends on the area to be lighted, but the AHLI recommends ¾ watt of fluorescent light or 1½ watts of incandescent light per square foot of kitchen floor. Off-center arrangements of track lights or fluorescent strip lighting can be used to provide parallel lighting to countertops. These lights should be spaced 18 inches to 2 feet from the wall cabinets. A strong downlight is needed over the sink for food preparation and washing dishes. Two lights approximately 18 inches apart, with 50 to 75-watt incandescent bulbs, or two fluorescent bulbs, each of at least 30 watts, are appropriate. Your range hood should take at least a 60-watt light bulb, so you can check the color and consistency of the food being cooked. If no range hood is in place, just follow the recommendations for sink lighting (Fig. 1-18).

The dining area can be made to seem more separate if you hang a fixture directly over the table (Fig. 1-19). Counter lighting may not be needed if you've installed offset lighting. If it is needed, install fluorescent lights, allowing 8 watts for every foot of counter.

Chapter 2

Tools

M ANY TOOLS ARE NEEDED WHEN WORKING ON kitchen. If you do the entire job yourself, you may need carpenter's, cabinetmaker's, plumber's, electrician's, and some mason's tools. I will try to indicate price ranges for good quality tools, but keeping up with the market is next to impossible. Prices of most tools have more than doubled in the past decade.

Let's start with the classic carpenter's tools, because some of them adapt to other crafts as well. Screwdrivers, for example, are needed for installing cabinets, wiring, and plumbing fixtures.

HAMMERS

Modern *hammers* have better striking faces than older hammers due to better metals and metal treatment. At one time only wood—usually hickory but sometimes white oak or ash—was available for hammer handles. Two types of steel hammer handles are readily found, and fiberglass-handled hammers are available. Wood-handled hammers offer good shock absorption, strength, and economy. The best head quality is found in hammers with fiberglass and steel handles.

Steel handles may be either solid or tubular (Fig. 2-1). They usually have porous plastic or rubber grips.

Strength is excellent, but even with the rubber or plastic grips, shock absorption is not as good as with wood. Tubular steel handles are better in this respect.

The strength of fiberglass handles approaches that of steel ones. The fiberglass handle shaft does a fine job of absorbing shock. Like steel handles, fiberglass handles usually come with plastic or rubber grips.

Replaceability is a consideration with hammer handles. Even a steel handle can be bent or broken without destroying the head. Plumb tubular steel-handled hammers use epoxy to hold things together. Fiberglass-handled hammers are bonded to the head in much the same way, while wood handles are fitted and wedges are driven to spread and hold them in place. Wood handles are generally the easiest to replace. You may have to work very hard to remove old epoxy bonding agents (Fig. 2-2).

Easco of Glen Burnie, Maryland, has developed a hammer called the *Hand Tastic*, with a 19½-degree arc or bend in it that reduces fatigue. The handle is hickory (Fig. 2-3).

Carpenter's hammers are available with head weights ranging from a light 13 ounces to a loaded 28 ounces. Each hammer is meant to do a particular job.

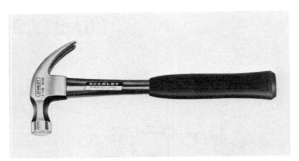

Fig. 2-1. A claw hammer with a steel handle (courtesy Stanley Tools).

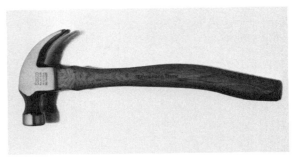

Fig. 2-3. The Easco Hand Tastic claw hammer (courtesy Easco Tools).

You will have no need for 22 and 28-ounce hammers in kitchen work. These hammers are meant for heavy framing jobs such as installing floor joists, ceiling joists, and rafters. The 22-ounce hammer is meant for the same type of work. General-use claw hammers are those with 16 and 20-ounce head weights, with the 16-ounce weight being the most common. I tend to prefer the 20-ounce head weight for general framing and even for most nailing. For light work, such as with window and door moldings and glue/nail joinery of cabinets, the light 13-ounce head is generally preferable.

Approximately 90 percent of the work in this book can be readily done with a 16-ounce head weight. The cheapest quality hammer, with a 16-ounce head and hickory handle, is going to cost about 12 or 13 dollars. The cheapest fiberglass-handled 16-ounce hammer is priced at 14 or 15 dollars. Steel-handled hammers cost about 16 or 17 dollars. You may pay as much as 20

dollars for a hammer (Easco's Hand Tastic is now retailing for about that), but you will seldom pay less than 12 dollars.

Don't use a *claw hammer* to pull nails that have been driven more than 1½ inches into wood. Do not pull any nails larger than 16-penny, partially driven or not. Do not use the hammer to break rock or brick, drive steel-handled chisels, or hammer masonry nails.

Soft-faced hammers are useful for many kitchen-related assembly and disassembly jobs. They are used when you want to mar a surface as little as possible, if at all. I have two soft-faced hammers with replaceable tips and one with nonreplaceable. One hammer is an old Craftsman, the other two are from Stanley, and all have wooden handles. The Craftsman hammer offers a choice of hard or soft plastic tips, but it has a head weight of only 12 ounces. The Stanley hammer with the solid head weighs 16 ounces. The head of the other hammer weighs 32 ounces (Fig. 2-4).

Shopsmith Inc. sells a hammer with a tightly rolled rawhide head. This is a 10-ounce head weight hammer with a 2-inch head diameter. Most soft-faced, plastic-headed handles cost under 10 dollars, while the rawhide-headed model is approaching 20 dollars.

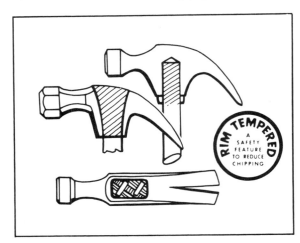

Fig. 2-2. Handle bonding (courtesy Plumb).

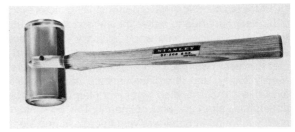

Fig. 2-4. Plastic head hammers are often useful to assemble items that might be damaged by steel heads (courtesy Stanley Tools).

Lignum vitae mallets are useful for kitchen remodeling work. Lignum vitae is a wood so dense that it will not float, and it is exceptionally strong.

SCREWDRIVERS

Screwdrivers are best chosen for hand fit and quality once the needed sizes are determined. If you plan on doing electrical work, only plastic-handled screwdrivers are suitable. For basic cabinetry and carpentry, you won't find better screwdrivers than those sold by Shopsmith and by Irwin. Shopsmith offers a set of screwdrivers, with a one-piece forged blade and handle and hickory grip inserts. The metal goes from tip to top, and the handle inserts are riveted on. The set of four includes a 4-inch shank model with a 5/16-inch tip, a 6-inch shank with a 3/8-inch tip, an 8-inch shank with a 7/16-inch tip, and a 10-inch shank with a 7/16-inch tip. Call 800-543-7586, or 800-762-7555 in Ohio, to check current prices.

A grip check is necessary, for a grip that is uncomfortable in your hand means a job that is likely to be done poorly. One type of grip found on plastic-handled screwdrivers is the basic fluted grip. It is found on most Craftsman screwdrivers from Sears, Roebuck and Company, as well as on Crescent and Stanley screwdrivers. The second type is a plastic grip with a cushion covering of rubber or plastic over it; it is offered by Crescent, Stanley, and Bernzomatic. Stanley also makes a handle that tapers down from the base (where the shaft of the screwdriver joins the handle) a modest amount. It is triangular in pattern, but the angles are not sharp at all. Because the handle tapers as your hand does, you get a very good, strong grip.

Regarding screwdriver tips needed for any kitchen job, you will need only the standard tip for slotted screws and, sometimes, a Phillips tip for hardware on various items you may need to assemble or disassemble (Figs. 2-5 and 2-6). You should have the three largest Phillips sizes and several standard tip screwdrivers.

Ratcheting screwdrivers are exceptionally handy when you have many screws to drive in wood. It's possible to use screwdriver bits driven with an electric

Fig. 2-6. Square shank slotted tip screwdriver (courtesy Stanley Tools).

drill for this work, but I prefer to do this only when metal is involved, for a single slip can tear up any wood surface. Stanley makes the Yankee screwdriver with manual or quick return ratchets. There are heavy-duty and regular-duty models, light-duty styles, and two Handyman styles. Stanley's regular-duty, quick return ratcheting screwdriver is excellent. As you end a stroke, the blade remains in the screw slot, but the handle returns to the driving position. The primary reason for selecting the regular-duty over the heavy-duty model is the wider availability of tips. There are six tip styles available only for the 130A model, and these tips will not fit the heavy-duty 131A model. The heavy-duty models are more expensive than the regular-duty styles (Fig. 2-7).

Ratcheting screwdrivers use 1/4-inch drive sockets (Stanley makes an adapter to fit them to the sockets). Some will also fit drill points for light drilling (these are the Handyman models).

SAWS

The base *handsaw* can trim countertops more neatly than a circular saw if the countertop is already laminated and has any kind of a lip or backsplash. You can cut from the top surface with a handsaw, while you have to turn the material over to make the cut with a circular saw. The handsaw cuts on the downstroke, thus leaving no tears and splinters on the top, visible edge. The circular saw cuts on its upstroke and may splinter top edges if the piece is not turned over. Because a saber saw cuts on its upstroke, visible edges may splinter. If you have no countertop trimming to do, then you probably won't need a handsaw. If you do,

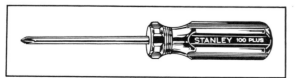

Fig. 2-5. Phillips tip screwdriver (courtesy Stanley Tools).

Fig. 2-7. The Yankee ratcheting screwdriver (courtesy Stanley Tools).

21

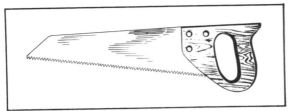

Fig. 2-8. A drywall saw is handy for cutting out receptacle holes and places for lights and other fixtures (courtesy Stanley Tools).

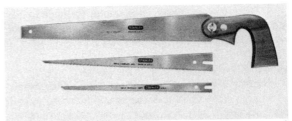

Fig. 2-10. A nest of saws provides keyhole, compass, and general-use saw blades (courtesy Stanley Tools).

select one with at least 10 teeth per inch for a smooth cut. Do not buy a handsaw with a plastic or poorly finished wood handle. Plastic is too slippery, and a poorly finished handle indicates that the rest of the saw is likely to be of poor quality. Hollow ground or taper ground blades are best, so that the kerf is wider than the top edge of the saw blade.

Check the entire saw for finish details. The blade should be highly polished and have teeth that look even when viewed from one end. The handle should be finished well and firmly riveted or screwed to the blade tang. The handle should fit your hand well, directing the force of the cutting motion into the cut. A good crosscut saw or rip saw is expensive. Good handsaws from Nicholson, Stanley, Disston, and Sears, Roebuck and Company will cost about 15 to 20 dollars.

Drywall, keyhole, and *compass saws* are useful for kitchen work (Figs. 2-8 and 2-9). These saws can cut smaller lines in areas where you may need to make a turn or install switch or receptacle boxes. In such cases, a nest of saws can be used (Fig. 2-10). A drywall saw is handy if you have large sections of plasterboard to cut and do not want to tear down entire walls. You can make sink cutouts with a compass saw, though the job is a lot easier and less time-consuming with a saber saw.

Hacksaws and Coping Saws

Hacksaws are used to cut mostly metals and plastics, but they are occasionally useful on wood projects. Select a hacksaw with a handle that directs pressure into its frame and the blade. Look for a sturdy frame and handle. Blades are selected to suit the thickness of the material being worked, with most hacksaw blades having from 18 to 32 teeth. Obviously, very thin metal or plastic is cut with the finer teeth, but it is best to clamp the work in some manner that prevents splitting.

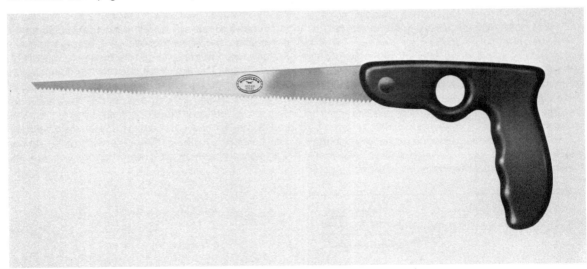

Fig. 2-9. For tighter cuts, a keyhole saw is necessary and can also be used in wood (courtesy Nicholson).

22

Coping saws are similar in general appearance to the hacksaw. They are much lighter and are used for cutting scroll designs and tight corners and for "coping" molding joints where a mitered joint won't work. Coping a joint is done by first marking the pattern of the molding already installed on the wall or floor on the molding to be installed. That pattern is then cut out with the coping saw, and the resulting joint is an accurate and tight fit. The fancier the molding, the more likely you need to use coped joints.

Miter Boxes

Miter boxes are closely tied to backsaws. They are most often used to miter joints for door and window, floor, and ceiling moldings, though they are also handy when building anything that requires joints at angles other than 90 degrees. Most can be set at a variety of angles, and some are already marked in the correct graduations for making 6, 8, 9, and 12-sided figures. A good miter box with backsaw should allow you to cut anywhere from 90 to 45 degrees. Some miter boxes will let you cut to about 30 degrees, though they tend to be very expensive. My own miter box/backsaw combination is a Stanley middle-of-the-range model intended for the home handyman (Figs. 2-11 and 2-12).

If you don't want to spend 60 dollars on a miter box and backsaw, there are several options. A popular choice is the maple miter box used with a fine-toothed (10 or 12 teeth per inch) handsaw. In addition, Stanley makes an inexpensive metal miter box that can use either a backsaw or a panel saw (85-114), and a plastic miter box that does the same job as the maple miter box, as well as a saw angle guide for panel saws (85-180). All are inexpensive options, though the cut accuracy won't be as good as with a miter box and backsaw. A *panel saw*, by the way, is nothing more than a basic handsaw.

Power Saws

Power saws are exceptionally handy tools in major remodeling or reconstruction. For kitchen remodeling work, you're unlikely to need more than a circular saw and a saber saw. You could do the job with some type of handsaw, but the power saws save time and energy and are usually worth the extra investment.

Circular saws are made by Black and Decker; Sears, Roebuck and Company; Montgomery Ward;

Rockwell International; Skil Corporation; and others (Fig. 2-13). Blades for the saws are made by companies such as Nicholson and Stanley as well as by the saw manufacturers. For light remodeling, you might get by with a 1½-horsepower, 7¼-inch circular saw. For more extensive use, though, you'll need one turning out 2 horsepower or more. It has been my experience in heavy cutting that the saws with less than 2 horsepower eventually burn out their motors. Gear-driven circular saws are expensive, but they are nice to have. Smaller, lighter saws are intended only for cutting plywood and lighter materials. These saws are cheaper, but their use is limited by blade size and a lack of power. Most won't cut much over 1½ inches, and the really light models have only a ¾-horsepower motor.

Blade choice for circular saws is important. You probably won't need a rip blade, but a good combination blade will handle most fairly long ripcuts and virtually all crosscuts (Fig. 2-14). You need either a planer blade or a plywood blade for smoother cuts. A plywood/veneer blade meant for use on countertops covered with laminate will reduce cut depth (usually to about 1¼ inches), but it will produce neater work and very smooth cuts (Figs. 2-15 and 2-16).

Flooring blades are used to make cuts in material where you might expect to run into nails and other items. Unless you're planning to cut out a floor or do cutting on old studs or other framing members, you really shouldn't need a flooring blade.

The power miter box is essentially a miter box with a circular saw attached to make mitering cuts. The price of this tool tends to be rather high. Sears also

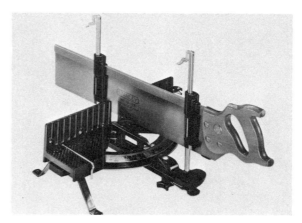

Fig. 2-11. A professional style miter box does many jobs quickly and well (courtesy Stanley Tools).

Fig. 2-12. Smaller backsaw and miter box combinations cost less than professional models and are useful to the home remodeler (courtesy Stanley Tools).

Fig. 2-13. The circular saw is a versatile tool (courtesy Rockwell International).

Fig. 2-14. These combination blades are carbide-tipped for long life (courtesy Nicholson).

Fig. 2-15. This plywood blade will provide for smooth cutting in veneered material (courtesy Nicholson).

Fig. 2-16. A plywood paneling blade works best in thin, veneered material (courtesy Rockwell International).

sells two miter guides for circular saws that should do any job the power miter box can do.

The saber saw in Fig. 2-17 is from Rockwell International and is a fine tool. The other companies listed earlier as making circular saws also make good saber saws. My particular saber saw is a PowerKraft from Montgomery Ward, with a manual scrolling setup. The two top-of-the-line saber saws from Sears are known as automatic scrolling models. When you move the saw forward, the blade cuts to the front. Move the saw sideways, and the blade turns to cut to the side. Move it backward, and the blade pivots to cut to the rear. Saber saws with no scrolling attachments of any kind will seldom run much more than 50 dollars.

Look for a saber saw with between ⅛ and ¼ horsepower, with a base that will tilt 45 degrees right and left. Consider whether or not you will ever want to make fancy cuts with the tool. If so, think about manual or automatic scrolling (manual scrolling means there is a knob on top of the saw that you must turn in order to change cut direction). Remember, though, that any saber saw can be used for scrolling and other fancy cuts by simply turning the saw so the blade points in the direction you must cut. A variable speed saw is your best bet. You can then adjust the speed for the material and blade in use, and the saw should have a stroke of at least ½ inch.

Blades for the saber saw are of top importance. You will find blades to cut metal, for flush cutting up to walls, for cutting rubber and leather, and for plywood and laminate cutting. These latter blades will usually have 10 to 14 teeth per inch and will work in material from ¾ inch to 2 inches in maximum thickness. Ten saber saw blades usually cost less than seven dollars.

MEASURING TOOLS

For remodeling purposes, you need such measuring tools as folding rules, measuring tapes, levels, and squares. Stanley and Lufkin make excellent tapes and rules, and Stanley has good levels and squares (Figs. 2-18 through 2-21).

Folding Rules

There are times when the *folding rule* is almost essential to a good measurement, and there are other occasions when it simply does the job more easily and readily than a tape (Fig. 2-22). Inside measurements of doors and windows provide one such use. Tape measures can be used in such instances, but they are a bit harder to accurately use than rules. Folding rules

need to be made of a wood that has some flexibility to prevent breaking. The rules must not be so flexible that they can't be held straight on a horizontal. Most folding rules are 6 feet long, usually with a 6-inch brass extension. Lufkin has an 8-foot model. The basic folding rule is marked in inches, with graduations down to 1/16 inch. Carpenter's folding rules will usually have 16-inch on-center markings for standard stud wall framing. You can also find rules marked to be read from either end and rules in metric sizing. You will find markings in tenths, hundredths, and sixteenths in engineer's rules. Plumber's rules are designed for easy figuring of pipe lengths at 45-degree angles, and mason's rules give modulars for masonry courses.

Tape Measures

Tape measures have improved considerably over the years (Fig. 2-23). When I first began using them, you had a choice of winding the tape back or watching the self-winding spring break about twice a day.

Fig. 2-17. Saber saw blades come in many styles (courtesy Rockwell International).

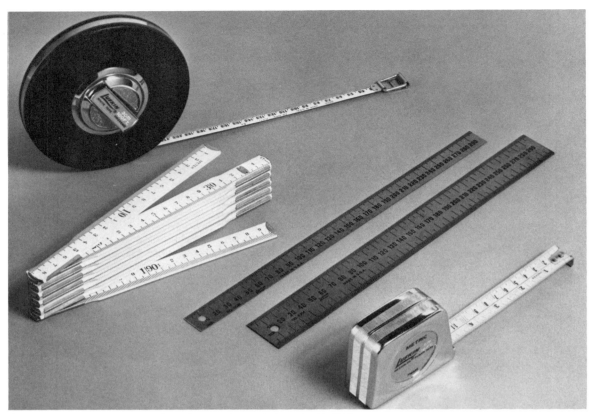

Fig. 2-18. Lufkin produces a variety of measuring tools (courtesy Lufkin).

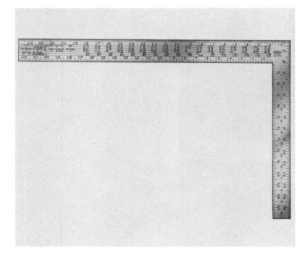

Fig. 2-19. Framing squares are relatively inexpensive, but they are essential for many jobs around the home (courtesy Stanley Tools).

Today, 25-foot tape measures are extremely reliable in their self-returning operation, and tapes have been redesigned for easy reading and use. Tapes up to 1 inch wide are used, and even today's ½-inch-wide tapes are far stiffer than the old ones. I use two Stanley Powerlock 25-foot models for most purposes. The last 7 feet of the 1-inch-wide blade have been stiffened so that one person can readily measure that distance horizontally. For longer distances, I have a Lufkin number 100 lightweight tape. This tape is very handy for measuring fence lines. It is rewound by hand.

Levels

A *level* is used to determine if everything on a job is plumb and horizontal. Buy a top-quality 2-foot level. My 2-foot level is an extruded aluminum Stanley +100 model. I also have a 4-foot Montgomery Ward Power-Kraft mahogany mason's level. This level is bound in brass (Fig. 2-24).

To check the accuracy of any level, you need only

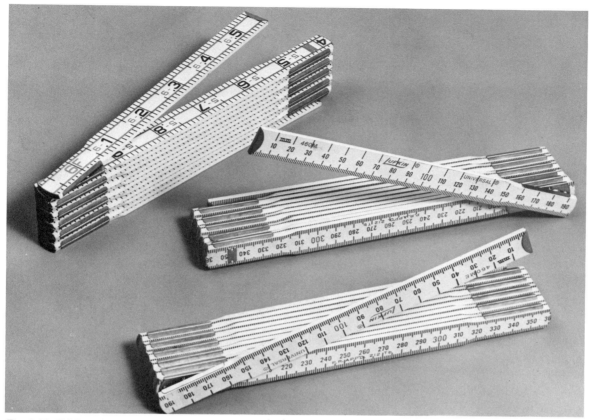

Fig. 2-20. Folding rules are useful in many situations (courtesy Lufkin).

a flat bench or floor space, the level, a pencil, and a grease pencil. Place the level on the flat surface and mark with the pencil the spots where both ends are resting. If the spot isn't level, use the grease pencil to mark the position of the bubble(s) in the vial(s). Simply reverse the level, end for end, placing it exactly between the marks made with the pencil. If the bubbles are in exactly the same place in the vials, then the level retains its accuracy. If not, you may have a level that is adjustable. Follow the maker's directions for adjustments. If the level is not adjustable, see if the vials can be replaced. You can check for accuracy of the plumb vials in the same manner, except that you will need to use a vertical flat surface instead of a horizontal surface.

Squares

You will need a *carpenter's square* (also known as a *framing square* and a *rafter square*) to check

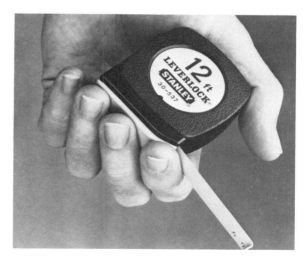

Fig. 2-21. Measuring tapes can be used to measure the diameters of circles and other items that do not have regular shapes (courtesy Stanley Tools).

29

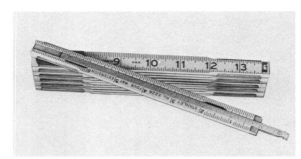

Fig. 2-22. Folding rules with brass extensions are handy items (courtesy Stanley Tools).

room corners for squareness, and possibly for use as a straightedge/square when trimming wall covering, resilient flooring, or other materials (Fig. 2-25). Rafter squares are generally available in both aluminum and steel.

Rafter squares will have a blade 2 inches wide by 2 feet long and a tongue 16 inches long by 1½ inches wide. The markings vary, but they are usually inches, broken down into sixteenths. The body of the square may be used to present various scales and tables.

The *try square* has its blade and handle solidly locked together. I prefer to use a try square instead of a combination square. I use Stanley's 46-526, which has a 12-inch blade on a 7¼-inch handle. The handle is cut so that you can also get short distance 45-degree angles when necessary. Try squares are used to check cut squareness and to lay out markings for square cuts. A 12-inch blade gives you just under a 24-inch capacity for marking if both sides of the piece are true (Figs. 2-26 and 2-27).

A try square is durable enough to remain accurate under some really intensive use. *Combination squares* may be nearly as well made, but with a sliding handle they cannot be as firmly set as a try square. The

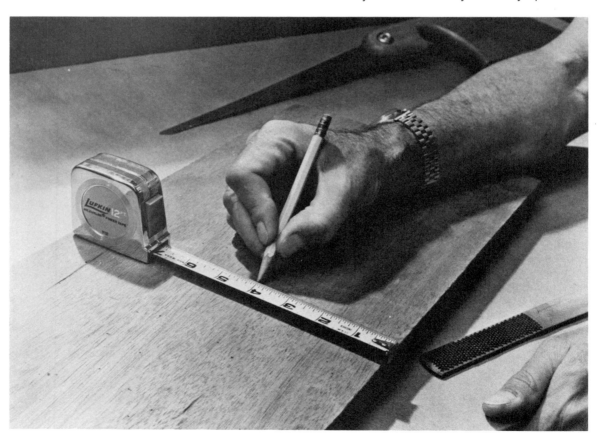

Fig. 2-23. Lufkin's 12-foot tape is also very useful (courtesy Lufkin).

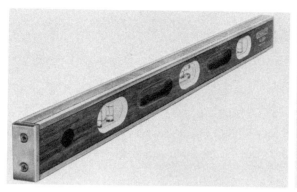

Fig. 2-24. Wood levels bound in brass are useful for all leveling and plumbing jobs (courtesy Stanley Tools).

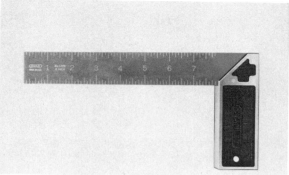

Fig. 2-26. Try squares are too often overlooked in the occasional remodeler's toolbox (courtesy Stanley Tools).

combination square does offer other options, such as greater ease of making 45-degree angle markings, and it can also be used as a marking device (Figs. 2-28 and 2-29). Many top-of-the-line combination squares come with a scriber built into the handle. Just unscrew it, set your square handle at the correct distance on the blade, and hold the scriber at the end of the blade as you move the handle along the edge. Many combination squares come with a level built into the handle. These levels, though, are soon knocked out of place. There's little or no price difference between a top-quality try square and a top-quality combination square, but I recommend that you get both.

The try square is related to the *sliding T bevel,* but the uses are different. A sliding T bevel usually has a wood handle and a metal blade with a slot at one end, extending about halfway along the blade. A wing nut loosens or tightens the blade on the handle, and it is used to determine or to mark angles other than 90 and 45 degrees. The sliding T bevel is very useful for determining angles in a corner and then transferring those angles to a section of countertop that needs to be fitted in that corner. Price is not extraordinary, though it will approach 10 dollars. Known angles can be set on the T bevel with a protractor and then transferred to the work surface.

The Center Square by Stanley is used as a protractor. It can also find the center of a circle (Fig. 2-30).

MARKING TOOLS

Marking devices include the *carpenter's pencil,* a flat pencil used to mark studs and other wood mem-

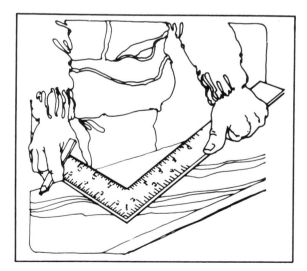

Fig. 2-25. This framing square is handy (courtesy Stanley Tools).

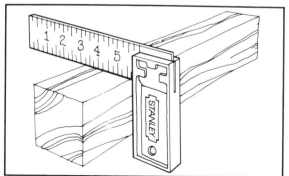

Fig. 2-27. Using a try square is simple (courtesy Stanley Tools).

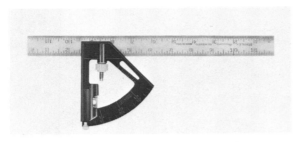

Fig. 2-28. While the combination square may not be as accurate as the try square, it does more jobs (courtesy Stanley Tools).

Fig. 2-30. The center square is invaluable when you have to work with round stock (courtesy Stanley Tools).

bers that will later be concealed. Pencils shouldn't be used to mark wood that will be finished naturally and exposed to view, as the graphite from the pencil lead tends to stay on the wood. Sometimes this mark can be removed by using an eraser—sanding only causes the particles to drop further down into the wood grain—but often part of it remains. Marking gauges are devices that have a locatable shoe on a bar with a scriber in its end. Most are made with scales on them, and in the better marking gauges this series of graduations will be accurate. In the cheaper ones, it pays to set the gauge from a rule or tape measure. The best marking devices are those such as Stanley's 47-065 with a hardwood body and shoe, and a brass faceplate on the shoe. The scribing pin is adjustable in this model (Fig. 2-31).

You can buy a cased chalk line with the case filled with powdered chalk, such as Stanley's Chalk-O-Matic. Either 50 or 100 feet of line are in the case with the chalk. The end of the line has a hook that can be attached to a projection or slipped in a slot, so one person can mark with a line. A chalk line is easy to use as long as you remember to lift the line, after it is tight, directly from the surface. Do not twist it to the right or left. Let it go, and the line will give you a mark for cutting or installation. With 50 feet of line, a good-quality cased chalk line will cost about five dollars, often with chalk included (Fig. 2-32).

KNIVES

A *utility knife* is used for trimming wall coverings, cutting gypsum wallboard and resilient floor tile, and other jobs. These knives come apart for blade replacement, and the blade type or shape can be varied to suit the job being done (Figs. 2-33 through 2-35).

An *electrician's knife* is a two or three-bladed knife. One blade is used as a screwdriver and is notched to make removing insulation from wire easier, while the other blade is a standard spearpoint pocketknife blade that is very useful.

DRILLS

If new plumbing or wiring is to be installed in the kitchen, you will be drilling holes through joists, studs,

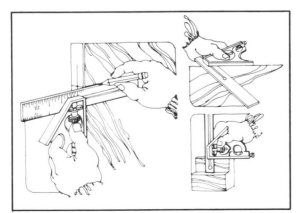

Fig. 2-29. The combination square in use (courtesy Stanley Tools).

Fig. 2-31. Marking gauges do a better job than if you mark by hand (courtesy Stanley Tools).

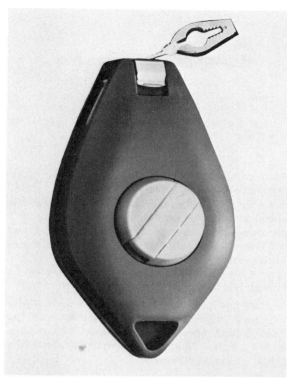

Fig. 2-32. The chalk line is excellent for marking long lines when laying ceramic or other tile and when installing flooring (courtesy Stanley Tools).

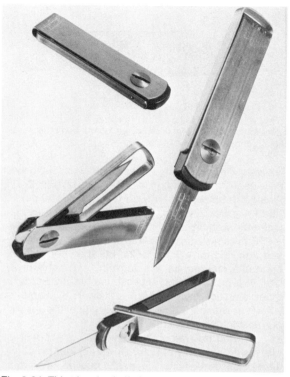

Fig. 2-34. This trimming knife folds so that it can be carried in your pocket (courtesy Stanley Tools).

Fig. 2-33. Trimming knives come in many shapes and sizes (courtesy Stanley Tools).

and floors. Even with some kinds of partially assembled cabinetry, you will need to drill the holes for the hinges and other hardware. Cabinet hanging will usually require drilling of walls to install anchor devices for hollow walls. Even installing prefabricated countertops will often require drilling to attach the top to the counter securely.

The electric drill is the tool you will most likely use. When working in homes, though, both the bit brace and the hand drill can be very handy.

The *bit brace* holds an auger bit, usually sized from ¼ inch to 1 inch or a bit more, and is turned by hand with a ratchet so it can be turned through part of the brace's circle when you're in an area short of space. Virtually all bit braces are of the ratcheting kind, and the most common will have a 10-inch sweep (bit braces with 6 and 12-inch sweeps are also available) (Fig. 2-36). Drill bits for the bit brace add to the relatively modest price of the brace itself, because drill bits require good-quality steel, even when used in wood. The *Irwin* or *solid core bit* is the cheapest good bit,

Fig. 2-35. A utility knife with a retractable blade will prove ideal for cutting resilient flooring, wallboard, and other materials (courtesy Stanley Tools).

Fig. 2-37. A solid core bit fits the brace. Sizes range for ¼ inch to well over 1 inch (courtesy Stanley Tools).

while the cleaner cutting Russell Jennings double twist bit is nearly double the price of the Irwin bit (Fig. 2-37). A single Jennings pattern wood bit can cost 30 dollars (the 1½-inch size). Such extravagance is only justified when the work involved must have very clean holes.

Bit braces don't take the number of accessories you can find for electric drills, but they can use expandable, countersinking, lockset, and screwdriver bits. The bit brace and accessories are invaluable in those situations where no electricity is available for whatever reason. They can be very useful even with an electric drill on hand.

A *hand drill* generally comes with a set of small bits inside a hollow handle. Sizes seldom go above 11/64 inch, though chuck capacity may be as great as ⅜ inch. Hand drills can be used to drill starter holes for wood screws. They are excellent for cabinetwork. A good-quality hand-drill, with eight drill bits ranging in size from 1/16 to 11/64 inch, should cost not much more than 20 dollars.

A good ⅜-inch chuck *electric drill* is an ideal investment. Sears, Montgomery Ward, Skil, Rockwell International and Black and Decker offer electric drills (Fig. 2-38). The cheapest go for less than 15 dollars, and the most expensive ones cost around 100 dollars.

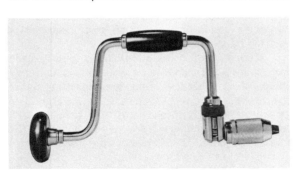

Fig. 2-36. When you're working without electric power, there is no substitute for a bit brace to make larger holes (courtesy Stanley Tools).

For most indoor remodeling work, you don't need a drill that also will serve as a rotary hammer. Reverse speed is handy for backing out stuck drills, and variable speed allows better work with different materials and accessories. The cheapest reversing variable speed drill I know of costs about 38 or 39 dollars. The impact feature is really only useful when drilling masonry, and special bits are required to take the impact (often as high as 25,000 shocks per minute).

Drill bits for electric drills come in several styles, with the twist drill bits being used for both wood and metal. Special wood-boring bits are available in sizes up to 1½ inches. Special bits drill and countersink the screw hole in one operation.

Circle cutters are to be used only with drill stands. They will cut circles in light sheet metals, laminates, hardboard, wood, and plywood (Fig. 2-39). Doweling jigs allow you to accurately align dowel holes, and drill guides help you to keep the holes being drilled straight up and down (Fig. 2-40). Stanley's drill guide has 13 hole sizes up to ¼ inch. It has a rubber backing to keep the drill bit from walking, so center punching is not needed. Other accessories include hole saws, sanding drums, contour sanders, buffing bonnets, and nut driver and screwdriver attachments. Drill stands and alignment guides are also available.

You don't even have to sharpen electric drill bits by hand. The cheapest sharpener is a drill attachment, while another sharpener has its own power source. Both accept drill bits in the following inch sizes: ⅛, 9/64, 5/32, 11/64, 3/16, 7/32, ¼, 9/32, 5/16, 11/32, and ⅜. You might want to consider the heavy-duty Craftsman model (now more than 200 dollars). This takes ⅛ to ½-inch bits.

PLANES AND CHISELS

Most chisels won't be too useful in kitchen remodeling unless you make your own cabinets and have to

Fig. 2-38. An electric drill can be used when remodeling a kitchen (courtesy Rockwell International).

clean out the bottoms of mortises. Often, though, you will need to trim wood or rip up portions of the floor or walls. Some type of chisel will be required.

Pry bars and flooring chisels will be used. The *flooring chisel* is designed to cut the tongue off tongue and groove flooring, so you can lift up a floorboard with minimal damage to the surface. It has a broad, straight blade, at least 1½ inches wide, and a long handle. The one shown in Fig. 2-41 has a 1⅞-inch-wide blade and an 18-inch-long handle. It is made of a silicon steel alloy.

Ripping bars can extend out to 3 feet and more. My Plumb ripping bar is a 3-footer. This bar has ripped off siding and a front porch. It has torn out many interior walls and portions of exterior walls. Flat pry bars such as Stanley's Wonder Bar are 13 to 14 inches long, with a width of about 1¾ inches. These serve as nail pullers, board lifters, chisels, and light ripping bars. All bars should be of some tool steel alloy (Fig. 2-42).

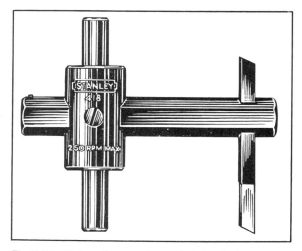

Fig. 2-39. Circle cutters can be useful when laying resilient flooring (courtesy Stanley Tools).

35

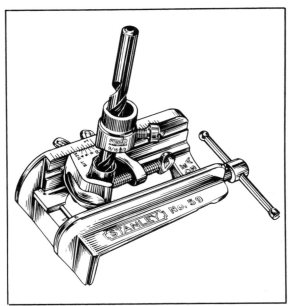

Fig. 2-40. Doweling jigs provide far greater accuracy than hand-guided drilling (courtesy Stanley Tools).

Fig. 2-41. The wide blade and long handle of the flooring chisel make it useful for removing older flooring without destroying large sections of the floor (courtesy Stanley Tools).

Standard wood chisels are not driven with a metal-headed hammer. Either plastic or wood mallets should be used to keep from destroying the chisel's handle. Socket and tang chisels are beveled chisels and good for removing wood. Japanese chisels are becoming more popular for woodworking in this country, even though they tend to be about 30 percent more expensive that comparable standard chisels. The chisels, because of their construction, take and hold a superb edge, and the handles are designed to withstand heavy mallet use. The hollow ground blades are easy to sharpen. These chisels are made of laminated metal, with a hard steel layer that registers very high on the Rockwell scale. A softer layer of steel is laminated onto this very hard but somewhat brittle layer to absorb the shock of blows during use.

Planes are easily adjusted. Make sure the adjustment is even across the base of the plane. Take your time and make your passes with gentle, firm pressure to keep from tearing off huge splinters of wood. Plane use could be required for interior doors that may not fit properly or for cabinet doors and drawers that stick.

There are basically two types of wood planes. The *bench plane* has a fairly large base (seldom under 9 inches and sometimes as much as 2 feet) and is used for smoothing wood surfaces running with the grain,

either on the face or edges of a board (Fig. 2-43). The plane iron or blade has a fairly high angle, and deep cuts can be made after you gain some basic experience.

Block planes have lower angles of cut, ranging from a cutter angle of 12 degrees up through about 21 degrees (Figs. 2-44 and 2-45). Block planes seldom exceed 6 inches in length and are meant for planing end grains and across grain, with the low angle model designed for use with hardwoods. Rabbeting planes sound different, but they are really bench planes meant to work close into corners and to rabbet boards for joinery. The blade extends all the way across the base plate of the plane, and in the bullnose model it is very close to the nose to allow work close to vertical surfaces (Fig. 2-46).

Surform tools from Stanley offer another choice

Fig. 2-42. A cat's claw pry bar is useful in many areas of remodeling (courtesy Stanley Tools).

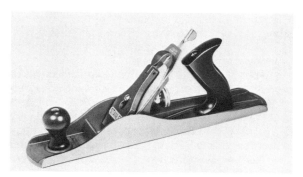

Fig. 2-43. The bench plane is ideal for removing shavings along the grain (courtesy Stanley Tools).

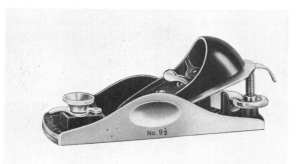

Fig. 2-45. An adjustable block plane is a handy tool (courtesy Stanley Tools).

when you need to remove material in a rush. These are similar to wood rasps, except that the teeth are cut individually in a replaceable blade, with holes behind each teeth through which material removed can pass. Material removal is quickest when the Surform is at a 45-degree angle to the direction of the stroke. Less material is removed by reducing that angle. A smooth surface results if you use the tool parallel to the work, while changing the angle against the direction of stroke tends to give a polishing effect. Surform tools come in many shapes and sizes, so material removal in all but the most confined areas is quite easy (Fig. 2-47).

NAILS AND WOOD SCREWS

The simplest device for making wood joints is the common wood *nail*. Nails are sized in pennies and styled in several ways. Common flathead nails are usually used in house framing. They come in sizes from 2 penny on to 60 penny. Anything over 60 penny

is a spike. A 2-penny nail is 1 inch long, and the 60-penny nail is 6 inches long. Box nails (similar to the common nail, but with a thinner shank), casing nails, and finish nails come in similar sizes. Casing and finish nails look very much alike, except that the casing nail has a countersink-shaped head, while the finish nail is designed to set below the work surface with a nail set. Brads are nails 1 inch and less in size. They are shaped like finish nails and are often used when assembling cabinets. See Fig. 2-48.

Wood screws provide much greater holding power than nails, but they are more expensive and take more time to use. It's not at all unusual to see few wood screws used anywhere in home construction except for hinges and other high-stress items. The most common wood screw head types are flat and round, though oval heads are also available. Most wood screws are made of mild steel, but there are brass and aluminum screws. Many screws will be painted to match a particular decor.

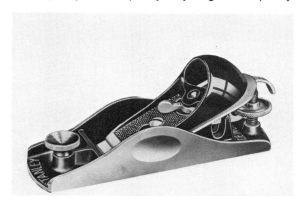

Fig. 2-44. The block plane removes end grain wood with its lower angle plane iron (courtesy Stanley Tools).

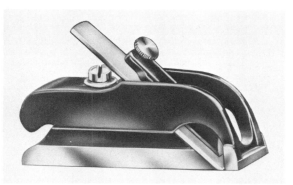

Fig. 2-46. A rabbet plane is useful for forming rabbets. The bullnosed models can work right up against obstructions (courtesy Stanley Tools).

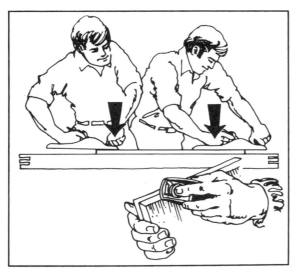

Fig. 2-47. Planes in use (courtesy Stanley Tools).

GLUES

Table 2-1 covers all readily available *glues* for today, explaining their uses and limitations quite clearly. Aliphatic resin glue (yellow glue) from United

Gilsonite Laboratories is one of the best of interior woodworking glues. Clamping time is short (about 1½ hours), and it dries overnight. It is a lot stronger than polyvinyl resin or white glues.

Apply the glue as the manufacturer directs. Make sure all surfaces being glued are clean and dry. Keep an eye on the temperature. Most wood glues work best at around room temperature or a bit higher, and very few glues work well under 60 degrees. If glue spreads out of the joint under clamping pressure, check the glue label. Most woodworkers' glues can be left to dry and are easily removed with a cabinet scraper.

Start all gluing by dry clamping the pieces to check the fit. Spread the glue, and then clamp for at least the time listed by the manufacturer. Use just enough pressure to hold the joints tightly. Too little pressure is when clamping leaves a weak joint. Too much pressure can bow the work and force glue out of the joints, making them "starved" and as weak as a poorly fitted joint.

CLAMPS

The *spring clamp* (Fig. 2-49) is good for light, small pieces. Deep throat *C clamps* up to about 4 inches are available, and the 4-inch clamp's throat

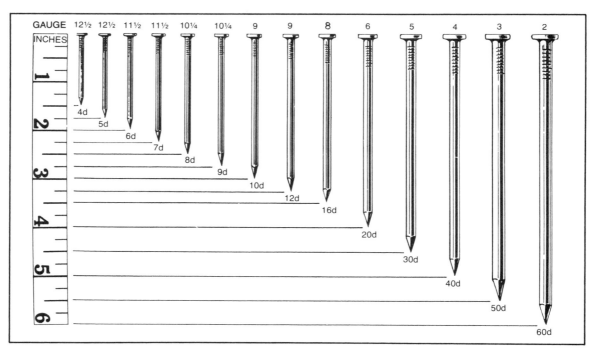

Fig. 2-48. Common wire nail sizes.

Table 2-1. Glue Selection Guide (courtesy Shopsmith Inc.).

Glue Type	Properties	Good For	Limitations
Polyvinyl resin (white glue)	Liquid, ready-to-use. Sets fast. Dries clear. Non-staining. (1½ hours clamping)	Gluing wood to wood and plywood, wood veneering, plastic laminates to wood, leather to leather and leather to wood.	Not good for high stress, lacks water resistance. Under heat, it will soften.
Aliphatic resin (yellow glue)	Liquid, ready-to-use. Very strong, tough, durable. Good heat resistance. Non-staining, bonds quickly. (1½ hours clamping)	Gluing wood to wood and plywood, wood veneering, plastic laminates to wood, leather to leather and leather to wood.	Lacks water resistance.
Contact cement	Liquid, ready-to-use. Water resistant. Adheres immediately on contact. (No clamping)	Wood veneering, plastic laminates to wood, leather to wood and rubber to wood.	Pieces cannot be shifted once contact is made.
Epoxy cement	Must be mixed. Bonds almost everything. Waterproof. (No clamping)	Gluing metal to wood, china repair, use in combination with tile, glass, metal and wood.	Not good for fastening wood to wood in large products.
Hot-melt glues	Must be heated. Sets fast. Waterproof. Flexible. (No clamping)	Mass production.	Not shock resistant. Will not take stain. Some cannot stand high temperatures.
Liquid hide	Liquid, ready-to-use. Reliable. Very strong. Resists heat and mold. (3 hours clamping)	Gluing wood to wood and plywood, wood veneering, plastic laminates to wood, leather to leather and leather to wood.	Not waterproof, must wait before clamping.
Powdered casein	Must be mixed. Strong, fairly water resistant. (3 hours clamping)	Gluing wood to wood and plywood, wood veneering, plastic laminates to wood. Good with oily woods.	Not good for outdoor uses. Will stain some wood.
Resorcinol resin	Must be mixed. Fully waterproof. Very strong. (16 hours clamping)	Gluing wood to wood and plywood, wood veneering, plastic laminates to wood, wood for marine and outdoor uses.	Dries to a dark coat and glue line.
Urea resin or plastic resin	Must be mixed. Water resistant. (8 hours clamping)	Gluing wood to wood and plywood, wood veneering, plastic laminates to wood, wood for outdoor uses.	Not good for oily woods. Becomes brittle if joints fit poorly.

depth increases from 2 to 5 inches (the price jumps about 30 percent, too) (Fig. 2-50). *Bar clamps* allow clamping of moderatley long pieces. *Pipe clamps* enable you to go considerably beyond the 2-foot bar clamp (Fig. 2-51). *Web clamps* are useful when clamping around chair legs or other irregular surfaces (Fig. 2-52).

The Maxi-Clamp from Shopsmith Inc. is a valu-able tool. Standard ⅜-inch threaded rods are used as the base for the system. Quick-acting knobs hold the various parts in place. You can tilt and slide the knobs along the threaded rod. As soon as you stop tilting, the

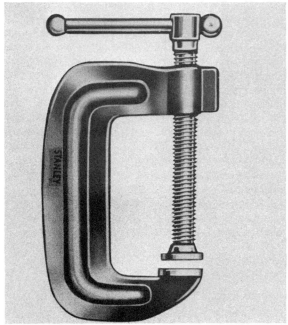

Fig. 2-50. C clamps can hold heavier items (courtesy Stanley Tools).

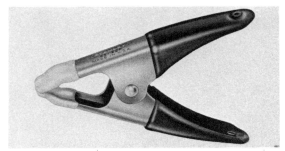

Fig. 2-49. Spring clamps hold light work for gluing (courtesy Stanley Tools).

39

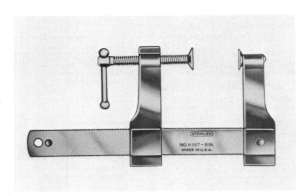

Fig. 2-51. Bar clamps fit longer items (courtesy Stanley Tools).

knobs engage the threads and can be tightened. Along with the knobs, there are pressure feet for the rod ends and clamping jaws, plus multi-hole junction blocks. Maxi-Clamp components can be used to make bench stops and bench dogs for holding work in place, or they can be assembled to form typical bar clamps. Coupling nuts are used to add length. To make a clamp to apply inside pressure, or to take apart glued items by slowly forcing the joints apart, an inside bar clamp can be made by turning the clamping jaws to face outward. Just turn the nuts with a wrench to apply as much pressure as is needed (Figs. 2-53 through 2-55).

T nuts can be used to make many clamping jigs for special shapes. Picture frames or other four-cornered assemblies can be done quite easily with the Maxi-Clamp. The system can be made into a gear and faucet puller, needing only a scrap of wood as an extra. It also makes a fine trammel point setup for scribing circles. With a bit of improvising, the same setup can be used to guide a circle-cutting saber saw. With the addition of jigs and of different length rods, this system can do many clamping jobs.

There are some points to remember concerning clamping. If the parts fit properly, the final job will be a lot stronger, so dry clamping is essential. If you're using bar clamps edge to edge to glue things, alternate clamps above and below the piece being glued to prevent buckling of the work. If you alternate the clamps every foot or so along the work, buckling should not be a problem. If your clamps don't have wooden faces, either use scrap blocks of wood or slip-on protectors to avoid marring the surfaces of the work being glued. Wood screws will collect glue on the jaws unless you keep them well-coated with boiled linseed oil or beeswax.

Bar clamps of extruded aviation aluminum alloy are available from Shopsmith in lengths of 2, 3, 4, and 6 feet. Clamp pads are also available, or you can make your own wood faces to prevent marring. These bar clamps are somewhat costly, but they are invaluable if needed for large gluing projects.

FINISHING TOOLS AND MATERIALS

Wood finishing requires a smaller number of tools, and much depends on the type of surface you desire. Cabinet scrapers and wood scrapers in other styles are readily available (Fig. 2-56). They do an excellent job in smoothing wood surfaces. Once the wood is prepared, you're ready to begin final finishing.

On old cabinets being renewed, start with a paint and varnish remover such as ZAR (Fig. 2-57). ZAR is one of the most highly rated paint and varnish removers, with a paste form to make working on vertical surfaces simpler. When the old finish is removed, select the type of stain you wish to use and apply it. Stains today are usually of the wipe-on type, and each manufacturer will supply specific application directions (Fig. 2-58).

The final finishing step is the application of either a wipe-on or a brush-on finish. For very highly polished surfaces, you'll probably most often use a brush-on

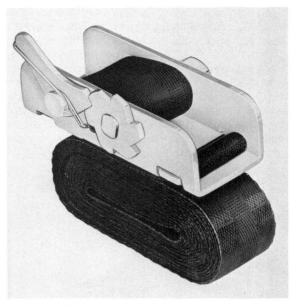

Fig. 2-52. Web or strap clamps are extremely useful for irregularly-shaped objects that must be clamped during gluing (courtesy Stanley Tools).

Fig. 2-53. The unassembled Maxi-Clamp (courtesy Shopsmith Inc.).

Fig. 2-54. The Maxi-Clamp can also serve as a gear puller (courtesy Shopsmith Inc.).

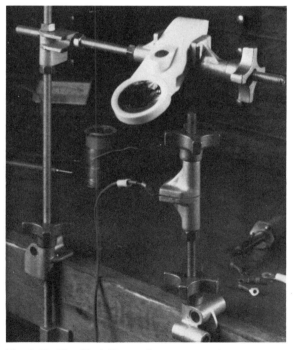

Fig. 2-55. The Maxi-Clamp also acts as a hold-down for electrical work (courtesy Shopsmith Inc.).

Fig. 2-56. Handled cabinet scrapers can be used to apply more pressure (courtesy Stanley Tools).

finish, though ZAR's wipe-on finish has a nice gloss and is resistant to most common chemicals. Brush-on polyurethane coatings provide the greatest possible protection today. Any finish that is also recommended for use on floors should withstand life on a cabinet door quite well. Wipe-on finishes such as United Gilsonite Laboratories ZAR tung oil are not for floor use, but they provide an excellent semigloss surface for cabinets and other spots (Fig. 2-59).

Always make sure any surface being finished or refinished is clean and dry. All dirt, oils, old wax, sanding dust, and grease should be removed with a solvent

Fig. 2-58. Wipe-on stain is probably your best choice (courtesy United Gilsonite Laboratories).

Fig. 2-57. ZAR paint and varnish remover is fast and easy to use (courtesy United Gilsonite Laboratories).

Fig. 2-59. For a glossier finish, use a brush-on product and a fine quality brush (courtesy United Gilsonite Laboratories).

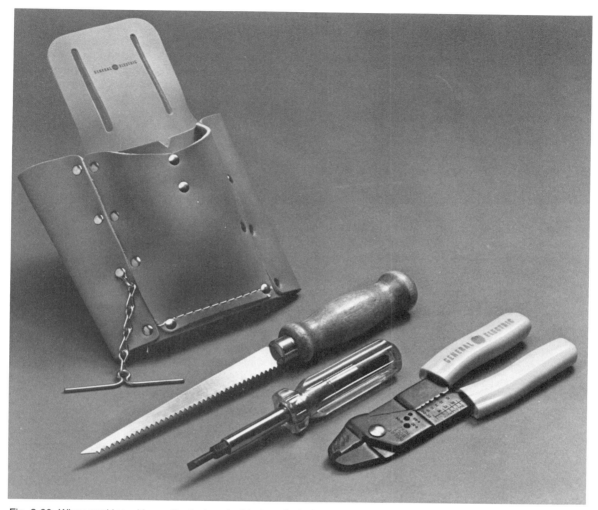

Fig. 2-60. When working with smaller tools, a belt holster for holding such items as a screwdriver, a hole saw, and a wire stripper is exceptionally handy (courtesy General Electric).

before the new finish is applied. Use either a tack rag or a soft rag dipped in paint thinner for wiping before application. ZAR polyurethane finishes take from four to six hours to dry. The first coat should always be thinned with 1 part mineral spirits to 2 parts of the coating. The final coat goes on at full strength, and floors should receive a third coat. Sand lightly and dust very carefully between coats. If three coats are applied, the first two are thinned as mentioned earlier. Stir the mixtures both before and during use. Use a brush to apply the coating, using as few strokes as possible.

PLUMBING TOOLS

Your selection of plumbing tools for kitchen installation work will vary according to the amount of work you plan on doing. If no new plumbing is being installed, and the old plumbing doesn't have to be removed, you can skip this part. If new cabinets are to be installed, old plumbing must usually be removed. Improvements you might consider making are the installation of cutoff valves under each appliance (in the water supply to the appliance) and swapping steel pipes for plastic ones. Genova, Inc. makes many adapters for working plastic pipe into older systems.

Copper tubing requires the largest number of tools for any type of plumbing today. You'll need a propane or MAPP gas torch and a flaring tool, a tubing cutter with a tubing reamer, a tubing bender, a hacksaw, solder and flux, and basic woodworking handtools for drilling holes and driving nails and screws. Adjustable pipe and strap wrenches are needed. The pipe wrench can usually be substituted for the strap wrench. A strap wrench is designed to remove chromed fittings without damaging their surfaces. A good pipe wrench will do the same job if you wrap the item to be removed with a couple of layers of duct tape.

Slide calipers are useful, though not essential, for measuring inside and outside diameters. You will need a top-quality tape measure or folding rule, or both. Pliers may or may not be needed. I like to keep a couple of pairs of locking pliers on hand for use as clamps when soldering joints that might move before the solder cools. Inside and outside pipe diameters can be easily measured with a rule, but circumferences require the use of a more flexible device such as a tape.

For working with thermoplastic pipe, you must have an electric or other type drill, drill bits in the required sizes, a hammer, measuring tape, a 2-foot level, utility knife, pipe wrench, appropriate adjustable wrenches, and possibly a handsaw, compass saw, and a hacksaw. Plastic pipe can be cut with any fine-tooth saw, but the best cuts are made with a backsaw and miter box. Genova *chlorinated polyvinyl chloride* (CPVC) and *polybutylene* (PB) pipe can be flared with a standard flaring tool. You will also need cement for the type of plastic being used and cleaner to remove dirt, grease, oil, and any other residues that might cause a joint to leak. Thermoplastic pipe will usually withstand up to 800 pounds per square inch (psi), but the joints, once cemented, are totally permanent and cannot be changed. Any skipping of steps can be fatal to long pipe runs if a joint starts to leak. Careful measurement and cutting, combined with correct assembly, will mean a long-lasting, economical plumbing system.

ELECTRICAL TOOLS

Tools needed for rewiring or wiring a kitchen include keyhold or compass saws, a drill and the appropriate bit sizes, a hammer, circuit tester, wire stripper, and an electrician's knife (Fig. 2-60). You will also want a fish tape on a reel if the walls are not to be opened up all the way.

Continuity testers, voltage testers, outlet analyzers, and volt-ohm-ammeters usually will not be needed. The more complex multimeters can provide useful information if there are circuit problems, but newly installed circuits, done properly, should have no problems.

Residential wiring should be planned well and done neatly according to codes and instructions. If your work is done in that manner, there should be no problems requiring expensive testing equipment.

Chapter 3

Plumbing

MOST PLUMBING IN MULTIPLE-STORY HOUSES today is done on the stack system, while one story homes get back-to-back systems. There are two reasons for keeping plumbing runs as short as possible. The first is to conserve materials. The second is to conserve energy. Short hot water runs lose less heat than long ones. Plastic pipe for plumbing runs is much cheaper than copper pipe.

You essentially have two water systems in your home—one for supplying water and one for disposing wastes. In both cases there will be several hundred feet of pipe in the average house, with fittings needed to join them to each other and to appliances. Urban water supply systems generally operate at about 50 pounds per square inch (psi) of pressure, so these pipes are relatively small in diameter. Suburban and rural water supply pressures may vary from 20 psi to 50 psi. The disposal system (also called the drain/waste/vent or DWV system) is gravity-fed and requires larger-diameter pipe to prevent clogging and backup. These two systems are never connected to each other, because waste water might back up and contaminate drinking water.

When you consider that every adult uses somewhere between 50 and 100 gallons of water per day,

the load on a DWV system and the attendant supply system can be readily understood. Your water supply system will use pipes usually no larger than 1 inch in size. Individual pipes supplying hot or cold water to sinks may be as small as ⅜ inch. Your water supply may be from a well or a city water supply. There is a main shutoff valve in either case. Locate this valve if you don't know where it is. The water runs into the house main from this main shutoff valve.

Your house main line is then run close to the water heater and branched off to deliver water to be heated and water to remain cold. The pipe that leaves the water heater is the start of your hot water system. Both hot and cold water supplies are then run to various fixtures by pipes called *hot water* and *cold water mains*. Branches from the mains lead to groups of fixtures and large water-using fixtures (kitchen sinks, dishwashers, laundry appliances bathtubs, and showers). Pipes running vertically through walls are called *risers*.

AIR CHAMBERS AND CUTOFF VALVES

Air chambers are foot-long lengths of pipe, capped at the top end, that run up beyond the fitting for the fixture (Fig. 3-1). Air chambers cushion the shock,

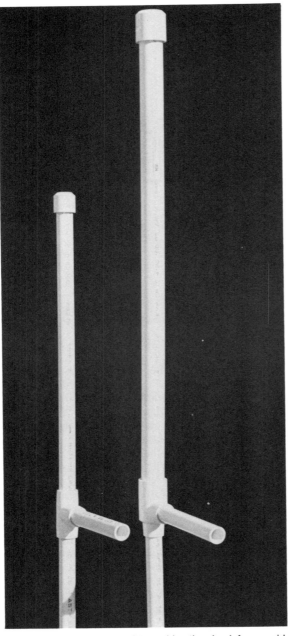

using trapped air, of water when it makes the quick turn to your faucet. This reduces or eliminates *hammering*. The pressure associated with water hammer is also hard on the faucets and on pipe runs.

In good-quality water supply systems, each fixture has its own cutoff valve just under the fixture or the floor beneath the fixture (assuming the floor is open from underneath). Such cutoff valves make it much easier to shut down one portion of a water system in order to make repairs to a toilet or sink. From the cutoff valve, a ⅜-inch diameter flexible riser tube or pipe provides water supply to the fixture. The risers may come from the floor or the wall.

Washing machines are connected to hot and cold water faucets with hoses that are usually supplied with the machines. You will get longer service from washing machine inlet valves if you turn off the taps after each use. Dishwashers are normally connected directly to the hot water supply main. A cutoff valve is used somewhere in the pipe, so the machine can be removed for repairs without cutting off the water supply to your house.

DWV PIPES

The drain/waste/vent system starts at the fixtures and appliances where the supply system ends. The DWV pipes must have a slight downward slope in order to assist the flow of waste. The turns are designed with corners slightly less than square, so the slope is more easily maintained. Water then flows from each fixture to the city sewer system or to a private disposal system. The first DWV pipe at the fixture or appliance is called the *waste pipe*. The toilet DWV pipe is called the *soil pipe*. Fixture waste pipes and toilet soil pipes enter a vertical pipe called a *stack* or *soil stack*. The lower end of the stack leads into the building drain. Any stack serving a toilet is called either a main stack or soil stack. Every residence has at least one, measuring 3 to 4 inches in diameter. The top end of any stack continues its run to the roof and is left open; this is the *vent*. A secondary or waste stack may measure as little as 2 inches, and a few are as small as 1½ inches (Figs. 3-2 through 3-10).

The building drain is a horizontal pipe, 3 to 4 inches in diameter, that collects waste water from all the fixtures and appliances in the house and then carries it out of the house. When the building drain is 5 feet beyond the house exterior, it becomes the house sewer (this house sewer must be below ground). The house sewer then slopes along underground to join the city sewer or your private septic field.

Fig. 3-1. Air chambers used to cushion the shock from rapid shutoff of running water are needed on all fixtures. The standard air chamber (left) is part of what plumbers call the fixture drop. The larger chamber is needed with extremely rapid shutoff appliances such as washing machines and dishwashers. Air chambers prevent pipe damage from water hammer (courtesy Genova, Inc.).

46

Fig. 3-2. Use a short section of pipe to mark for a new DWV pipe (courtesy Genova, Inc.).

Fig. 3-3. Cut out excess material. Be careful not to hit wires or other plumbing runs (courtesy Genova, Inc.).

Fig. 3-4. Material is drilled out to make cutting easier. Power saws will usually not fit into such areas, though a reciprocating saw may work (courtesy Genova, Inc.).

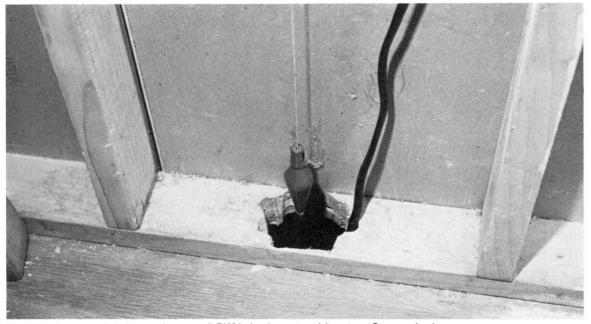

Fig. 3-5. Use a plumb bob to make sure all DWV pipe is centered (courtesy Genova, Inc.).

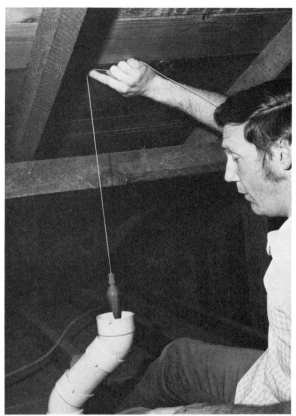

Fig. 3-6. Use of the plumb bob must continue right on up to the roof area and beyond, as the pipe must line up exactly (courtesy Genova, Inc.).

Fig. 3-7. Vent stacks run through the roof and are cut off at the correct height. Make sure they are at least 18 inches above the roof surface (courtesy Genova, Inc.).

DWV TRAPS

Traps are U-shaped and water-filled sections of pipe that allow water to pass. Traps keep gases and vermin from getting inside the DWV pipes at the fixtures and appliances. Every appliance and fixture in the house must have a trap. Toilets have built-in traps. The water inside is part of the trap seal and is replenished by a water supply in the tank. Other fixtures and appliances need separate traps, usually with the traps set underneath the fixture and concealed. Sinks and lavatories will have either S-shaped or P-shaped trap pipes, which include a U-section, with one end connecting to the fixture drain and the other to the DWV system's waste pipe. The trap diameter must be as large as the diameter of the tailpiece coming down from the fixture or appliance drain. Slip joints are used. They are made gastight and watertight by soft ring gaskets.

Bathtub and shower traps may be either large P-shaped units or drum types. Any trap must provide access in case of clogging. Most toilet and sink or lavatory traps can be cleaned topside through the drain for the fixture. Some bathtub and shower traps may be cleaned the same way. The best P and S-shaped traps are built with a cleanout plug at the lowest part of the U-section (Fig. 3-11).

VENTING

Venting is necessary with P and S-traps, because water rushing through a pipe causes a vacuum or suction. Siphoning action is often powerful enough to suck all the water from a trap and leave it almost dry. Venting prevents siphoning in your system's other traps. All venting is done to the outside, above the roof. Venting also prevents pressurization in the DWV sys-

Fig. 3-8. Genova's Snap-Fit kit comes in sizes to fit vent pipes from 1-¼ inch to 4 inches in diameter. It is a two-piece unit. The bottom piece fits under the shingles (courtesy Genova, Inc.).

Fig. 3-9. When the top piece of the Genova Snap-Fit is in place, you have a leak-free vent pipe (courtesy Genova, Inc.).

Fig. 3-10. Genova's Raingo spray paint can be used to color the vent pipe to match the roof (courtesy Genova, Inc.).

tem that, if not prevented, could force gases past the trap's water seals.

A waste pipe from a fixture can be drained and vented through the same pipe. Known as *wet venting*, this happens to all fixtures for at least a short distance. The wet-venting length is limited by plumbing codes. If the wet-vented length is too long, some form of alternative venting must be provided. Adding a vent that runs up to the roof is one way. Reventing is the most common solution and involves adding a stack closer to the branch vent or fixture. The revent is a vent-only pipe leading upward from the fixture waste pipe. It bends as needed to meet and connect with the stack above the point where the highest fixture waste pipe enters the stack. The stack entered need not be the same one into which the fixture drains.

Stacks and vents are usually of the same size pipe used to drain a fixture, although a vent a size or two smaller is occasionally allowed. No vent or waste pipe is ever under 1¼ inches in diameter. More recent construction uses nothing smaller than 1½ inches.

Drain/waste/vent systems will offer cleanouts to allow you to remove inside-the-system stoppages. Every horizontal drainage run must have cleanout access, usually provided by a cleanout opening at the higher end of the run. Genova, Inc., provides special

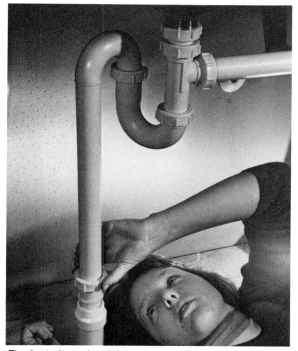

Fig. 3-11. An under-sink trap is essential (courtesy Genova, Inc.).

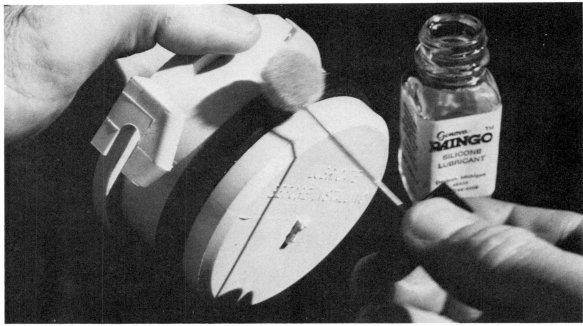

Fig. 3-12. The Twist-Lok gasket is coated with Raingo lubricant before it is installed (courtesy Genova, Inc.).

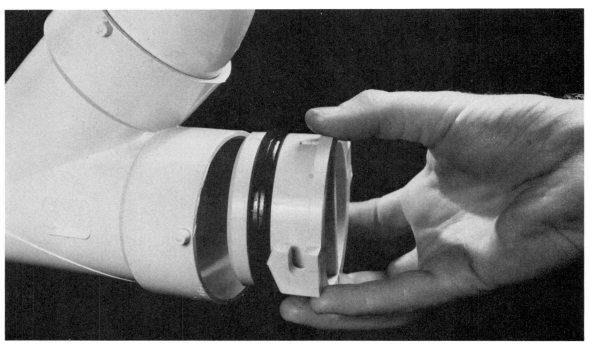

Fig. 3-13. The Twist-Lok is inserted in any Genova hub of the same size and twisted until its ears lock over the hub's pins (courtesy Genova, Inc.)

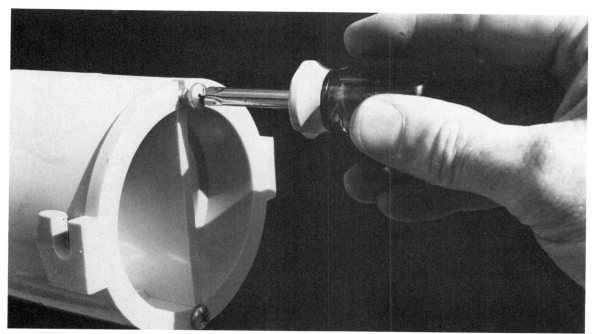

Fig. 3-14. When no pins are available, two sheet metal screws are used to hold the Twist-Lok in place (courtesy Genova, Inc.).

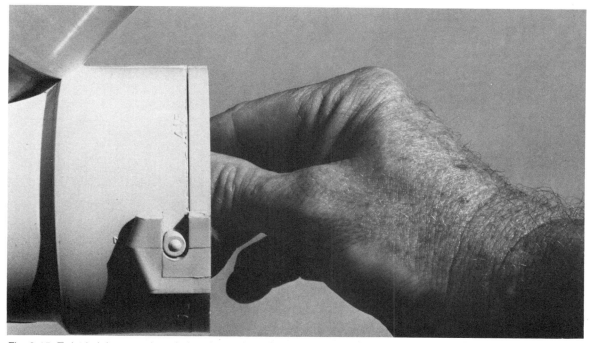

Fig. 3-15. Twist-Lok is, to my knowledge, the easiest of all cleanouts to install and use (courtesy Genova, Inc.).

Twist-Lok covers that require no tools for removal and reinstallation. They have no threads. You also need a cleanout opening in the house sewer line (Figs. 3-12 through 3-15).

DWV FITTINGS

Drain/waste/vent fittings are not made in quite the same way as are those used for the water supply.

Drainage fittings have gentle bends to aid gravity flow by cutting resistance to that flow (Fig. 3-16). Water supply fittings of all kinds make abrupt 90 or 45-degree changes in direction. The changes are much less abrupt in DWV fittings. Common DWV fittings are elbows, tees, wyes, and various kinds of couplings.

CODE COMPLIANCE

Code compliance is of extreme importance.

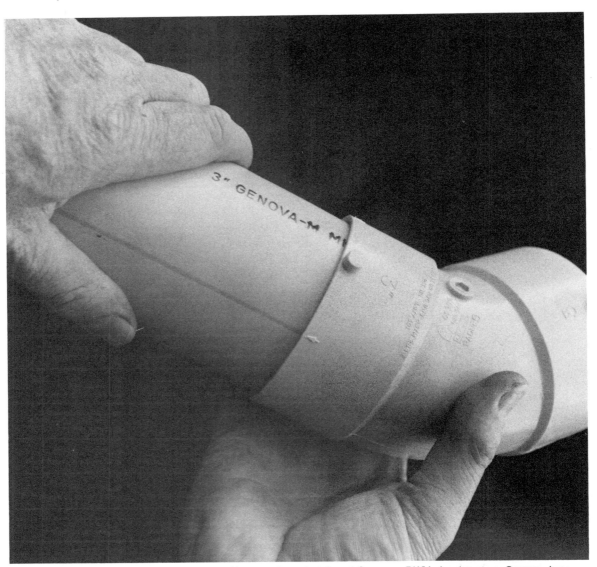

Fig. 3-16. Gentle bends and an alignment marking are characteristics of Genova's DWV pipe (courtesy Genova, Inc.).

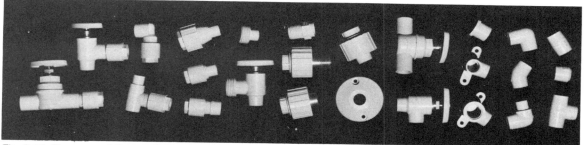

Fig. 3-17. The array of Genova fittings is wide enough to do any home plumbing job (courtesy Genova, Inc.).

Building inspectors can rescind a certificate of occupancy for noncompliance in materials or methods. Plastic pipe can now be used in most locations. Some codes are open to various interpretations, but it is best to get things straightened out before starting work.

SUPPLY SYSTEMS

Chlorinated polyvinyl chloride (CPVC) is almost universally accepted as a supply (and DWV) system material, and CPVC is a tougher version of the older *polyvinyl chloride* (PVC). For unprotected outdoor

Fig. 3-18. Any fine-toothed handsaw can be used to cut rigid plastic pipe (courtesy Genova, Inc.).

Fig. 3-19. Flexible PB pipe combines well with CPVC rigid pipe to make plumbing jobs easier (courtesy Genova, Inc.).

use, polybutylene (PB) is used. *Polybutylene* is a heat-resistant flexible thermoplastic that is also approved for interior use.

Pipe

Chlorinated polyvinyl chloride pipe is rigid and light beige in color. Diameters available are ¾ and ½-inch, in 10-foot lengths. These are easily cut to size with any fine-toothed handsaw and are readily solvent welded (Figs. 3-17 and 3-18).

Polybutylene pipe is a flexible beige pipe for hot and cold water supply use. It is available in 1, ¾, ½, ⅜, and ¼-inch diameters in 100-foot coils and, except for the 1-inch diameter pipe, in 25-foot coils (Fig. 3-19). It can be cut with a knife and joined with special PB/CPVC adapters, as well as regular CPVC solvent weld fittings. Genova even supplies some CPVC fittings with PB adapters already in place (Fig. 3-20). Both types of plastic are accepted by the Federal Housing Administration.

The diameters specified are for the inside diameter in most cases. Pipe with a ¾-inch inside diameter will have an outside diameter of ⅞ inch, while PB with a 1-inch inside diameter will measure 1⅛ inches.

Plastic pipe is self-insulating and noncorrosive. Because the plastic pipe doesn't conduct electricity, there is no dielectric action between dissimilar metals to eat away pipe.

Chlorinated polyvinyl chloride is made by adding an extra atom to the molecular structure of PVC. This increases overall toughness and heat resistance, making the CPVC particularly good for pressurized pipe systems. When selecting plastic pipe and fittings, choose from a list provided by one manufacturer. Fitting tolerances are quite wide in the industry standards for inside and outside diameters. Each manufacturer

Fig. 3-20. Both PB and CPVC pipe fit adapters (courtesy Genova, Inc.).

designs and produces fittings and pipe that work well together. The fittings and pipe may not work well with those from another manufacturer.

Genova is the oldest and largest manufacturer of CPVC pipe and fittings. Their CPVC pipe comes in the natural color of the plastic, with no fillers, and is made to rigid tolerances. Leaking joints are rare (Fig. 3-21).

Solvents

Solvents used to weld joints are just as important as the pipe when it comes to quality. Always use the solvent recommended by the manufacturer of the pipe and fittings; normally, that manufacturer will also produce the solvent. Solvent welding is a relatively easy job, but it should always be carried through fully with no skimping (Fig. 3-22).

Measuring the Pipe Run

Begin the plumbing job with careful measurement of the pipe run. Allow for the depth of the fitting socket, which varies from fitting to fitting. You must allow for

this depth on both ends of pipe runs. Start the fitting job by making a square cut to the properly marked length, using a fine-toothed saw or a tubing cutter with a special vinyl wheel (Fig. 3-23). Use a sharp knife or sandpaper to remove all burrs from the cut edge, and then use a clean rag to apply primer (cleaner) (Figs. 3-24 and 3-25). Check the assembly for position and fit. Disassemble and give the fitting a sparing coat of solvent. Give the pipe a liberal coating of solvent. (Immediately push the pipe into the socket, using a slight twisting motion until the pipe bottoms in the socket. Make the alignment adjustment immediately on bottoming of the pipe, or the solvent will set up with things turned the wrong way (Figs. 3-26 and 3-27).

If your system already has threaded or sweat soldered metal pipes installed, you don't have to replace them in order to use plastic pipe in the new sections. Transition fittings do the job. Because metal and vinyl have different rates of expansion, specially designed adapters are required—especially on hot

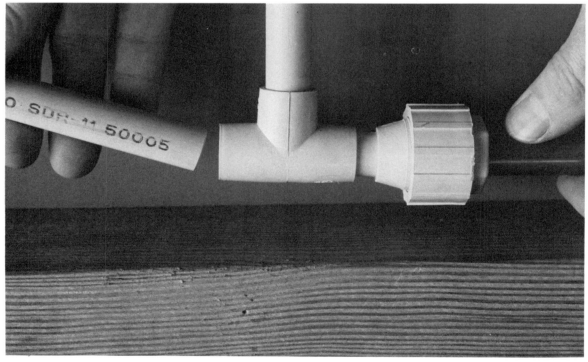

Fig. 3-21. Close tolerances are as essential to a leak-free fit with plastic pipe as with any other kind. Make sure pipe and fittings are all bought from the same manufacturer (courtesy Genova, Inc.).

58

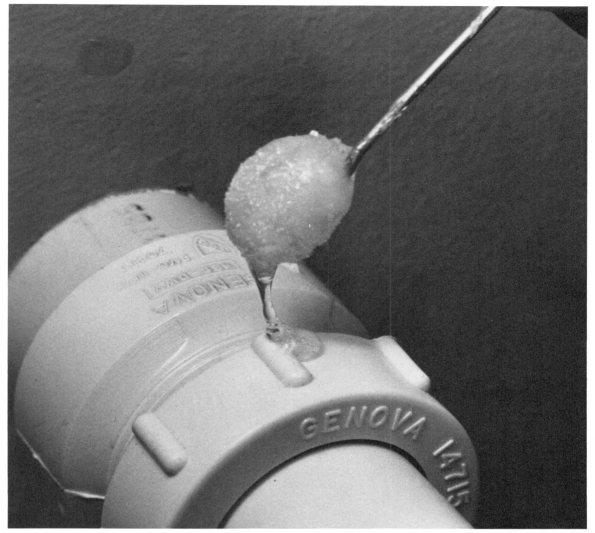

Fig. 3-22. Solvent welding assures a tight joint if carried out correctly (courtesy Genova, Inc.).

water pipe runs. Genova's transition fittings provide two faces that meet across a rubber gasket. Each face is able to expand or contract at its own rate, so leaks are eliminated. Transition fittings are also useful as unions because they provide easy disassembly of the connections at any time (Figs. 3-28 through 3-34).

Make-up dimensions add some difficulty to the taking of measurements for pipe runs, because you need a measuring device that will slip into the socket of the fitting to get the socket depth. Some Genova fit-

tings provide make-up dimensions. For other fittings, you will still need to take depth measurements. Always subtract for center-to-end make-up dimensions. You are getting the measurement for overall distance, including the full size of the fitting, and then you are subtracting the amount of the fitting that is not socket depth. For fittings in position, you can measure face-to-face of each pair of fittings, and then add socket depth of ½ inch for ½-inch inside-diameter (ID) pipe and 11/16 inch for ¾-inch ID pipe.

Fig. 3-23. Rigid CPVC cuts easily and squarely with a fine-toothed backsaw in a miter box (courtesy Genova, Inc.).

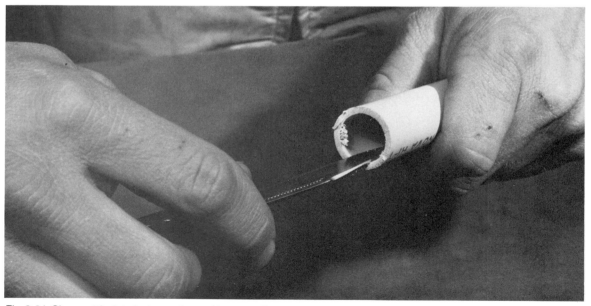

Fig. 3-24. Clean out the interior burrs after making a cut. The burrs will impede waterflow if not cleaned away (courtesy Genova, Inc.).

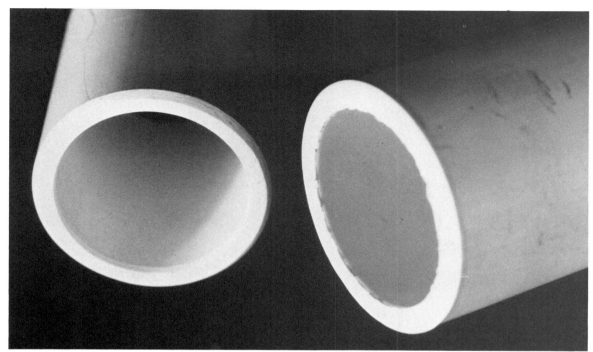

Fig. 3-25. Properly chamfering the outside and inside edges of ends to fit in fittings reduces water flow resistance. Make sure no cleaning is done on the area of the pipe to be run into or solvent welded to the fitting (courtesy Genova, Inc.).

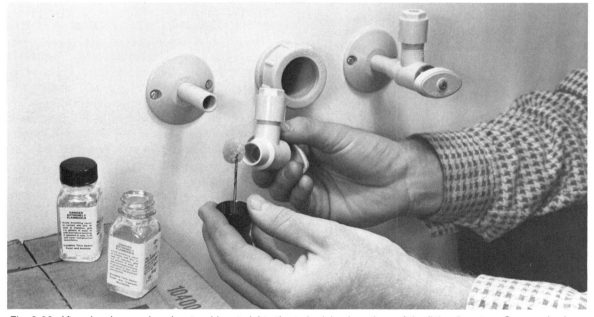

Fig. 3-26. After cleaning, apply solvent weld material to the to-be-joined sections of the fitting (courtesy Genova, Inc.).

61

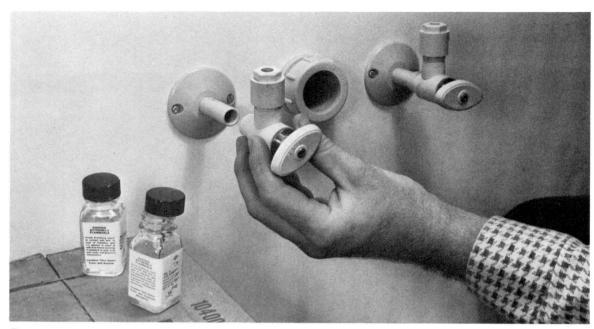

Fig. 3-27. Make the joint immediately after applying solvent weld (courtesy Genova, Inc.).

Dry Disassembly of Components

A dry disassembly of major components to check for overall fit is an excellent idea. It is best to do dry assembly of no more than three fittings per run. Use a grease pencil to make the correct mark for fitting position (on the outside of the fitting and above the solvent line on the pipe). Putting together an entire run of 12 or more dry fittings is almost a sure way to guarantee that you will forget to take one joint apart. Once that happens, you will leave a dry joint that will leak. It will then have to be disassembled, dried, and solvent welded after you drain the system.

System Design

System design is another factor in long life and good operation. Polyvinyl chloride pipe is rated to withstand 100 psi of water pressure at 180 degrees Fahrenheit. Using air chambers at all fixtures and water-using appliances is one way to keep pressures from building up too much. Plastic pipe cannot be restrained against thermal expansion and contraction. You must allow for some movement. Start by using the correct pipe hangers, at 32-inch intervals, for the brand

of pipe you are using. These will be designed to allow the pipe to slide freely. When installing long runs of plastic pipe, don't have them touching walls or framing at the end. Leave a little room for expansion (Fig. 3-35). Use foot doglegs to provide an offset in pipe runs more than 35 feet long. Such dogleg offsets will bend enough to allow for expansion needs. The CPVC risers coming off CPVC mains should be unbound and long enough from the main to the point of entering the wall or ceiling to allow for slight movement of the main. Eight inches is usually sufficient. The PB risers don't need the allowance, because they are flexible. In general, allow ¼ inch of end-to-end expansion room for every 10 feet of CPVC pipe.

Polybutylene (PB) pipe is a fairly high temperature thermoplastic that allows you to install flexible hot and cold water lines. The flexibility of PB is great enough that long pipe runs may be installed with no joints, elbows, or other fittings. Any expansion of the pipe is absorbed by the flex. The PB pipe can simply be threaded through walls (Fig. 3-36).

The PB pipe from Genova is used with Genogrip fittings. These fittings seal off the water, and then they mechanically hold the pipe. An *O-ring* of elastomeric

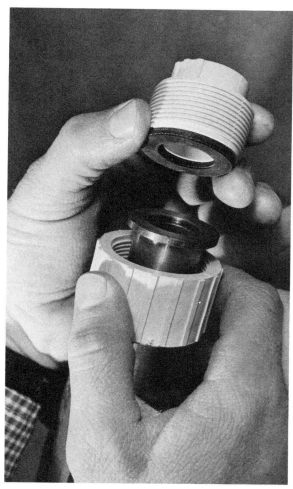

Fig. 3-28. Bring the parts of the transistion fitting together, after the lower portion has been set on the metal pipe (courtesy Genova, Inc.).

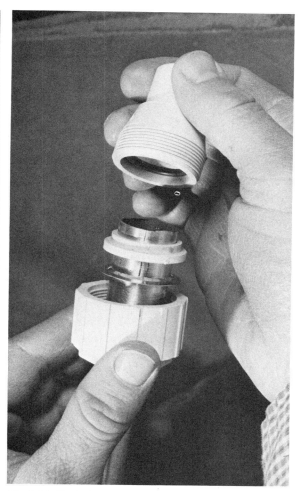

Fig. 3-29. Gasketing material is pushed down onto the metal pipe (courtesy Genova, Inc.).

material acts as a water seal, while a split grab ring of Noryl holds the pipe in place mechanically. Noryl is a springy form of plastic (Figs. 3-37 through 3-40).

The PB pipe is inserted through the O-ring to bottom out on the shoulder inside the fitting. When the fitting nut is tightened, a cone-shaped inner surface on that nut puts the lock on a cone-shaped outer surface on the grab ring. Then a ridge on the inside of the grab ring digs into the pipe, making a slight groove and locking the fitting on the pipe. This connection has been tested to hold up under 200 psi at 180 degrees Fahrenheit for a period of 11.2 years. The burst

strength of the fitting exceeds that of the pipe. The nut can't be overtightened as it bottoms out first. The fitting can be taken off and reconnected as often as necessary. Assembly is simple. Make a square cut on the PB pipe with a knife, leaving about 1½ inches to enter the fitting. Simply insert the pipe into the fitting and hand-tighten the nut.

Genova adapters for PB pipe come in ⅜, ½, and ¾-inch sizes, so the flexible plastic piping can be used almost anywhere in your supply system. These items also adapt to Genova's CPVC fittings.

Genova's Poly Risers are ⅜-inch PB pipes used

Fig. 3-30. The units are then joined (courtesy Genova, Inc.).

Fig. 3-31. The fitting is then set up with solvent cement (courtesy Genova, Inc.).

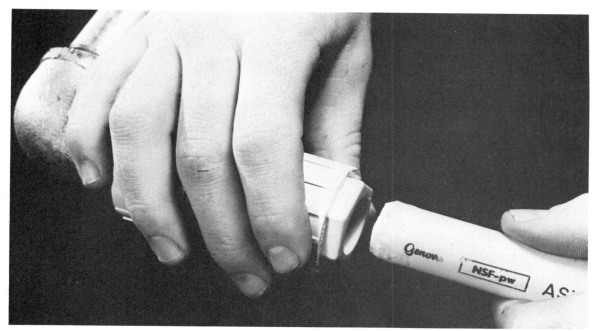

Fig. 3-32. The new line is now inserted (courtesy Genova, Inc.).

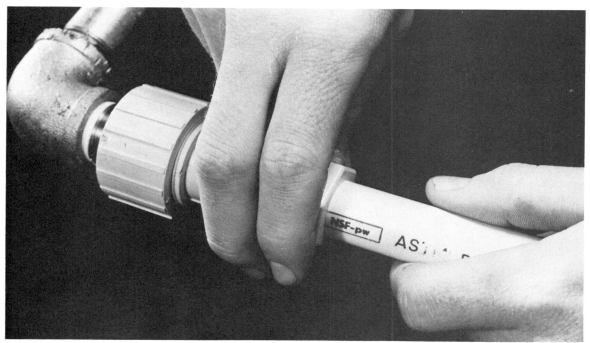

Fig. 3-33. Everything is tightened down (courtesy Genova, Inc.).

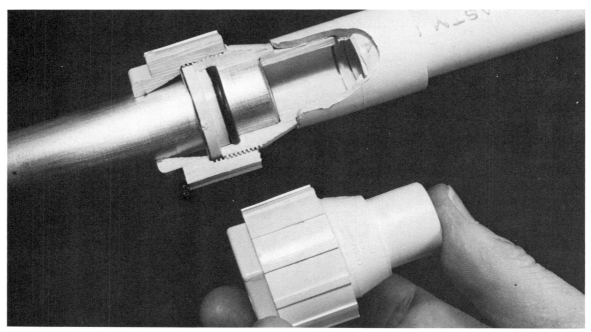

Fig. 3-34. This cutaway photo shows the insides of one type of transition fitting (courtesy Genova, Inc.).

Fig. 3-35. This elbow is too close to the joist. At least ¼ inch of clearance is needed to allow for expansion and contraction (courtesy Genova, Inc.).

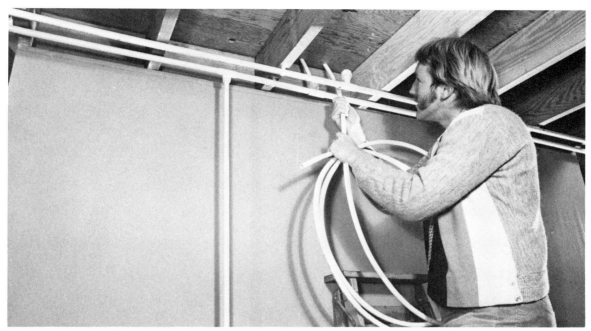

Fig. 3-36. Polybutylene pipe's flexibility makes it the easiest to use in remodeling work where walls must be threaded. It comes in 25 and 100-foot coils and can be used for both hot and cold supply runs (courtesy Genova, Inc.).

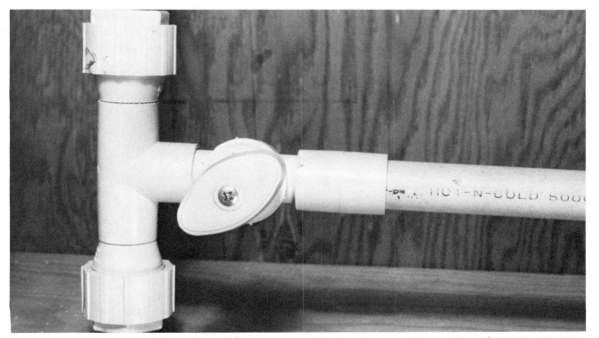

Fig. 3-37. Tap-off with Genova's Genogrips, using two on a copper line. No soldering is required. The tee is ¾ inch, with a ½ by ¾-inch line-stop valve, and ¾-inch coupling and ¾-inch supply running to the add-on kitchen (courtesy Genova, Inc.).

67

Fig. 3-38. When a solvent welded joint has set, a flexible Poly-Riser fixture supply tube can be pushed into the Genogrip fitting and hand-tightened so it is leak-free (courtesy Genova, Inc.).

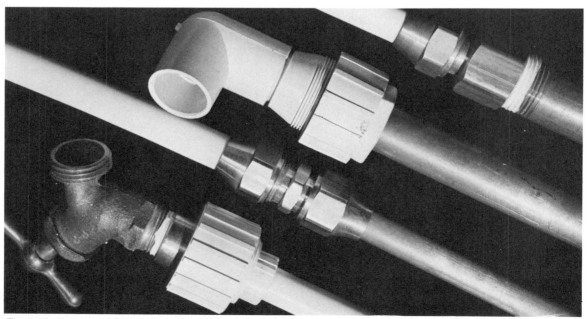

Fig. 3-39. An array of Genova transition fittings (courtesy Genova, Inc.).

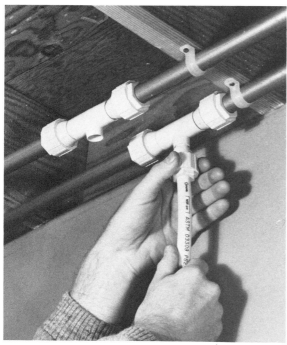

Fig. 3-40. Genogrip adapter and CPVC tees make tapping in for the new supply easy (courtesy Genova, Inc.).

to hook up fixtures and provide a connection that can withstand 800 psi. Poly Risers come in two styles. One style has a bullet nose for connecting sinks and lavatories, and the other has a flange end for connecting toilets. They are available in 12 and 20-inch lengths. Lavatory types are also available in 3-foot lengths (Figs. 3-41 and 3-42).

Both CPVC and PB pipes can be used for any water supply purpose inside the house. The PB pipe can be laid in trenches below ground from a well or the city water main. The slightly cheaper CPVC pipe can be used for most indoor purposes that do not require flexibility. Switch to PB pipe when flexibility is needed. The PB pipe is most useful for remodeling jobs when you can't reach the interiors of all the walls where plumbing runs must be located, and for riser installation beneath fixtures. Because PB can be used to turn corners (with a minimum bend radius of 2 inches for ⅜-inch PB pipe), no corner fittings are needed.

Drain/waste/vent systems have characteristically been made of cast iron, but plastic is easy to work with and more durable than cast iron. Chemical plants have found plastic pipe suitable for carrying very strong acid or alkaline solutions. The light weight of plastic pipe also is an advantage. A 2-inch PVC-DWV pipe, 10 feet long, weighs only 6 pounds. The smooth interior of the

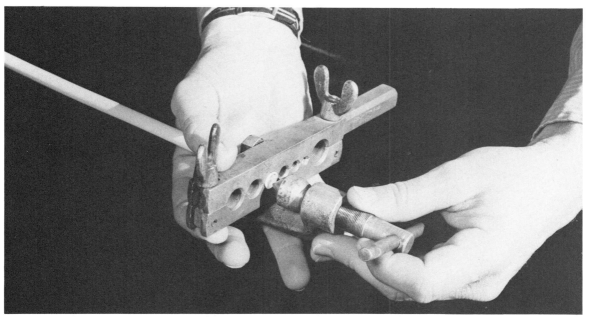

Fig. 3-41. Polypropylene riser tubes are easily fitted to nonstandard plain copper tube faucet tailpieces by flaring both. When the riser tube is flared, it can then be joined to a flared faucet tailpiece with a simple flare coupling (courtesy Genova, Inc.).

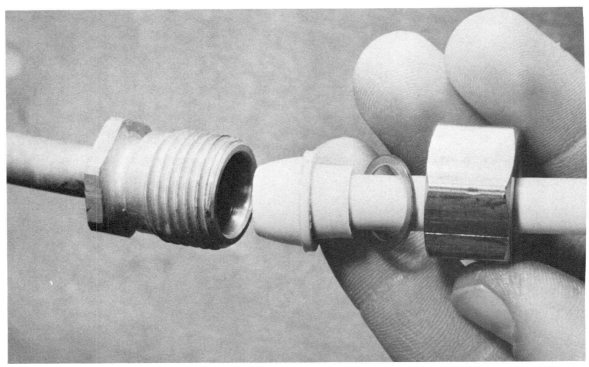

Fig. 3-42. The bullet-nosed end at the top of a polypropylene riser tube fits directly into most faucet tailpieces. It is held in place with a ½-inch faucet nut and, sometimes, a brass washer (courtesy Genova, Inc.).

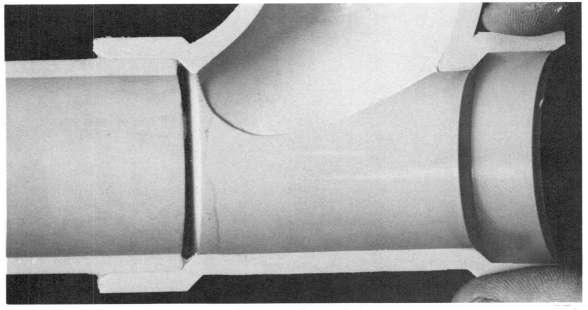

Fig. 3-43. Genova DWV pipe has a smooth interior (courtesy Genova, Inc.).

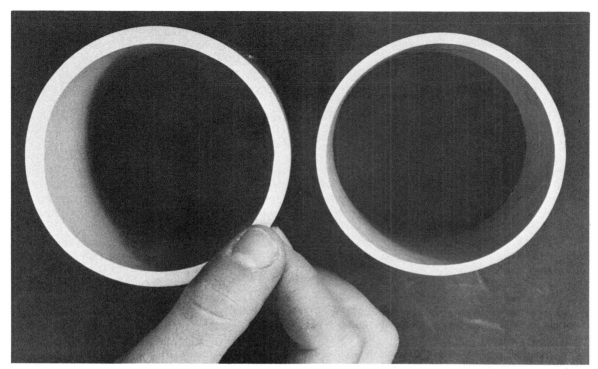

Fig. 3-44. Schedule 40 DWV pipe (left) requires 1-inch furring to fit inside a stud wall, while the Schedule 30 pipe (right), with the same interior diameter, will fit inside a standard 2 by 4 stud wall with no furring (courtesy Genova, Inc.).

pipe allows for better flow characteristics, even in a gravity system (Fig. 3-43). Most DWV pipe can be 6-inch, 4-inch, 3-inch, 2-inch, and 1½-inch diameters. Genova has developed two lines. Schedule 40 is the standard pipe, while Schedule 30 is meant specifically for do-it-yourself work and is known as the in-wall system. Schedule 30 pipe has somewhat thinner walls than does standard pipe, so that the 3-inch stack will fit inside a 2 by 4 stud wall (the Schedule 40 will not). Schedule 30 comes only in the 3-inch size (Fig. 3-44).

Again, fittings and pipe should be bought from the same manufacturer. The tolerances are much closer, and there is less chance of leakage in the system.

The DWV pipe is cut to size in the same manner as CPVC supply pipe. Make sure the cut is square (using a fine-toothed saw for the cutting). Deburr the works with sandpaper or a knife. Use a cleaner next. Apply solvent welding compound liberally to the pipe and sparingly to the socket. Push the two together with a slight twisting motion and immediately align the fitting.

You get best results using a miter box with this larger pipe, and the pipe should be kept off the floor or ground after cleaning. Check each pipe end for cracks, deep gouges, and abrasions. Cut off any damaged parts. If you use a file or coarse grit sandpaper to chamfer the edge of the pipe to about 45 degrees, it will slide more easily into the fitting socket. Support pipe runs every 4 feet, and make sure you've left expansion allowances. Provide a slope of ¼ inch per foot toward the drains (Fig. 3-45). If you are mixing plastic types, use less cement to make the joints than with PVC joints. Remember that acrylonitrile-butadiene-styrene (ABS) plastics are not as resistant to chemicals as PVC plastics.

Kitchen waste systems are installed using plumber's putty under both sides of the bowl flanges, around the drains, and beneath faucets not having base gaskets. Tailpiece size from the sink drain will be 1½ inches; the trap size is the same.

WASHERS

Many homes don't have plumbing installed for setting up automatic washers. When the location is chosen, you have a fairly easy job when you use CPVC and PVC pipe for the installation.

The drainpipe is run first. The PVC-DWV pipe and vent are used. You have a choice of adding a standpipe or setting up a laundry tub into which the washer can drain. A standpipe should reach about 3 feet above floor level and have a P-trap below to keep the gases outside the house. Vent as needed, either with a wet vent or with reventing, depending on distance. Tie the drain into a drain stack.

Water supply is run after the drain is in. It requires a pair of ½-inch CPVC or PB hot and cold water pipes on the wall behind the washer. Use threaded hose bibbs to end the supply runs. Place ¾-inch CPVC air chambers 18 inches long above them, capping them at the tops. The washer solenoid valves are extremely fast-acting and close rapidly when filling is complete. The air chambers prevent damage to the plumbing from the rapid cutoff.

During plumbing installation, some cutting of joists and studs may be needed. Do not reduce joist strength by more than allowable limits, so that any notching or drilling required for pipe runs may only be done in specified areas of the material. Holes may be drilled in the joist if they are near the joist centerline (horizontally), but no joist can be notched in its middle half. The maximum hole size is a quarter of the joist depth, and the maximum notch depth is a quarter of the joist depth. Holes or notches any larger than this mean you must brace the joist with 2 by 4s on both sides. Notches should have the bottom sides braced with 2 by 2s or metal strapping. Studs can be notched up to 2½ inches square if you use a metal strap brace, but unbraced notches can be more than 1¼ inches square.

Refrigerators and washing machines should be placed over doubled joists. You may have to install an extra joist to take the extra weight of appliances. Use solid blocking between the present joists and the new framing member. Make the new joist the same size as the old. If the present framing is 16 inches on center, install the new joist at 8 inches on center. If the present framing is 2 feet on center, install the new joist at either 8 inches or 1 foot. Blocking should go in at 2 to 3-foot intervals.

DISHWASHERS

A *dishwasher* installation is not just a plumbing job. It requires some wiring and cabinetry as well. Dishwasher plumbing can come directly off the kitchen

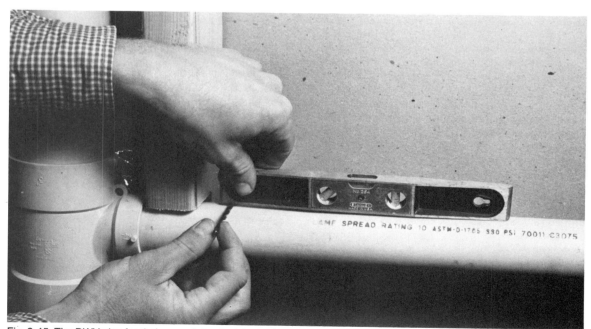

Fig. 3-45. The DWV pipe for drains needs to slant down about ¼ inch per foot. Use a drill bit and a short level to make sure it does (courtesy Genova, Inc.).

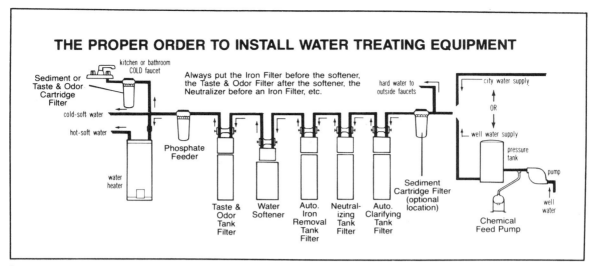

THE PROPER ORDER TO INSTALL WATER TREATING EQUIPMENT

Always put the Iron Filter before the softener, the Taste & Odor Filter after the softener, the Neutralizer before an Iron Filter, etc.

Fig. 3-46. Order of installation for water treatment equipment (courtesy Sears, Roebuck and Company).

sink hot water supply line, with the waste plumbing running to the kitchen sink drain. There must be a cutoff valve installed in the line, using 3/8-inch copper or plastic pipe.

Electrical wiring must be installed according to code, which will mean a separate junction box on a separate 15-ampere circuit for almost all installations. Wiring details are covered in the next chapter. Special applications, such as those kitchen sinks having a dishwasher and garbage disposal unit attached, are generally furnished with the dishwashers. Special kits are available with most brands to make the work go more easily.

The dishwasher must be located as close as possible to the kitchen sink. This saves plumbing materials and generally simplifies the installation, while cutting down on heat loss in long plumbing runs.

Check opening sizes carefully. Most full-sized dishwashers are 24 inches wide, requiring a 24 1/8-inch-wide opening about 24 1/4 inches deep. The height of the opening may vary 1/2 inch from 34 to 34 1/2 inches.

WATER SOFTENERS

Whether or not you need a *water softener* depends on the type of water in your home. Free analysis is available from Sears stores and other places that sell water softeners. A water softener, though, may not be the only piece of treatment equipment you need. Much depends on the quantities of various substances found in your home water supply.

If your water contains too much iron, the analysis will determine whether or not you need a filter to remove it. Acid, alkaline, or corrosive water problems can also be determined by analysis, which will let you determine what kind of neutralizing filter or crystal feeder you may need. Taste and odor problems can also be corrected with various kinds of filters, as can turbidity. See Fig. 3-46.

Water softeners generally require a minimum water pressure of 20 psi at the softener inlet. You must allow for losses if in-line filter equipment is installed before the softener. A maximum of 120 psi is normal. Anything more than that will require that you install a pressure reduction valve in the supply line ahead of the softener. You need a minimum flow rate of 2 gallons per minute.

To install any water softener, you must shut down the system, because you need to cut into the cold water supply ahead of your water heater. Make sure the water heater is cut off so electrical coils don't burn out, or gas heat doesn't ruin the base of the water heater tank. You will also need a grounded, plug-in electrical outlet clost by. It it usually best to locate the softener as close as possible to the point at which you cut into the cold water line. Because adequate drainage is also needed, it may be cheaper to extend an existing line so you do not have to install a new drain.

The CPVC pipe is the easiest material to use when making water softener installations. Start by moving the softener into position. Use flat cedar shim stock to get the softener level. Measure the pipe needed. Double check all measurements.

Shut down the hot water heater. Shut off the water at the main supply valve. Open both the highest and lowest faucets in the system. You must drain the pipes, or you can't work on the system.

Once the water has drained for the lines, you can start installing the take-off piping to the softener. When that is done, install the take-off pipe back into the supply line. Install the valve drain and salt tank overflow hoses, usually using 7/16-inch (ID) flexible hose. Slide the hose over the softener outlets. Use clamps to secure the hose in place. Allow an air gap at the drain end of the hose, and make sure there are no kinks.

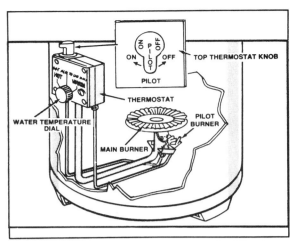

Fig. 3-48. Lighting the gas hot water heater after filling (courtesy Sears, Roebuck and Company).

Check for secure fittings. Turn the system water back on (after closing the opened faucets) and start the water heater. Fill the salt storage tank and program the softener to fit your needs. Finally, plug the unit into the grounded electrical outlet.

WATER HEATERS

Revamping a kitchen can also mean revamping the hot water system. Changes in hot water heaters are usually rather simple, straightforward jobs. Placement is important, along with proper venting of gas models and installation of electric heaters. If placement is not already determined by a present hot water heater, select a spot that will give at least 2 inches of clearance at the back and sides. Location should be in a spot not subjected to freezing temperatures. Keep any vent and hot water lines as short as possible. It is against all codes to install any gas hot water heater in bathrooms or any occupied room that is normally kept closed. Make sure there is adequate ventilation.

Water pipes are installed as in most other types of built-in appliance installations. Make sure the gas or electricity is cut off. Cut off the main water supply, and release the water in the system by opening the highest and lowest taps and letting the lines drain. Drain the old heater, if there is one, and move the new one into position.

All male threaded pipe must have pipe joint compound applied to it for sealing. Be sure that the cold water supply has a cutoff valve and union installed. The relief valve must be installed to meet local code

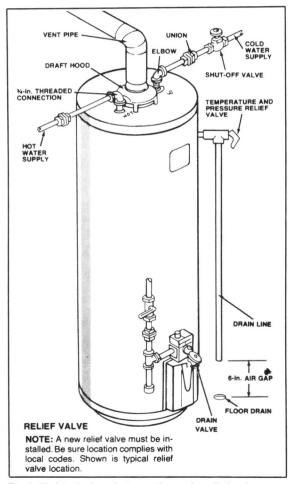

Fig. 3-47. A typical gas hot water heater installation (courtesy Sears, Roebuck and Company).

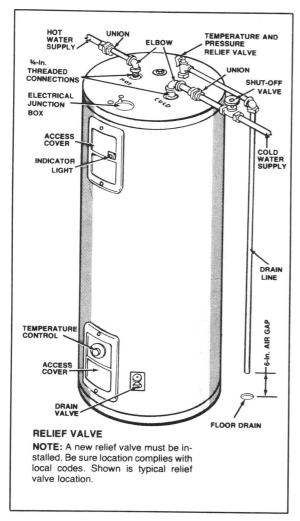

HOT WATER SUPPLY

UNION

ELBOW

TEMPERATURE AND PRESSURE RELIEF VALVE

¾-in. THREADED CONNECTIONS

UNION

SHUT-OFF VALVE

ELECTRICAL JUNCTION BOX

ACCESS COVER

INDICATOR LIGHT

COLD WATER SUPPLY

HOT

COLD

DRAIN LINE

6-in. AIR GAP

TEMPERATURE CONTROL

ACCESS COVER

DRAIN VALVE

FLOOR DRAIN

RELIEF VALVE

NOTE: A new relief valve must be installed. Be sure location complies with local codes. Shown is typical relief valve location.

Fig. 3-49. Typical electric hot water heater installation (courtesy Sears, Roebuck and Company).

requirements. A pipe is run from the relief valve outlet to a suitable drain. The relief pipe must be of the same size as the valve outlet. The relief pipe does not have a cutoff valve; nor is it threaded, capped, or plugged in any manner (Fig. 3-47).

Gas supply piping is needed, and it must conform to local codes. All gas connections must be tight. Check by applying a mixture of liquid soap and water and looking for bubbles at all fittings and joints. Flexible gas connector lines can be obtained.

Venting of a gas hot water heater is essential. Use new vent pipe of the correct size for your installation and keep the pipe run as short as possible. The vent pipe run can not be more than 15 feet. The vent pipe is run vertically as high as possible before running it into the chimney. Vent pipe must clear all combustible surfaces by a minimum of 6 inches and enter the chimney above any furnace flue pipe.

To fill a new hot water heater, close the drain valve. Open the cold water supply to the heater and leave it open. Open a nearby hot water faucet to allow the air in the heater tank and in the line to escape. Keep the faucet open until water comes through, then close it. Make a check for leaks. You can then light the hot water heater according to the directions attached to the heater's jacket (Fig. 3-48).

Electric hot water heaters have the same location needs, except regarding ventilation requirements. If a new hot water heater is replacing an old one of the same size, simply position the new one, connect the plumbing and wiring, and fill it (Fig. 3-49). The National Electrical Code requires that a heater with a wattage rating of 3800 use a size 12 wire and a 20-ampere fuse or circuit breaker. A 5500-watt hot water heater requires number 10 wire and a 30-ampere fuse or circuit breaker.

New model hot water heaters will have several features to save you money. Thicker insulation will be provided for better heat retention. Some gas hot water heaters offer easily adjustable vacation temperature controls. Annual savings for such units have been estimated to average as high as 45 dollars when electricity costs are just under 5 cents a kilowatt hour, and over 90 dollars when electricity costs 10 cents a kilowatt hour.

Chapter 4

Wiring

RESIDENTIAL ELECTRICAL WIRING IS NOT REALLY complex. Neatness counts when wiring any part of a house. There are few other jobs around the home that can prove as dangerous if not handled carefully.

CIRCUITRY

Most of the kitchens built more than 15 years ago have inadequate wiring systems, which means that some wiring will be needed to get the lighting and appliance circuits up-to-date and able to handle modern loads. On-counter accessories such as microwave and toaster ovens can save energy. Thus, the need for appliance circuits has increased.

For today's kitchen, you will need at least a single appliance circuit handling nothing else but toasters and other small appliances. Some more appliances can be handled by a second circuit shared with a dining area. Kitchen lights are on the same circuit as the living room outlets. Another appliance circuit is needed for the washing machine. You will need a separate 240-volt, 50-ampere circuit for an electric range, and a seperate circuit for an electric dryer, which will be 240 volts and usually 30 amperes. Dishwashers and disposal units each need separate 15-ampere circuits.

Most houses require at least two dozen circuits. Circuit loading must be considered, though, before planning the wiring on graph paper. You need extra capacity if you want to get full use from your appliances. Overloaded circuits, even with circuit breakers in place, can be a danger. Obviously, not every appliance on a single circuit will be in use at the same time. Even 20-ampere circuits have a total wattage load capacity of only about 2200, while 15-ampere circuits shouldn't be loaded beyond 1650 watts at any one time. With the average toaster drawing some 1100 watts, a tabletop or countertop rotisserie oven needing 1400 watts, and a refrigerator requiring 250 watts, it's easy to see the problems you can encounter with a single circuit for appliances (Fig. 4-1).

Once the circuit needs are determined, you can decide where to place the outlets. For kitchen use along countertops, a double receptacle outlet every 4 feet is almost a must. Even closer spacing of alternated appliance circuits will allow the use of more appliances when needed. Lighting circuits are required, with one 15-ampere circuit for every 375 square feet of floor space. Placing a split lighting circuit in a room can save problems. If all the lights in a room are on a single circuit, one blown fuse will put the entire room in darkness. Make sure that all the outlets on a single floor, even in a very small two-story house, are not on a single circuit.

You will need at least two 20-ampere appliance circuits in the kitchen and dining areas, plus another circuit for laundry appliances if they will be in the kitchen. In addition, you must have a lighting circuit shared with the living room outlets. No lighting is installed on any appliance circuit.

Dishwashers and waste disposal units each draw about 1500 watts. Each unit must have a separate 15-ampere circuit. The appliance circuit for the washing machine should be a 20-ampere circuit, so a 700-watt automatic washing machine may be shared with an 1100-watt iron when needed. Electric range and dryer circuits are separate, and each requires a different kind of receptacle. The different receptacle pattern prevents the electric range from being plugged into the electric dryer circuit. Virtually all electric ranges require a 220/240-volt, 50-ampere circuit, while dryers need a 30-ampere circuit of the same voltage. Water heaters are wired directly into the circuit and also need an individual 220/240-volt circuit, usually 30-ampere.

Circuits for 15 amperes may be wired with number 14 copper cable. Twenty-ampere circuits require heavier number 12 cable. Circuits for a 30-ampere load will need a number 10 cable, and electric ranges require a number 6 cable to handle the 50-ampere load. High-speed electric dryers (drawing about 8500 watts) will need a 50-ampere hookup, as does the electric range.

SERVICE ENTRANCE PANEL

Once you've decided on the circuitry to be added, take a look at the electric *service entrance panel* for your home. The panel may have to be replaced so that you can modernize the kitchen. A subpanel may have to be wired into the house, or the panel may be adequate with only minor changes. The electric service panel connects the main service cable to the branch circuits (general purpose and appliance). It is either fused or has circuit breakers installed. In recent years, fused service panels have just about disappeared. Circuit breakers save money, energy, and aggravation.

Today's minimum service entrance panel capacity is 100 amperes for residences up to 3000 square feet. The older standard of 60 amperes is too small for modern homes and should be replaced or supplemented with a subpanel. The 150-ampere service allows for a range, an electric water heater, a high-speed dryer, central air conditioning, small appliances, and lighting. When electric heat is installed, you must go to a 200-ampere service.

Most 15-ampere circuits could withstand four units at one time. To install 150 or 200-ampere service panels, or to add a subpanel to update an older electrical service to that level, the service entrance cable must be a 1/0 or 3/0 using type RHW insulation. If you are unable to determine the size and type of entrance cable used, check with your local utility. Service to the meter is the responsibility of the utility company. Services beyond the meter are the responsibility of the homeowner (Fig. 4-2).

EQUIPMENT

If you find the installation of a service panel or a subpanel necessary, some work must be done near hot circuitry. You should never do this work near hot circuitry while you are standing on a damp basement floor or surface. Wear insulated gloves and rubbers or rubber-soled shoes.

Most service panels have two power take-off lugs set between two left and two right fuses of the plug-in type. In order to add additional circuits, a new panel can be installed. Two black wires are run to the power take-off lugs, and the white wire is connected to the neutral strip. This gives you 120 volts between the black and white wires or a 240-volt circuit between the two black wires at the new panel. The new panel is required for circuit protection. You must use wire not smaller than number 10, three-wire cable. The power take-off is now fused at 60 amperes in the main disconnect (Figs. 4-3 and 4-4).

Electrical services installed today must be grounded. There are three ways to do the job, depending on whether metal conduit is used in an urban or rural system. The neutral wire (white) is grounded, and grounds are never fused.

A number 4 wire is sufficient ground for most systems of up to 200 amperes capacity. In most urban systems, the ground wire is run from the service panel to the water pipes using an armored ground conductor. The water meter is jumped (Figs. 4-5 and 4-6). For rural electrical systems, a ground rod must be driven and attached to the ground wire. The ground rod must be at least 8 feet long and, if copper, at least ½ inch in diameter. If steel or galvanized iron pipe is used, the diameter must be at least ¾ inch. Ground rods must be

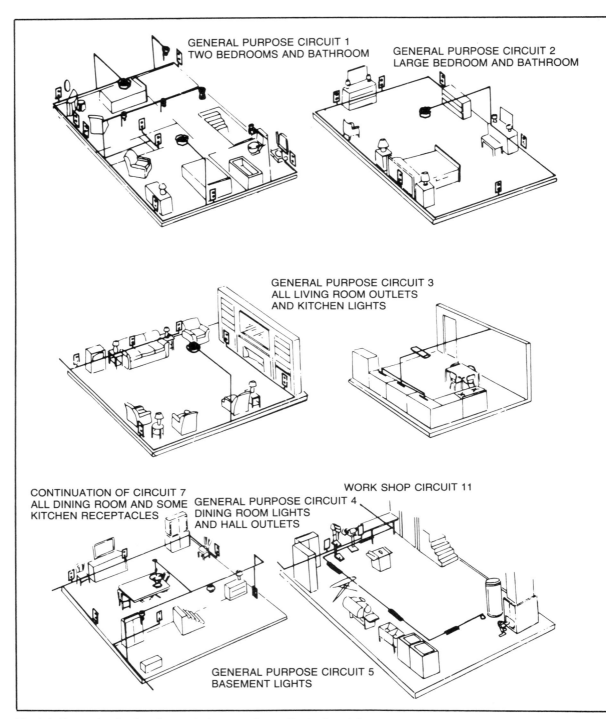

Fig. 4-1. House circuits placed properly (courtesy Sears, Roebuck and Company).

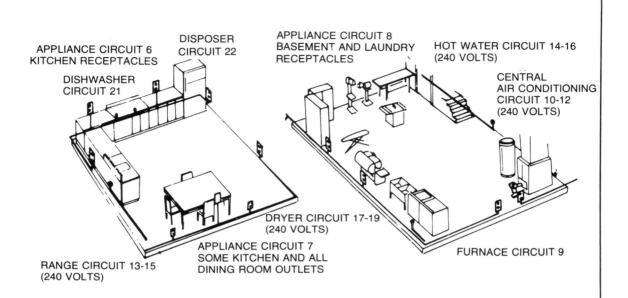

APPLIANCE CIRCUIT 6
KITCHEN RECEPTACLES

DISPOSER
CIRCUIT 22

APPLIANCE CIRCUIT 8
BASEMENT AND LAUNDRY
RECEPTACLES

HOT WATER CIRCUIT 14-16
(240 VOLTS)

DISHWASHER
CIRCUIT 21

CENTRAL
AIR CONDITIONING
CIRCUIT 10-12
(240 VOLTS)

DRYER CIRCUIT 17-19
(240 VOLTS)

APPLIANCE CIRCUIT 7
SOME KITCHEN AND ALL
DINING ROOM OUTLETS

FURNACE CIRCUIT 9

RANGE CIRCUIT 13-15
(240 VOLTS)

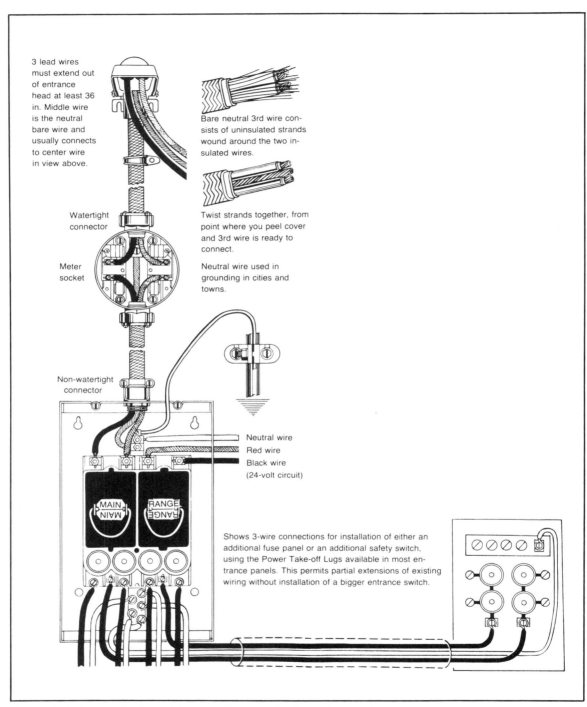

3 lead wires must extend out of entrance head at least 36 in. Middle wire is the neutral bare wire and usually connects to center wire in view above.

Bare neutral 3rd wire consists of uninsulated strands wound around the two insulated wires.

Twist strands together, from point where you peel cover and 3rd wire is ready to connect.

Neutral wire used in grounding in cities and towns.

Watertight connector

Meter socket

Non-watertight connector

Neutral wire
Red wire
Black wire
(24-volt circuit)

MAIN

RANGE

Shows 3-wire connections for installation of either an additional fuse panel or an additional safety switch, using the Power Take-off Lugs available in most entrance panels. This permits partial extensions of existing wiring without installation of a bigger entrance switch.

Fig. 4-2. Main fuses and subpanel (courtesy Sears, Roebuck and Company).

Fig. 4-3. Service panels (courtesy General Electric).

located a minimum of 2 feet out from any building and driven so that the top is a foot below the surface, at which time a grounding clamp is used to attach the wire to the rod (Fig. 4-7).

ACCESSORIES

The service box and its heavy cable are only the beginning of any residental wiring system. Cable and outlet boxes, among other accessories, are vital.

Cable

Cable for residential wiring comes in three basic forms; only two are used commonly now. The old metallic armored or *BX cable* is not used in new installations and remodeling. Most cable used today is copper, sheathed with plastic, with an inner jacket of either plastic or plastic and heavy paper. When running cable through areas that may become damp, you need an outdoor, all-plastic sheathed cable. Dry locations can use the indoor cable. Outdoor cable can be used either outdoors or indoors, while indoor cable cannot be used outdoors. The indoor cable generally costs from 30 to 35 percent less than the outdoor cable, so it doesn't pay to wire dry areas with outdoor cable. If wire run interruption isn't too big a problem,

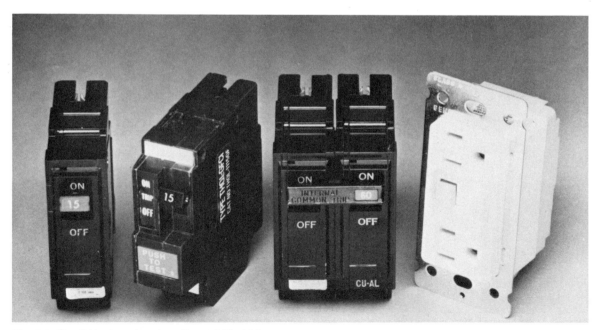

Fig. 4-4. Circuit breakers (courtesy General Electric).

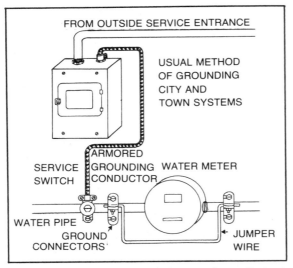

Fig. 4-5. Urban system grounding (courtesy Sears, Roebuck and Company).

you may run outdoor cable under bathroom and kitchen flooring.

Thin-wall or rigid conduit is seldom needed in residential construction. Plastic sheathed cable is usually used in underground outdoor wiring (Fig. 4-8).

Nonmetallic cable is easy to install and goes in quickly for runs even in old construction where it must be fished through walls, over ceilings, and under

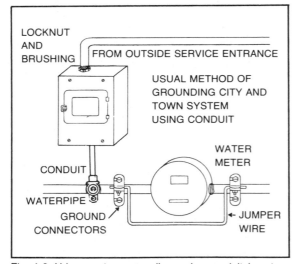

Fig. 4-6. Urban system grounding, using conduit (courtesy Sears, Roebuck and Company).

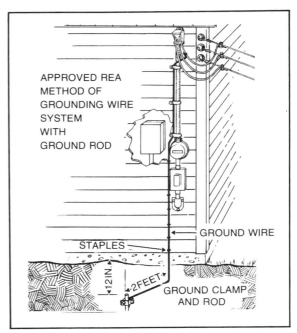

Fig. 4-7. Rural grounding (courtesy Sears, Roebuck and Company).

floors. The cable will run from outlet box to outlet box and then to the main service panel, or to the new add-on panel. Grounds are attached to metal outlet boxes or to each other when the boxes are plastic. No ground is interrupted or fused (Figs. 4-9 and 4-10).

Boxes

Outlet, receptacle, or switch *boxes* come in many styles and sizes (Fig. 4-11). Box depth is often far more important than overall size (box size is determined by the number of wires you must connect in the box). Boxes for switches are generally rectangular. They

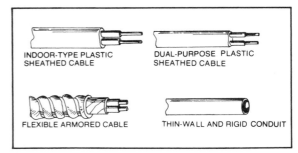

Fig. 4-8. Cable types.

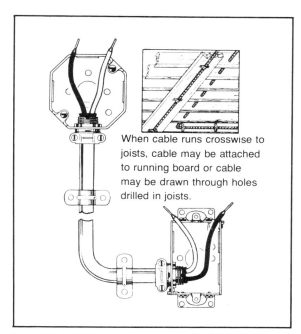

When cable runs crosswise to joists, cable may be attached to running board or cable may be drawn through holes drilled in joists.

Fig. 4-9. Installing nonmetallic cable (courtesy Sears, Roebuck and Company).

may be as shallow as 1½ inches or as deep as 2½ inches. In new construction and for standard framing in remodeling, the deeper boxes are used. The more room there is in a box, the easier it is to work within the box. Shallow boxes are ideal when you must install circuits in areas where full depth framing isn't possible, such as on basement walls, when 2 by 2s are used to frame over concrete or concrete block.

Box shapes include rectangular, octagonal, and round. Octagonal sizes generally reach 4 inches, and most round boxes are 3½ inches in diameter. Boxes come in sectional steel models, one-piece steel models, and one-piece plastic models. Sectional steel switch boxes are needed when you must *gang* or attach more than one box in order to install several receptacle sets or switches. All boxes must be covered when wiring is done. They must be securely attached to framing, wallboard, or some other attachment point. Various kinds of mounting brackets are available. Many boxes also can be attached by driving nails through them and into the framing member against which they are placed.

Wire Nuts

Solderless wire connectors or *wire nuts* are read-ily available. They should be used for making wire-to-wire attachments inside switch and outlet boxes. These screw-on connectors save time. Most wires, from about number 18 to number 10 can be readily connected by using wire nuts. The price is quite reasonable. Both Vaco and General Electric make these nuts, and these companies also make wire ties that slip around wires and hold them together.

Electrician's Tape

You should have stretchable, electrician's plastic tape. Rubber tape must be overwrapped with friction tape. Friction tape has poor adhesive qualities and doesn't stretch well to make a smooth coating.

Staples and Cable Straps

Insulated *staples* are used only on small wire, and staples for NM and larger cables are not normally insulated. Experts disagree on whether staples or *cable straps* are better as holders for long wiring runs. Staples are faster to apply, but they require care when being driven to keep from damaging the cable's insulation. Cable straps require you to drive a couple of small nails. The straps take slightly longer to install, but they are far less likely to cause cable damage.

Ground Fault Circuit Interrupters

When you're looking through the usual service panel/circuit breaker assortment, consider installing *ground fault circuit interrupters* on at least two circuits. Ground fault circuit interrupters are required to meet codes on bathrooms, and they are a good idea in

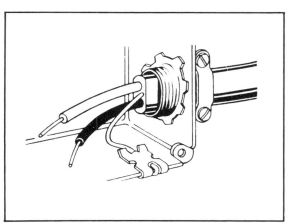

Fig. 4-10. Installing rounds (courtesy Sears, Roebuck and Company).

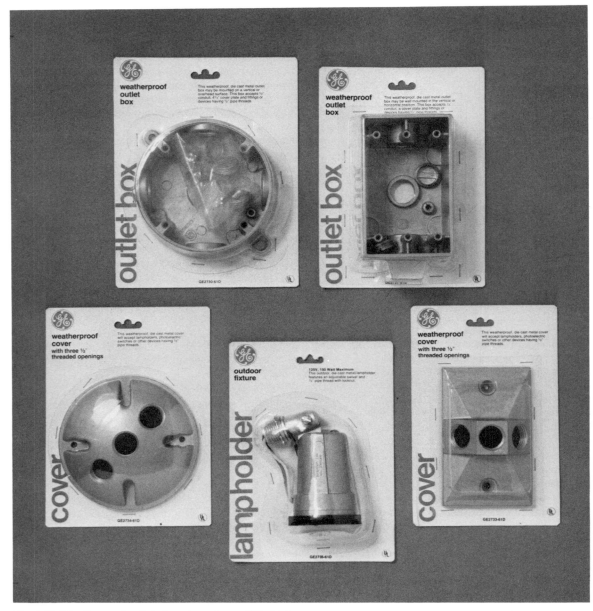

Fig. 4-11. Weatherproof outlets (courtesy General Electric).

kitchens. They cost more than circuit breakers—usually at least 10 times as much—but you do not need as many.

Ground fault circuit interrupters come in three styles. The cheapest one is portable and can be moved from outlet to outlet where it is simply plugged in. Another is installed in the outlet and protects all outlets on the circuit past and including itself. The third type replaces the circuit breaker and protects all outlets on that particular circuit. These interrupters trip the

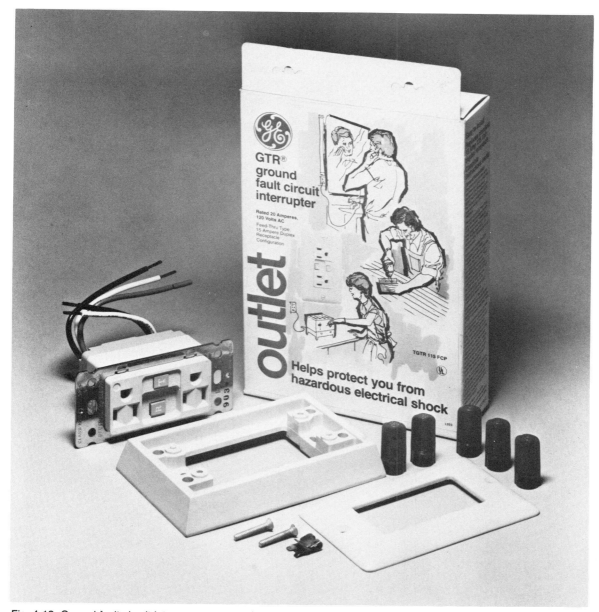

Fig. 4-12. Ground fault circuit interrupter receptacle kit (courtesy General Electric).

circuit with a 5-milliampere fault and take under a half second to do so. Circuit-breaker-replacing interrupters are available in 15, 20, 25, and 30-ampere sizes at 120 volts and 240 volts. Plug-in receptacle styles are normally 15-volt models, with receptacle (outlet) re-placement interrupters available in 15 and 20-ampere, 120-volt models. If you want the outlet replacement model to protect later outlets on the circuit, make sure it is a feed-through type and not a termination type (Fig. 4-12).

TECHNIQUES

The techniques of stripping a wire become exceptionally important when the wire end must lead into a wire nut or onto a terminal on a switch, an outlet, or a fixture. Too much distance allows dirt to build up and increase resistance. If corrosion builds up as well as dirt, resistance may be even higher. Cutting cable sheathing incorrectly and stripping away too little or too much insulation will also ruin the job.

Wire needs a little slack at each connection to allow for expansion and contraction, so you have the room you need to make connections cleanly. Cable runs must also have support where they don't run through joists, studs, and other framing members. The cable runs should be covered with protective plates when they do run through studs. Clamps are used at each box to keep wires or cable from being pulled loose inside the box.

When you've decided on wire runs and box locations, get the cable coil out and make the runs. Leave 8 inches at each box where a run must be connected—whether to a switch, light, or other fixture. The 8 inches give you sufficient room to work. The boxes should be installed by this time (Fig. 4-13). As the cable is run, it should be strapped at intervals no longer than 4 feet. A strap should also be used within 1 foot of all outlets and switches. You can use staples, but take care when hammering them into place. If you are doing work where cable must be fished through a wall or other area that remains enclosed, strapping or staples need only be used on exposed portions of the work. New construction must be supported as above before the work is inspected and the walls, ceilings, or floors are closed. If the cable is to remain exposed, then you must strap it at intervals no greater than 3 feet.

Use a running board of 1 by 2 material to support cable spanning open spaces, or draw the cable through holes in joists or other framing members. Attic-installed cables should be at least 7 feet from the floor, on the rafters, or across the top of floor beams. Protect them with strips nailed on each side of the cable.

Stripping and Splicing Wire

Strip cable sheathing with a cable ripper or an electrician's knife. Most wire strippers won't strip cable easily. Wire can be stripped with an electrician's knife or a wire stripper. Strip wires so that the remaining insulation tapers towards the bare wire, exposing about ½ inch of the wire. For bigger terminals, with

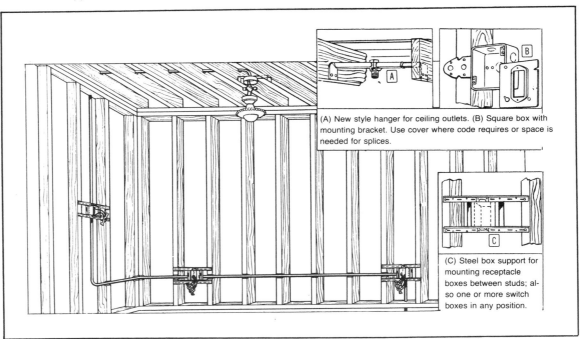

(A) New style hanger for ceiling outlets. (B) Square box with mounting bracket. Use cover where code requires or space is needed for splices.

(C) Steel box support for mounting receptacle boxes between studs; also one or more switch boxes in any position.

Fig. 4-13. Cable runs (courtesy Sears, Roebuck and Company).

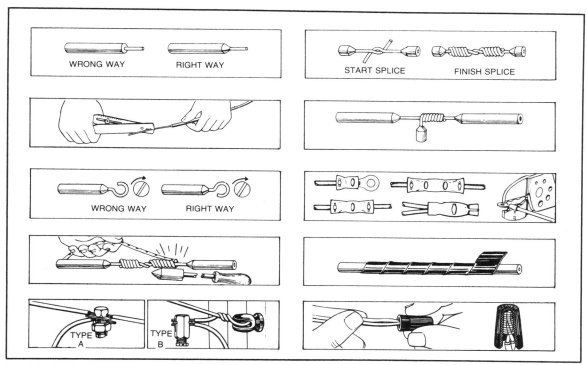

Fig. 4-14. Wiring techniques for neatness and safety (courtesy Sears, Roebuck and Company).

larger cable and wire sizes, you may need to go to ¾ inch, and even to 1 inch or more with larger sizes. Take a pair of needlenose pliers and make a loop in the end of the stripped wire to fit over the terminal screw. Leave an opening of about a quarter to a third of the circumference of the circle you make. Turn the wire so that its open end will be closed by the terminal screw as you screw it down. You may have a switch or other fixture that requires you to simply insert a stripped wire end in the correct terminal (Figs. 4-14 and 4-15).

If wires must be spliced, use wire nuts. You may need to splice a wire with solder, especially if you have to run a tap splice. Take off about 3 inches of insulation from each wire, and cross the wires about 1 inch from the remaining insulation. Make six to eight turns using pliers to complete the dry splice. Go ahead and use the solder. Coat the wires with a nonacid paste flux. Heat with a soldering iron or torch. Let the solder touch the splice and flow into each crevice. Take the heat and the solder away. When cool, wrap the splice at least three times with plastic electrician's tape.

Solderless terminals can sometimes be used in residential wiring and might be especially handy if you're building your own cords for ranges, hot water heaters, and other appliances. Standard insulated solderless terminals are available in wire sizes from number 22 to number 10. Uninsulated terminals can be had in wire sizes to number 6.

Installing Switch Boxes

Switch boxes at walls and outlet boxes are easily installed in old paneling, plaster, or gypsum wallboard. First (on plaster or gypsum wallboard), check for stud location. Either rap on the wall with your knuckles or use a magnetic stud finder. If that doesn't work, select a small drill and make holes in the wall every 2 inches. Make the holes as small as possible, and position them just above the baseboard if you don't want to do a lot of refinishing work. Once the stud is located and the box location is determined, cut away the plaster (mark the wall with the box placed against it, using a pencil). You will likely find lath behind old plaster and nothing behind gypsum wallboard. Lath will have to be drilled at all four corners and sawed out. Gypsum wallboard will readily come out with a saw, after drilling at four corners, or it can be cut out with a utility knife or the

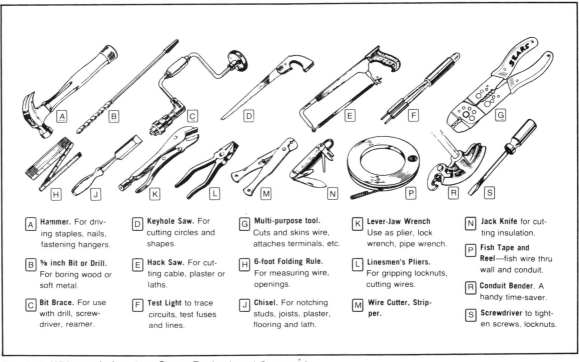

A Hammer. For driving staples, nails, fastening hangers.	**D** Keyhole Saw. For cutting circles and shapes.	**G** Multi-purpose tool. Cuts and skins wire, attaches terminals, etc.	**K** Lever-Jaw Wrench Use as plier, lock wrench, pipe wrench.	**N** Jack Knife for cutting insulation.
B ⅝ inch Bit or Drill. For boring wood or soft metal.	**E** Hack Saw. For cutting cable, plaster or laths.	**H** 6-foot Folding Rule. For measuring wire, openings.	**L** Linesmen's Pliers. For gripping locknuts, cutting wires.	**P** Fish Tape and Reel—fish wire thru wall and conduit.
C Bit Brace. For use with drill, screwdriver, reamer.	**F** Test Light to trace circuits, test fuses and lines.	**J** Chisel. For notching studs, joists, plaster, flooring and lath.	**M** Wire Cutter, Stripper.	**R** Conduit Bender. A handy time-saver.
				S Screwdriver to tighten screws, locknuts.

Fig. 4-15. Wiring tools (courtesy Sears, Roebuck and Company).

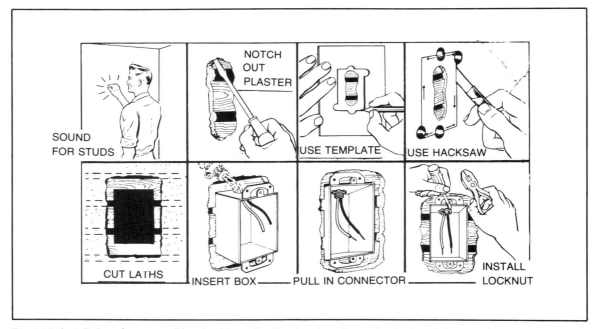

Fig. 4-16. Installation of a new wall box in old construction (courtesy Sears, Roebuck and Company).

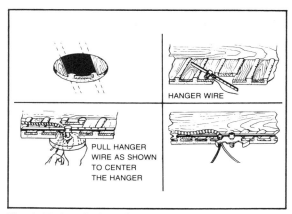

Fig. 4-17. Installation of a ceiling box (courtesy Sears, Roebuck and Company).

Cut-Zum Knife from Hyde Manufacturing Company. When the cable is fished, draw it up and out of the hole about 8 inches. Slip it through the correct knockout plug in the box, clamping it in place. Insert the box using whatever connectors needed to hold the box firmly in the wall. Strip the wire ends. Install the switch or fixture. If a fixture doesn't cover the box, install the cover plate (Fig. 4-16).

Ceiling boxes in old construction are most often installed using a coat hanger wire run through the center of the threaded stud. The hanger and stud are held above the ceiling, and the hanger wire is pulled to get the hanger in place. The cable is connected to the box and pulled through the ceiling. The hanger wire is pulled through, and the locknut is installed after the box is in place (Fig. 4-17).

Running Cable

To run new cable around door frames and headers, start by removing the baseboard and trim. Notch the wall and spacers between the framing and the doorjamb. If the new outlet or switch is to be placed beyond the first upright or stud, use a bit with an extension on it to drill past any extra studs. Not all walls have headers. If headers are in the wall, you can go past them by notching away the stud both above and below the header, or by cutting a notch in the header itself. This may require removing wallboard or plaster and patching the hole afterward.

Running cable along basement floor joists (for the first floor) is a simple matter, with the hole for the new outlet or switch cut first. Interior partition walls usually let you drill straight up through the wall sole plate at the point desired. Exterior walls force you to come in at an angle from the inside edge of the foundation wall. If cable is run perpendicular to joists, drill holes in the joists to run it. If the cable runs parallel to the joists, use staples or cable straps every 3 feet to secure the cable to the sides of the beams or joists.

Wiring from a Wall Switch to a Baseboard Outlet

Wiring run from a wall switch to a baseboard outlet is done by first removing the baseboard in the area to be worked on. Mark the spot to be opened. Cut the hole for the drop of the wire at the correct level and directly under the already installed switch. Keeping level, move over to a point directly under the new outlet location and cut a hole a few inches down from the spot. Cut the hole for the outlet box, punch out the correct knockout plug, and drop the cable down from

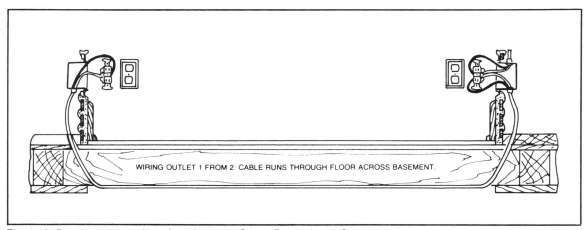

Fig. 4-18. Running cable under a floor (courtesy Sears, Roebuck and Company).

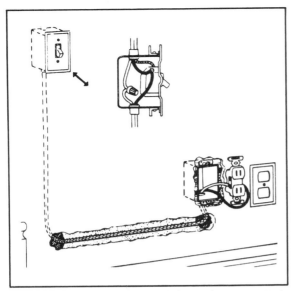

Fig. 4-19. Wiring from a wall switch to a base receptacle (courtesy Sears, Roebuck and Company).

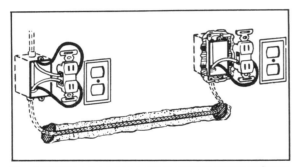

Fig. 4-20. Wiring from one outlet to another (courtesy Sears, Roebuck and Company).

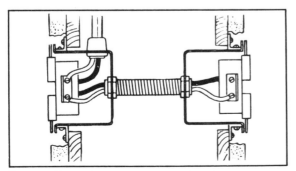

Fig. 4-21. Wiring from back-to-back outlets (courtesy Sears, Roebuck and Company).

the switch box in the wall, using holes already cut to guide the cable to the new box (Figs. 4-18 through 4-22).

If the wall is plaster, you can sometimes just notch a channel across. Wiring new baseboard or near-baseboard level outlets is done similarly. The procedure can also be used to move one outlet into a new room, wiring it to an outlet in the adjacent room. Keep black wire attached to black wire and white to white in all installations.

FISHING

Fishing is a hot, sweaty job and can be frustrating at times. Refer to Chapter 5. The job is much easier if you have a knowledge of house framing.

If the attic or basement is accessible, the job will usually be more easily accomplished. In an attic or upper room that has been finished, start by pulling off the baseboard over the proper section. Drill a diagonal hole downward far enough to penetrate the top plate(s). If this is not possible, drill a diagonal hole upward from the opposite room. Drill in horizontally until the holes meet.

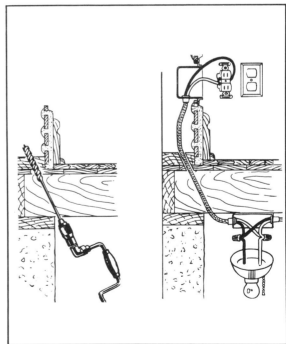

Fig. 4-22. Running cable through a floor (courtesy Sears, Roebuck and Company).

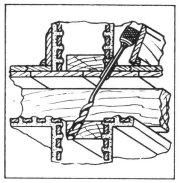

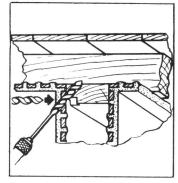

If you can get into attic or upper room, simply remove the upstairs baseboard. Then drill diagonal hole downward as shown.

Drill diagonal hole upward from opposite room. Then drill horizontally till holes meet. This method requires patching plaster.

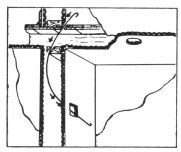

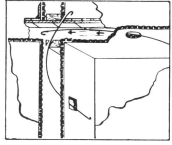

Push 12-foot fish wire, hooked at two ends, through hole on 2nd floor. Pull one end out at switch outlet on 1st floor.

Next, push 20-25 foot fish wire, hooked at both ends thru ceiling outlet (arrows). Now fish until you touch the first wire.

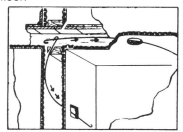

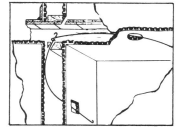

Then withdraw either wire (arrows) until it hooks the other wire; then withdraw second wire until both hooks hook together.

Lastly, pull shorter wire thru switch outlet. When hook from long wire appears, attach cable and pull thru wall and ceiling.

Fig. 4-23. Fishing cable (courtesy Sears, Roebuck and Company).

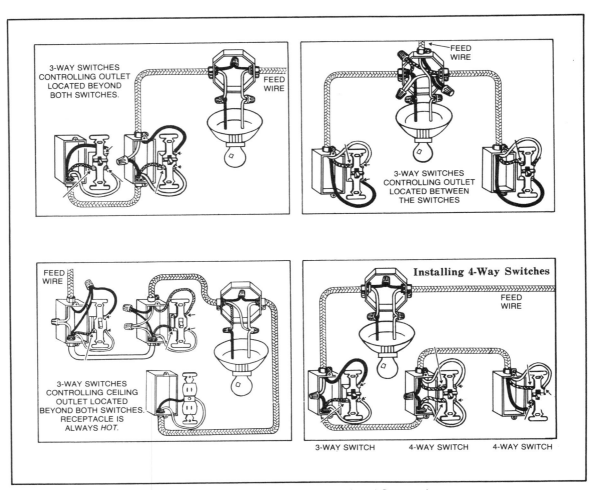

Fig. 4-24. Wiring three and four-way switches (courtesy Sears, Roebuck and Company).

Insert a short fish wire with two end hooks through the top hole, and bring it down until you can feed it out through a switch outlet on the lower floor. Hook on a longer fish wire through the ceiling outlet by feeding it in until the two wires touch. Pull either wire until it hooks the other, and then pull the shorter fish wire through the switch outlet. When the hook on the longer fish wire shows up at the wall outlet for the switch, hook on the cable and pull it to the new outlet (Fig. 4-23).

If there are headers in the walls, you will probably have to make several more holes in the walls, which will require later patching, in order to feed the cable through. In cases where a number of studs or other framing members must be passed through, cut out the wall and chisel a notch in the framing member. When

getting ready to close up the wall, always use a TECO protection plate over the newly installed cable.

DIAGRAMS

A three-way switch setup gives you two points of control, not three. The outlet may be located beyond both switches, between the switches, or beyond the switches with a receptacle added. A four-way switch provides three control stations for an outlet and can be used to add even more control points. The basic three-station setup requires two three-way switches and a single four-way switch, but further control stations require only the addition of a four-way switch for each.

You must follow the diagrams exactly when you

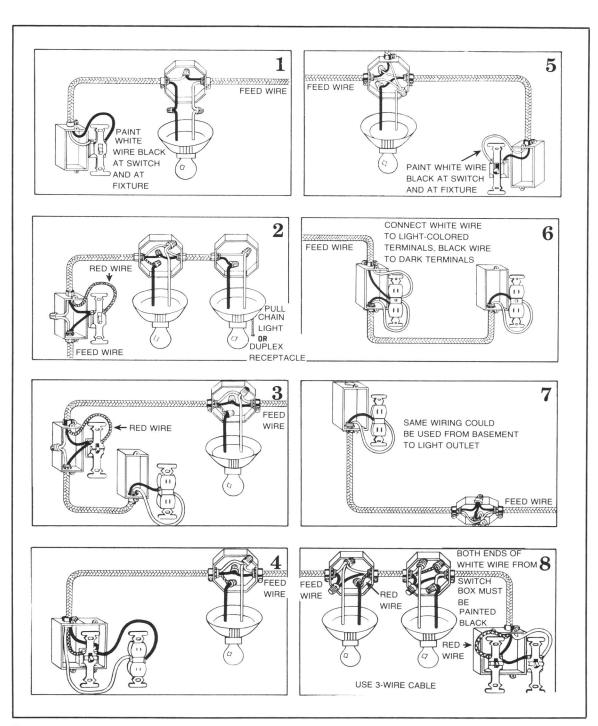

1 FEED WIRE
PAINT WHITE WIRE BLACK AT SWITCH AND AT FIXTURE

2 RED WIRE
FEED WIRE
PULL CHAIN LIGHT **OR** DUPLEX RECEPTACLE

3 ←RED WIRE
FEED WIRE

4 FEED WIRE

5 FEED WIRE
PAINT WHITE WIRE BLACK AT SWITCH AND AT FIXTURE

6 CONNECT WHITE WIRE TO LIGHT-COLORED TERMINALS, BLACK WIRE TO DARK TERMINALS
FEED WIRE

7 SAME WIRING COULD BE USED FROM BASEMENT TO LIGHT OUTLET
FEED WIRE

8 BOTH ENDS OF WHITE WIRE FROM SWITCH BOX MUST BE PAINTED BLACK
FEED WIRE
RED WIRE
RED WIRE
USE 3-WIRE CABLE

Fig. 4-25. Installation of some simpler switches (courtesy Sears, Roebuck and Company).

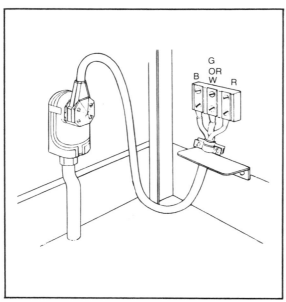

Fig. 4-26. A typical range wiring installation (courtesy Sears, Roebuck and Company).

junction box can be used as a current source for a new outlet. New switches and light fixtures can be added to an existing circuit with a light fixture on it. These light fixtures would, if wired as detailed, be switched separately (Fig. 4-25).

Heavier (240-volt) circuits require some different wiring techniques, but these are really no more difficult to carry out than 120-volt circuitry wiring. The basic 240-volt circuit takes two 120-volt circuits, so that there are more "hot" wires involved. Three-wire cable is required. Figure 4-26 shows a typical wiring setup for a range or dryer. Check local electrical codes to make certain your intended setup conforms to those codes. You will usually need a three-wire, number 6 cable to handle 50-ampere circuits, which will provide enough load-carrying capacity for even a high-speed, heavy-duty electric dryer. Standard dryers usually need a 30-ampere, 240-volt circuit, instead of the 50-ampere one required with high-speed appliances.

Most water heaters use two thermostats on two heating coils to bring temperatures up quickly, though single element water heaters are still readily available. If there is no circuit breaker available in the main service panel for the water heater, you will need to install a fused safety switch in the line. Most electric water heaters will use a 30-ampere, 240-volt circuit.

connect three and four-way switches. Light-colored terminals receive red and white wires, and the dark-colored terminals receive black wires. If you must use three-wire cable, paint the white wire black both at the switch and at the light outlet (Fig. 4-24).

Some wiring and rewiring jobs are simpler than those where three and four-way switches are needed. Adding a wall switch to control a ceiling light is reasonably easy. To add a one-way control at the end of a run, start by fishing the cable (two-wire). Connect the black lead to the black lead on the light fixture. Connect the white, new cable lead to the black lead at the already installed fixture. Paint the lead black at the switch and at the fixture. The job is done when the switch is installed. Painting of white wires is also needed if the switch is added in the middle of the circuit run. You will find yourself with three white leads in a single wire nut, three black leads in another, and two black leads in the last.

Two lights can be installed on a single line, with one controlled by a switch and the other by a pull chain. If you want to add an outlet and a switch past an existing light, then you will need three-wire cable (with one red wire). The switch and outlet can also be contained in the same box with no more complexity in the wiring, while new outlets are readily added beyond those already installed and on the same circuit. A

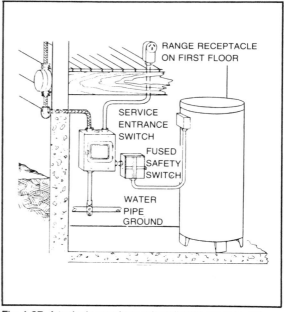

Fig. 4-27. A typical water heater installation (courtesy Sears, Roebuck and Company).

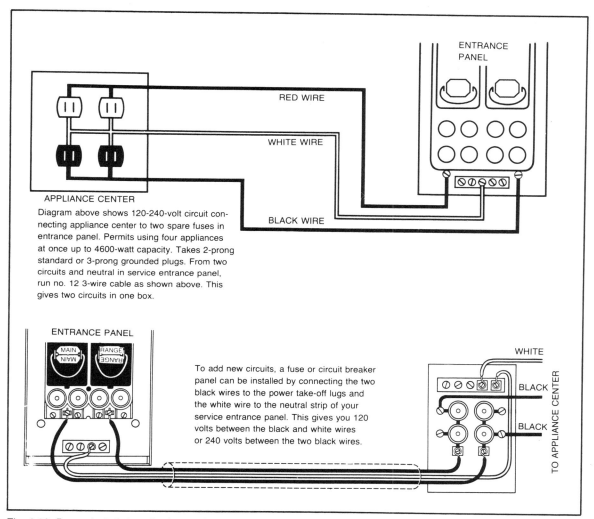

RED WIRE

WHITE WIRE

BLACK WIRE

ENTRANCE PANEL

APPLIANCE CENTER

Diagram above shows 120-240-volt circuit connecting appliance center to two spare fuses in entrance panel. Permits using four appliances at once up to 4600-watt capacity. Takes 2-prong standard or 3-prong grounded plugs. From two circuits and neutral in service entrance panel, run no. 12 3-wire cable as shown above. This gives two circuits in one box.

ENTRANCE PANEL

MAIN

RANGE

To add new circuits, a fuse or circuit breaker panel can be installed by connecting the two black wires to the power take-off lugs and the white wire to the neutral strip of your service entrance panel. This gives you 120 volts between the black and white wires or 240 volts between the two black wires.

WHITE

BLACK

BLACK

TO APPLIANCE CENTER

Fig. 4-28. Proper installation of a four-outlet receptacle (courtesy Sears, Roebuck and Company).

Check with your local utility company to make sure you're using the correct circuitry for a particular type of water heater (Fig. 4-27).

Overloading of appliance circuits in the kitchen is not unusual. A tap plug is often used to hold the appliance cords from an electric iron, toaster, blender, and one or two other small appliances. The two-circuit, four-outlet design in Fig. 4-28 is both safe and convenient. Use only a number 12, three-wire cable to run the double circuit into the four-outlet unit. You will then have a 4,600-watt capacity for small appliances, probably more than you will ever need at one time.

Chapter 5

Walls and Floors

B ASIC WALL FRAMING TECHNIQUES ARE NOT DIF-
ficult to learn and apply (Fig. 5-1). Even wall removal and replacement is relatively simple, assuming
there are no load-bearing walls to be taken out.

PARTITION WALLS

To install partition walls, you must decide first
where everything is going to be located. Make your
measurements and mark the interior edge of the new
wall. Decide on framing on-center distances. Check
local codes; some codes are still restrictive enough to
require 16-inch on-center distances even for partition
(non-load-bearing) walls. Others allow you to erect
such walls with on-center distances of 24 inches and,
sometimes, of 2 by 3s instead of 2 by 4s. Interior
partition walls should be of 2 by 4 construction. Any
paneled wall opened up to 24 inches on center should
have an underlayer of at least ⅜-inch gypsum
wallboard before paneling is installed. Any partition
wall with paneling is sturdier and looks better, if an
underlying support of gypsum board is laid in place
and properly nailed. Seams on tapered edges need to
be taped. Unless nail holes are dished deeply, the
other finishing steps can be avoided (Fig. 5-2).

Partition walls are framed using a sole plate and at
least a single top plate. Studs are toenailed or installed

using TECO anchor plates at the sole plate. You can
cut studs to length and nail the top rail in place before
tilting the wall unit up. Nail the top plate in relatively
small sections, because the studs are hanging loose at
the bottom end. Make sure the studs are plumb when
preparing to nail. It generally doesn't work too well to
try and frame the entire partition section, sole plate,
studs, and top plate.

LOAD-BEARING WALLS

When you must remove a load-bearing wall to
increase room size or change room layout, check local
codes carefully. You will have specific on-center distance limitations on stud spacing. That spacing may be
16 or 24 inches, but you cannot exceed it and get a
certificate of occupancy. On-center spacing will be
tighter for wall construction. You will almost certainly
need a doubled top plate, too. Door installation may
require specific header sizes and an extra stud in the
rough framing.

Take care when removing the present wall. You
will certainly need bracing. If the ceiling and upper floor
(if any) are not braced, you will probably see sagging
as work proceeds. This is one spot where no mistakes
are allowed during construction.

Fig. 5-1. Attractive walls are readily created with today's wallcovering (courtesy Thomas Strahan/Broyhill).

Make sure the old ceiling is structured well before the bracing is removed. You cannot simply remove a load-bearing wall and let things hang. A new wall, or a new set of framing members, must be designed and installed to provide the support that is being removed with the old wall.

A beam that is too light to brace the upstairs load will cause problems. Floors sagging away from walls and baseboards in the upstairs are among these problems. Many codes will specify the minimum beam size for a particular span.

BRACING

When I've removed old, load-bearing walls, the bracing has ranged from none to 2 by 4s spaced on 12-inch centers, run at an angle, to 2 by 4s run into 2 by 6 plates set under the ceiling and holding joist ends. You do not have to use support on removal jobs if the section of load-bearing wall is relatively small, say, 6 feet. Support is not needed if you are opening a passageway or installing a sliding glass door. If the span approaches 8 feet, though, you need some support.

The type of support will depend on the area in which the wall is being removed.

Recently I pulled out about 19 feet of load-bearing wall that rested directly on the basement/floor system girder, with the attic central beam resting on the load-bearing wall. That required a little thought. The ceiling joists all ended in the area from which I was taking support. Any sag during removal would be disastrous. I ran a 2 by 4, doubled, along the ceiling about 8 inches to one side of the load-bearing wall. I did the same on the other side of the load-bearing wall. I then supported each of those top plates with 2 by 4s wedged in at about 3-foot intervals. There was no sag whatsoever when I removed the wall. Once the central beam was cut and installed, I was able to simply knock the wedging free, dodge the falling top plates, and finish the job.

There are many ways to remove old walls. Pull all pipe, tubing, and wiring out of the area. Rip off the plaster or plasterboard. If good-quality paneling has been used, I like to try and save it by using a tool that looks like a flat ripping bar. You will also want a 3-foot ripping bar like my Plumb model and a sledge hammer of either 8 or 10-pound head weight. If you want to save some of the lumber used to frame the old wall, you will also want a smaller engineer's hammer or cross-peen hammer with a 3-pound head weight. If a wall has been in place for several years, though, the wood will be so dry around the nails that it will split and splinter no matter how carefully you work. Any pieces of framing left can be used as short sections.

Span is a problem when you're working with opened-up bearing wall sections. Use only grade number 1 wood, no matter the species. Firs, yellow pine, Southern pine, and other softwoods are best for strength. Avoid hemlocks, cedars, and other weak woods. Doubled spanning girders can add strength. Some newer homes have 7-foot ceilings, and a very tall person will have a problem if you open up a span so wide that you have to use anything larger than a 2 by 8. If you double a frame member when spanning wide areas, work with either double 16-penny nails, two placed every 2 feet, or carriage bolts or lag screws positioned every 2 feet.

Using braces at the ends—at 45-degree angles—will help reduce the span. You can open up more than 12 feet, then slip in nailed or cut-in bracing from one upright to the beam to reduce the span. The braces make great plant hangers, too.

Any new beams added must be supported well at their ends. Using even doubled 2 by 4s is seldom

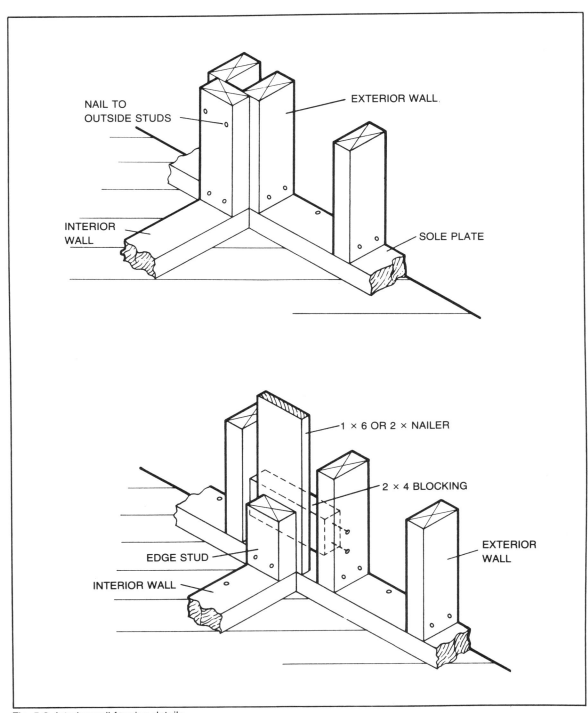

NAIL TO
OUTSIDE STUDS

EXTERIOR WALL

INTERIOR
WALL

SOLE PLATE

1 × 6 OR 2 × NAILER

2 × 4 BLOCKING

EDGE STUD

INTERIOR WALL

EXTERIOR
WALL

Fig. 5-2. Interior wall framing details.

enough. You will usually need 2 by 6s, doubled, if the span is more than 8 feet. A lumber dealer should have complete span strength lists for any wood that he sells, when looking at strength listings, remember that allowable deflection is always 1/360. The span can deflect 1 inch for every 360 inches of length. You need to know the floor load to use a span chart; to be safe, figure at least 40 pounds for the floor load.

DOOR OPENINGS

Door openings in partitions require a doubled studding at the hinge side and are best served with a double stud on the latch side as well. Door headers for partitions may be doubled 2 by 4s, though 2 by 6s are used if the door is more than 2 feet wide. Door framing must be done to the rough opening size of the prehung door unit that you will be installing. You can still buy and assemble separate doors and door casings, then install your own hinges and locksets. The work involved is tedious, though, and requires great accuracy (especially in mortising for the hinges and cutting the holes for the lockset). Special mortising kits for use with routers are available, but the cost of the router, bit, and hinge jig is far more than the price of prehung doors.

Toenailing of studs is done with 12-penny nails, and face nailing is accomplished with 16-penny nails. If you use TECO framing anchors, they come with appropriate nails specifically designed for each anchor to provide the greatest holding power. Screws for hinges will be supplied. For light interior doors, you will seldom need hinges larger than number 12. Exterior doors, though, often use a number 16 screw as much as 2½ inches long.

WALLBOARD

Wallboard is simple to install. Lengths up to 16 feet are available on order, although 8-foot ones are standard (the sheet is 4 by 8 feet, either ⅜ or ½ inch thick). Wallboard is nailed at 8-inch intervals along the borders—using ring-shanked nails to prevent nail popping—and at 16-inch intervals along the interior, using doubled nails. When using doubled nails, you will be finished more quickly because you don't have as many dimples to fill with joint compound (Fig. 5-3).

Wallboard can also be installed using fewer nails and an interior construction adhesive. The adhesive, produced by Franklin Chemical Industries, comes in cartridges for use with cartridge guns. This glue and adhesive combination can also be used with interior

paneling, and it provides a wall that is as strong as one put up conventionally with nails only. Finish problems are also reduced, because most nails can be set in areas to be covered with molding, either at the top or the bottom. In many cases you only need to tape the joints for a smooth wall finish.

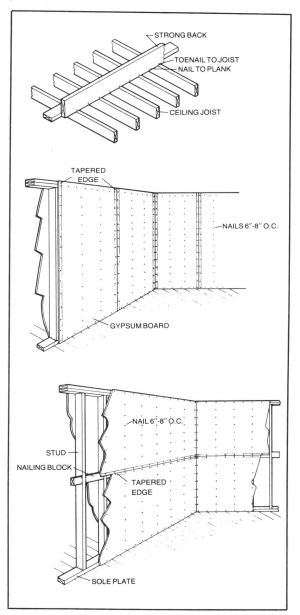

Fig. 5-3. Installing wallboard.

99

Joint taping on wallboard is a chore. Joints must be taped in a three-step, two-day process. Begin by spreading a layer of joint compound thick enough to accept the joint tape. Use a new model joint tape with a mesh design instead of the old paper tapes. The newer mesh tapes are easier to use and form a stronger joint. Spread the first layer of joint compound smoothly, and then use a 1½-inch or 2-inch flexible putty knife to press the tape into the compound. Apply a second coating of joint compound before the first coat has a chances to dry. The second coat should be considerably less thick that the first coat (Fig. 5-4).

If you use the widest taping knife available, then you have far less work to get a really smooth joint at the tape lines. Hyde Manufacturing Company makes a ten-inch-wide taping knife and a corner taping knife. Interior joints on wallboard are especially difficult. A straight taping knife tends to slide over and cut into one surface after it has been smoothed, or you have to wait until the first finished surface is dry. To save time, a joint taping knife has a blade set at 103 degrees to finish both sides at one time. Wide knives come in widths to a foot in Hyde's JT series. Another knife has a slightly offset 10-inch blade. The Blue Steel Hyde series includes knives 8, 10, and 12-inch sizes. Hyde's offset or JT knives are fine, and the Blue Steel knives are best for professionals (Figs. 5-5 and 5-6).

If you use a wrung-out sponge to wipe the second coat of joint compound about 15 to 30 minutes after it is applied, the finish will go more easily. Keep a large water bucket on hand to keep the sponge rinsed well, and wipe only lightly in the direction of the joint. The final layer of joint compound is relatively thin and is applied after the first and second coats have dried. If necessary, give the second coat a light sanding before applying the last coat. Sand the final coat no sooner than 24 hours after application, and you should have a wall appearing almost seamless.

Wallboard is cut with a utility knife. You can snap chalk lines or use a wallboard square (a slightly offset T square with a 4-foot aluminum blade to mark the board. Cut the finish surface side first. Score deeply enough to break through the paper, and then snap down firmly. Cut the back paper along the line. A saw is used to cut wallboard only when very small or interior cuts are to be made (Fig. 5-7).

Finish sanding on wallboard joints and nail holes should be light. Major depressions should be filled. Horizontal tape joints are less likely to reflect light in a way that will show up as a seam. In most cases, then, it is best to run wallboard horizontally.

Most new construction codes will require at least ½-inch-thick wallboard. Some codes prefer double-thick ⅜-inch wallboard, with a fairly heavy adhesive layer between the two sheets. You can use 5-penny ring-shanked nails (about 1¾ inches long) for wallboard installation and expect a solid job. When you double the thickness of the wallboard, though, go to at least a 6-penny ring-shanked nail.

If you use gypsum wallboard for ceilings, you need a T brace made of 2 by 4s to support the wallboard as you lift it and prepare to nail. Make the T brace yourself. Tape and fill nail dimples for ceilings just as you would with walls (Figs. 5-8 through 5-13).

FLOORING MATERIALS

Kitchen floors are vulnerable spots (Fig. 5-14). Check kitchen floors carefully, even if you have to remove portions of a basement or another ceiling. Joists running parallel to walls where heavy appliances, such as refrigerators and freezers, are to be located must be doubled. Use joist members the same size as original members of the floor system. Continue them across the full span, just as the original members are carried across. You may have to trim extra joist ends to fit into close quarters, and you may also have to detach plumbing or wiring runs to bring them through holes drilled or notches cut in new framing members. It is definitely worth the extra effort even if local codes don't require the extra strength. The floor installed to finish the job will last longer with less subfloor flex; the subfloor will last longer, too. There is also far less chance of a joist cracking under the heavy appliances.

When framing any new floor, remember that the allowable span for any wood is determined by the grade and species of wood almost as much as by the on-center distance of the construction. The American Plywood Association (APA) standards allow for an 8-foot, 2-inch span with Douglas fir, using nails only. The span can be 9 feet, 1 inch when using glue and nails. As the grade of wood decreases, so does the allowable span.

Plywood

Plywood is the most common modern subflooring material. The subfloor grades are listed by the APA as Structural 1 and Structural 11. Many people also use a C-C Exterior grade. Always buy kitchen subflooring with exterior glue to reduce problems from water spills.

A system known as MOD 24 includes a single-layer, ¾-inch tongue and groove plywood on 24-inch centers, over the joists, with glue and nails. If you use a structural finish floor of wood at least 25/32 inch thick, then ½-inch C-D plywood is suitable. This is for wood strip flooring only—not for parquet or other wood block styles. Any plywood used as subflooring should be installed so that the grain of the top ply runs at right angles to the joists, and the end joints must be staggered so that breaks occur over different joists. Plywood subflooring should always meet on joists, too, or you will have to install special blocking (solid) for

support of the edges. Use 8-penny, ring-shanked nails plus glue. Nail the plywood at 6-inch intervals along the outer edges and at 10-inch intervals along inner joists. If the flooring is to be single layer (without a structurally rigid finish floor), all nails should be at 6-inch intervals.

Tongue and groove plywood is designed to fit, but butt joints on plywood mean you must allow for expansion and contraction. The APA recommends ⅛ inch at the edges and 1/16 inch at the ends of each sheet. If conditions are damp, make sure the plywood is Ex-

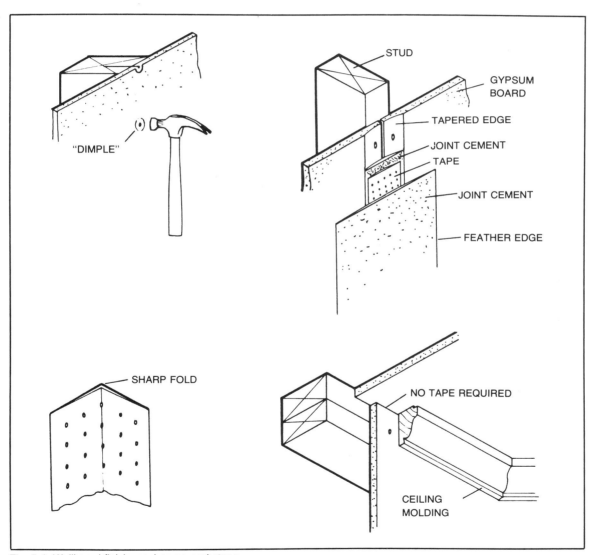

Fig. 5-4. Wallboard finish requires several steps.

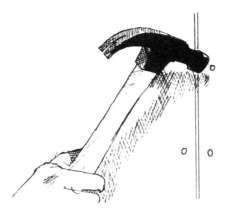

Inspect joint carefully before application of joint compound for taping. See that nails are set, joints straight, if joint space is wider than ⅛″ fill with compound. When nails are set too deep fill in holes with compound. Use a 3″ No. 02350 flexible Hyde Scraper to fill.

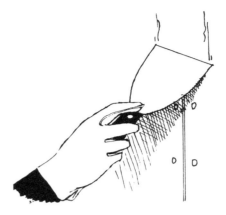

Apply compound filling valley or hollow of boards at joint. Use a Hyde 4″ flexible Joint Knife No. 02550 or 5″ size No. 02750. Be sure and spread evenly, no skips, or tape will not adhere, thus resulting in blisters.

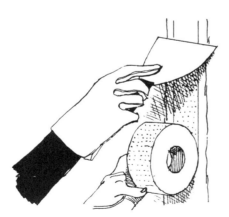

Following the first application imbed tape into compound, down the joint, make sure tape is straight and on center, press firmly with Hyde Joint Knives 4″ or 5″ size as indicated in the preceeding instructions. Hold roll of tape as shown.

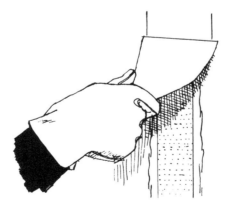

After first coat is thoroughly dry apply another coat using a 6″ Hyde Joint Knife No. 02850 feathering out compound and leveling any depressions or skips. Allow to dry thoroughly before applying finish coat.

Fig. 5-5. Wallboard finishing tips (courtesy Hyde Manufacturing Company).

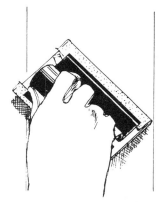

To finish use a 10″ wide Hyde Joint Knife, No. 09100 stainless steel or No. 09710 blue steel or No. 09210 stainless steel. Feather out compound with one of the broad joint knives selected. The better the feathering the less sanding is required for a smooth wall.

Sanding is extremely important to smooth joint project to blend with wall. Light sanding when joint is completed and thoroughly dry will finish the joint for painting or wallcovering. Check product information on joint compound package and see your local retailer.

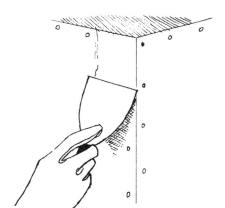

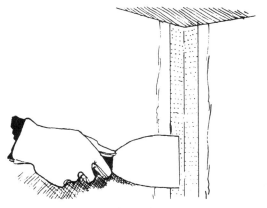

Inside or interior corners should be finished following the same procedures as doing the joints on flat wall surfaces. Apply joint compound to make a bed for the dry wall joint tape using Hyde Joint Knives as indicated for flat wall joint job.

Taping an inside corner requires the folding or creasing of tape to fit snugly in the corner over the application of joint compound. Tape is imbedded into joint compound using a Hyde Flexible Joint Knife to press tape, or use Hyde Corner Tool No. 09410, see next page.

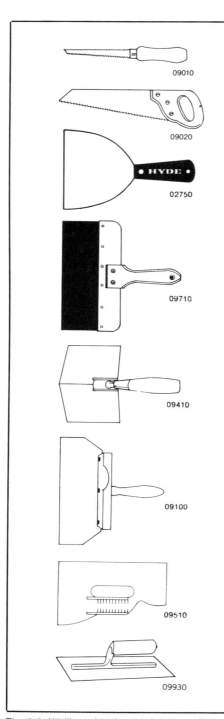

09010

09020

02750

09710

09410

09100

09510

09930

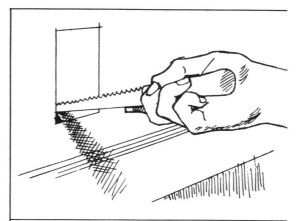

Keyhole saw.
Small sharp teeth slim saw blade to saw out openings for light switches, outlet boxes, pipe bolts, etc. Measure area for opening, drill holes within area to start sawing. No. 09010.

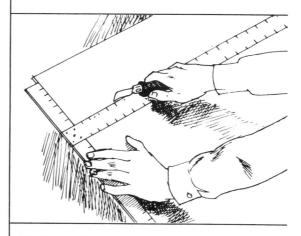

Wallboard T square.
Made of spring aluminum, used to accurately measure standard 48″ wide wallboard to be cut into desired lengths. Top cross piece with lip to hold in place and vertical strip have easy to read markings. No. 35400.

Fig. 5-6. Wallboard tools and their uses (courtesy Hyde Manufacturing Company).

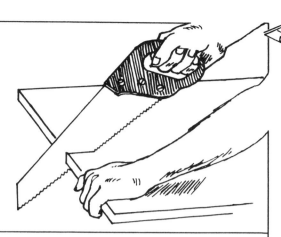

Wallboard saw.
Sharp deep teeth blade to cut sections from wallboard. Blade measures 15½" long with point for easy entry. No. 09020. Use Hyde giant wallboard T square to accurately measure.

Pan for joint compound.
Sturdy, hand-held plastic container holds dry-wall joint and patch compounds. Features two steel wiping blades at the top sides. Blades are handy to wipe knives clean, save and keep compounds off floor. No. 45480.

Long-handle pole sander.
The answer to sanding ceilings and high walls. This pole sander has a lightweight swivel head that attaches to a pole. Die cast aluminum sander has foam rubber pad, clamps, several sheets of sandpaper, measures 9⅜" x 3¼". A real timesaver, stand on floor to do ceiling sanding. No. 35400.

Trowels for drywall.
Some prefer use of curved trowel No. 09930. Use tool after first coat is dry to build up compounded joint. When dry, sand smooth. Use trowel No. 09900 with compound to finish joint, sand smooth and feather edges.

Finish inside corners with a special tool for best results. The Hyde Corner Tool No. 09410 is used for tape application as well as the application of the final coat of joint compound. Tool has 4" wide flexible stainless steel blades with 103° angle to fit tightly into corners.

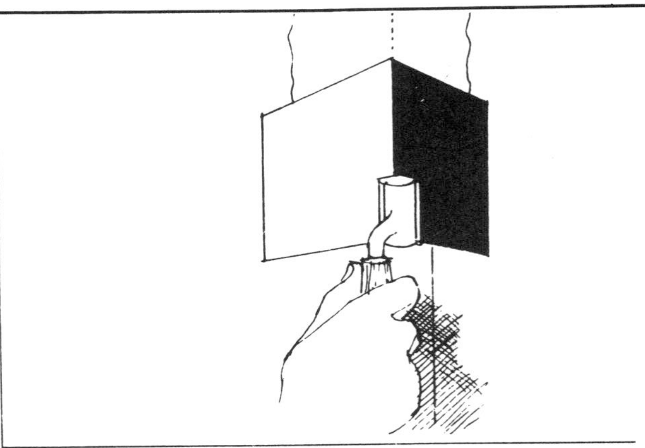

Outside corners in rooms follow the same first step procedure as flat wall joints. Apply joint compound on both sides of corners for imbedding of metal bead. Use Hyde Joint Knife to apply compound.

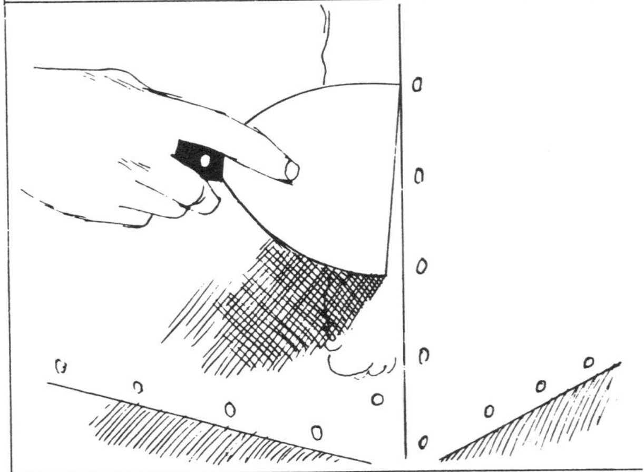

Press metal bead strip into joint compound and allow time for thorough drying before proceeding to next step.

Fig. 5-7. Taping tips will make the job faster and the finish smoother (courtesy Hyde Manufacturing Company).

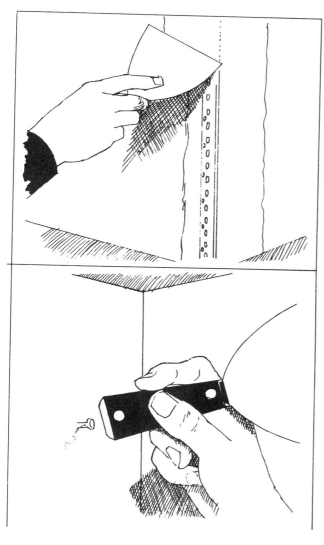

Apply compound to cover metal bead, feather compound out from corner. Use No. 02550, 4″ or No. 02750, 5″ flexible joint knives. Sand to smooth and blend when compound is dry.

Popped nails at joints can be tapped in and dimples leveled with the special end cap of Zamac, a zinc metal, on handles of the Hyde Hammer Head Joint Knives. Tool numbers are 4″ size No. 08550, 5″ No. 08750, 6″ 08850.

terior type and double the spacing at edges and ends, because expansion and contraction will be greater. These situations occur most often when you build over crawl spaces and slabs.

Resilient Tile

You need a finish floor for your kitchen that will resist water, grease, and wear. Select a floor that can be easily cleaned and will last a long time. Most kitchen floors today are some form of resilent tile or carpeting. A ceramic tile floor, if properly laid, will outlast any kitchen carpet. Good tile with modern grouts should never have to be replaced, unless it is broken by a heavy, hard object. Regrouting may have to be done every decade or two, but that is easy compared to relaying carpet every five or six years (Figs. 5-15 through 5-19).

Wood

Wood flooring for kitchens is a bit unusual, but it shouldn't be dropped from consideration. A wood strip floor of oak, maple, beech, birch, or even hard pine can be extremely attractive if wider boards are used for a rustic or colonial look (Fig. 5-20). Today's wood finishes reduce your worries about water spills and heavy wear. A finish such as ZAR Imperial polyurethane gloss from United Gilsonite Laboratories is going to wear a long time. It is basically impervious to water spills as well as grease and kitchen chemicals. Refinishing is messy but relatively cheap, fast, and easy compared with replacing an entire floor of another material.

Ceramic Tile

Ceramic tile flooring is about the hardest to install properly, because special cutting and trimming tools are essential to a good job. Ceramic hole saws and drill bits make the installation easier, and new adhesives eliminate a lot of work. New grout styles are far easier to apply than older joint fillers. Most styles can be wiped over a fairly large surface area. The residue is simply cleaned from the tile surfaces with a damp cloth.

Ceramic tile is also the most expensive type of flooring to use. The cost of ceramic tile is often the reason for its use only in smaller areas such as bathrooms. You should consider using ceramic tile in the kitchen because of its amazing durability and beauty. Ceramic tile will cost from 1½ to 6 times as much as resilient tile per square foot. Resilient tile is approxi-

mately the same price as top-quality indoor/outdoor carpet.

Wood flooring varies widely in price. Most prefinished wood flooring is not really suitable for use in wet areas. So you can thus add in the cost of polyurethane coatings, with most floors probably needing at least 1 gallon.

FLOOR INSTALLATION

Your first step in laying any floor is to determine the amount of material required to do the job. The material requirements will include the correct number of square feet of finish flooring, any adhesive, and any base moldings to go around walls and cabinet sides. If you're measuring tightly, allow 5 percent for waste and breakage with ceramic tiles and wood, and the same amount for extra tile when laying resilient tile (for tiles that get broken or torn in use).

When installing any finish floor, vacuum the subfloor thoroughly. When adhesives are used to install flooring, be sure there is no dust to interfere with the finished floor. Go over the subfloor and make sure all nailheads are driven in. Check nailing patterns to ensure that the subfloor won't lift under the finished flooring. With board flooring, check for loose boards and nail where needed.

Wood Strip Flooring

Wood strip flooring is normally laid at right angles to the joists underneath. The subfloor, if not plywood, must be covered with builder's felt. Staple the builder's felt ½ inch out from the wall where you will start to lay the strip flooring; this is usually the outer joist end wall. Lay the grooved side (with tongue and groove flooring) toward the wall, and face-nail the strip close enough to the wall so the baseboard will cover everything when it is installed. A standard baseboard with a half-round shoe will extend out about 1¼ to 1½ inches. Your next strip is laid, groove to tongue, against this starter strip. It is driven as hard against the starter strip as possible, so that any cracks between strips are eliminated. The second strip is then toenailed, just at the top of the tongue, using flooring nails. A nail set is useful. If you are not used to laying strip flooring, dividing the room into at least four sections with chalk lines is probably a good idea (Fig. 5-21).

Run chalk lines showing where the joists lie under the subflooring. Make sure nails are driven through the subfloor and into the joists. This helps to prevent squeaking. Penetration into the joists need not be

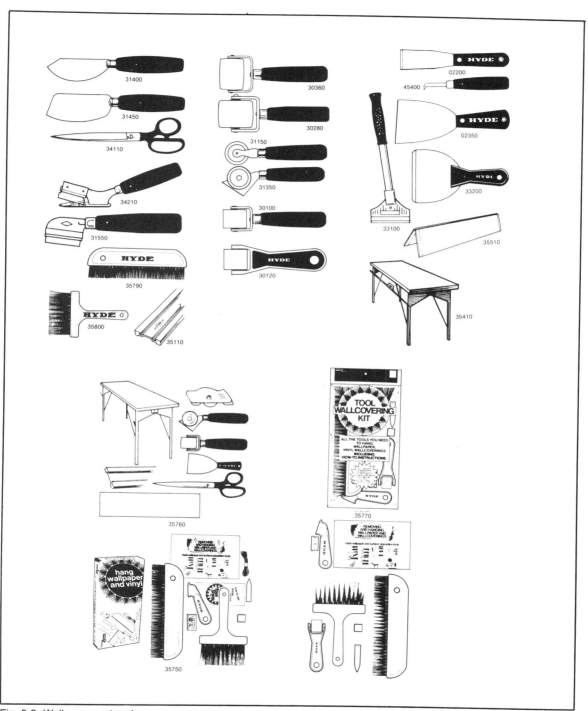

Fig. 5-8. Wallpaper and surface preparation tools (courtesy Hyde Manufacturing Company).

DESCRIPTION AND USE OF HYDE WALLPAPER AND WALLCOVERING TOOLS.

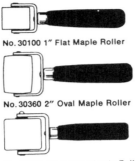

No. 30100 1" Flat Maple Roller

No. 30360 2" Oval Maple Roller

No. 30270 1⁹⁄₁₆" Flat Plastic Roller

No. 30280 1⁹⁄₁₆" Oval Plastic Roller

Hyde presents 2 types of seam rollers as illustrated. Plastic rollers are preferred by many as the rollers are easier to clean, however, they should be used with care on certain papers to avoid shinny look. The flat rollers are used to smooth areas on each side of seams. The oval rollers are for the seams, they press and join seams together for a tight bond. The oval rollers help to prevent spreading of paste on paper from seams. The plastic rollers are produced in the sizes shown above. The hardwood line of seam rollers are popular with many, they are not as easy to clean, however, they do the job as required. The flat rollers are for large areas on the paper to roll out ripples, etc. The oval rollers are for seams to press down papers together for a tight snug seam. See all sizes with tool numbers above. When flocked or certain material papers are used a material may be used over flat rollers to prevent crushed designs. Material cut to exact width and held to roller with double face tape, butt material on roller to prevent a bumpy roller, the roller should have a consistent smooth surface.

An unusual and handy 2-in-1 1¼" flat maple roller. Use for flat wall as packaged, change axle with screw driver and reverse roller and tool becomes a corner roller. Hyde No. 30250.

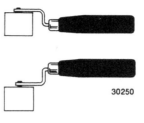

30250

30120

An inexpensive flat 1¼" maple roller held by a plastic handle. Hyde No. 30120.

No. 31150 Smooth blade

No. 31350 Ser. Casing and Corner Knife

Casing knives are used to trim wallpaper on walls while wet before paper dries around windows, door frames and baseboards. There are 3 kinds of blades on these knives, smooth wheels, serrated and a combination casing and corner knife. The salvage is trimmed at ceilings and baseboards with these tools using a guide for straight trimming.

Fig. 5-9. The variety of wallcovering tools is wide (courtesy Hyde Manufacturing Company).

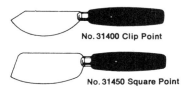

No. 31400 Clip Point

No. 31450 Square Point

Wallpaper knives may be used to trim paper on paste table with straight edge as a guide or on walls at ceiling and baseboard.

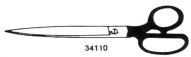

34110

Shears are used to trim paper around light switches, ceiling fixtures. There are 2 kinds of shears, forged steel with 12″ blades, No.34110 and cast iron steel with 12″ blades, No.34160. The forged steel shears are considered to be the better shears.

31550

The razor knife is an all purpose trimming tool for wallpaper. Tool holds replaceable single edge razor blade. Hyde No.31550. Use knife with guide, straight edge or a 6″ wide Hyde joint knife for trimming.

32110

Chalk line holder and dispenser. This tool holds 50′ of line which is chalked in holder. Hyde No.32110.

HYDE TOOLS 15000

Single edge industrial type razor blades are used in Hyde tools to cut and trim wallpaper and wallcoverings. Hyde provides these blades in standard packages of 5 each and in bulk lots.

34210

This Hyde tool is a vinyl wallcovering trimming knife. It holds a disposable single edge industrial razor blade. Sometimes called a "seam buster" tool cuts overlapped seams for a perfect butt seam. Instructions for use are found on back of tool package. No. 34210.

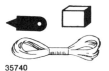

35740

Hyde provides a plumb bob, chalk cake and 12′ of mason's twine in a plastic bag for the hanging of wallpaper and wallcoverings. The plumb line is important to start right with the first roll of material on the wall.

No. 45810

A versatile long blue plastic guide with a 24″ stainless steel blade especially designed to be used as a large paint shield, smoothing device for heavy wall coverings, a straightedge for trimming, a wall smoothing tool, etc. Attractive red, white and blue labels identify and show the many uses of this tool.

111

Wallpaper may be removed first by soaking the paper with a sponge using a 'wetting agent' a commercial liquid wallpaper remover. Paper that has been painted will require the scratching of the surface so the chemical agent or water will penetrate the paper.

Spraying the surface of the wallpaper with a hand sprayer containing water or liquid wallpaper remover will penetrate to paste for removal. Use plastic drop cloth to protect floor when removing paper.

Remove soaked paper with the Hyde No. 33200 special wall scraper tool. Tool has a sturdy 4½" wide extra sharp blade with rounded edges. Push scraper upwards at an angle, starting at base of wall, into wet wallpaper.

This 11" long handle wallpaper shaver tool holds a replaceable 4½" wide razor sharp blade. Wallpaper may be shaved off wall wet or dry. Start at base of wall and push tool upwards at an angle into wallpaper. Hyde Tool No. 33100. See tool package for information.

Sponge wall with wall cleaner to remove paste and bits of old paper. See your paint and wallpaper store for wall cleaner and instructions to prepare wall for repainting or application of new wallpaper.

Fig. 5-10. Removal of old wallcoverings and proper surface preparation are essential to a good job (courtesy Hyde Manufacturing Company).

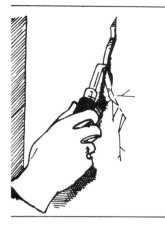

Cracks should be opened, cleaned out and patched. Hyde No. 45400 is a special crack opening tool with sharp steel wedge point that opens cracks easily for patching.

Cracks and pucks on walls should be filled with patching compound, use a Hyde Flexible Putty Knife No. 02100 or combination crack opener and application tool No. 45450. Sand filled cracks when compound is dry.

Dimples on the walls can be smoothed out with the use of the Hyde No. 45810 Super Guide. This large plastic tool holds a 24" long stainless steel blade. Tool is moved over wall surface in a sweeping motion. Tool has many other uses; trim guide, paint shield, etc.

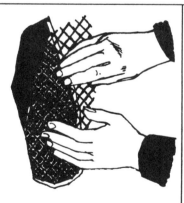

Larger holes may be filled with patch compound after holes are backed with wire mesh. The mesh cut oversize is pushed into hole and held in place with an epoxy glue or tape against back of wall. See other hole patching systems in this book.

Many cloth back vinyls and some acrylic coated papers are strippable simply by starting at a corner and carefully peeling the entire strip from the wall. Prepare walls for painting or wallpapering following wall clean-up and patch-up procedures.

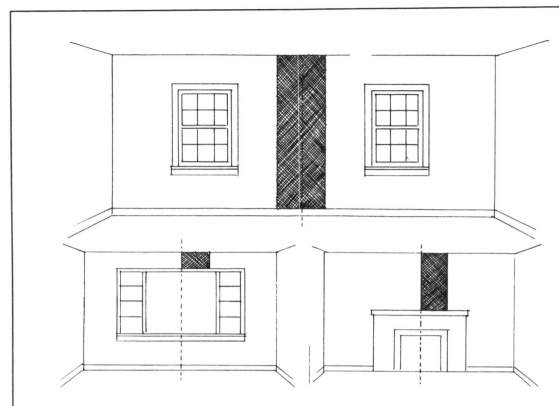

WALLPAPER AND WALLCOVERING TIPS USING HYDE TOOLS.

Be sure walls are in proper condition for hanging of wallpaper or wallcoverings. See preceding pages for wall surface preparation. If old paper is not removed be sure seams are tight. Loose paper should be pasted down or removed and paper around area sanded lightly to smooth and blend with bare wall. Thick overlapped seams should also be lightly sanded. Where wallpaper has been removed wash down and size wall, speak to your wallpaper sup-

plier about these procedures. There are many different types and kinds of wallpaper and wallcoverings on the market today and the handling for hanging of anyone of these varieties should be discussed with your wallpaper dealer. In many instances where prepasted paper is used it is not necessary to work on a paste table, however, non-pasted paper requires the use of a wallpaper table. The butt joint is the most popular, however, there are lap and wire edge joints. Where adhesives are required ask advice from dealer and read instructions on

Fig. 5-11. When the surface is prepared, you can hang the new wallcoverings (courtesy Hyde Manufacturing Company).

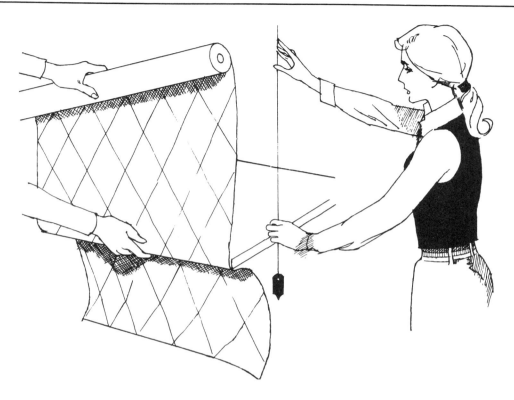

the packaged materials.

Where to start the first strip.
Study the room and decide where to hang the first strip. Generally the first strip is hung on the center of a wall which is most noticed in the room. Start between 2 windows, fireplace, picture window or if there are no outstanding openings, the first strip may be hung starting at a corner where an overlap is required into the corner.

Using the plumb bob.
When the decision is made where to start drive a tack into wall about 2" from ceiling. Bob should hang around 2" from floor. When bob stops swaying make a mark on wall above baseboard. Chalk line, hold line on mark and pull line out at center and release to make a vertical mark on wall. First strip of paper should align with mark. Plumb line each wall to keep paper vertical.

Preparing the paper.
It is necessary to uncurl the paper by holding the roll up in one hand and pulling down on a section of the paper over the edge of the table with the other hand.

WALLPAPER AND WALLCOVERING TIPS USING HYDE TOOLS.

Cutting the first strips.

Two sections of the paper must be cut to match pattern from ceiling to floor allowing 2″ of trim at ceiling and baseboard keeping in mind the matching of the designs in the paper.

Paste application.

Place the two sections of the matched paper on the table, patterns down, paste on thoroughly to cover all areas to prevent unpasted spots, except for 2″ at the top for trimming at ceiling. Fold first section of paper, carry to the wall for hanging. Do not paste more than two sections of paper at a time.

Hanging the first strip.

Unfold paper and place in position on wall using chalk line as guide allowing 2″ trim area at the top. Paper may be slid around to fit the area as planned. Starting at the top brush paper down to smooth out wrinkles unfolding the paper as you go down the wall reaching the baseboard at the bottom where 2″ of paper has been allowed for baseboard trim.

Fig. 5-12. Wallcovering tips (courtesy Hyde Manufacturing Company).

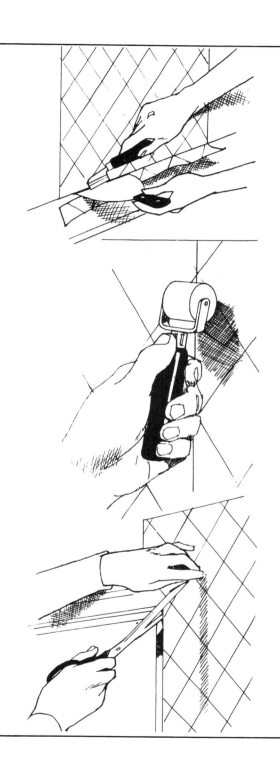

Trimming at the ceiling.
Paper trimmed where wall meets ceiling using Hyde Super Guide No. 45810 with Hyde No. 31550 Razor Knife. Follow the same procedure for the second strip of paper matching the pattern where 2″ has been allowed at the top and bottom on the basis of the matched patterns.

Rolling the paper and seams.
Roll seam with Hyde Oval Plastic Seam Roller No. 30280 or No. 30360 hardwood roller. Use No. 30250 side arm roller to roll both sides of corner. Blisters or raised paper may be gently rolled out with a Hyde flat roller No. 30270 plastic or No. 30310 hardwood roller. Pin prick covering to allow air to escape.

Baseboard trimming.
The paper at the base may be trimmed with a Hyde No. 31350 serrated casing and corner knife or Hyde Casing Knife No. 31150.

Trimming around doors and windows.
Concerning doors and windows, paper should be cut and trimmed as indicated using shears and Hyde casing and corner knives.

WALLPAPER AND WALLCOVERING TIPS USING HYDE TOOLS.

Papering around light switches—outlets—etc.

Lighting fixtures and plates for electrical outlets should be removed, the paper cut and trimmed with care as indicated, electricity should be turned off.

The hanging of vinyl wallcoverings.

Follow pattern line up and pasting as indicated for wallpapering—see your wallcovering dealer for correct adhesive and read carefully instructions on package.

The butt joint procedures for the hanging of vinyl wallcovers.

Use Hyde Tool No. 34210 Vinyl Knife a trimmer that holds a single edge razor blade securely in place to cut double and single layers of all types and weights of wall coverings, including vinyl, clothbacked and waterproofed materials.

Overlapped seams.

Overlapped seams are accomplished as follows with the Hyde No. 34210 Vinyl Trimmer and

Fig. 5-13. More wallcovering tips (courtesy Hyde Manufacturing Company).

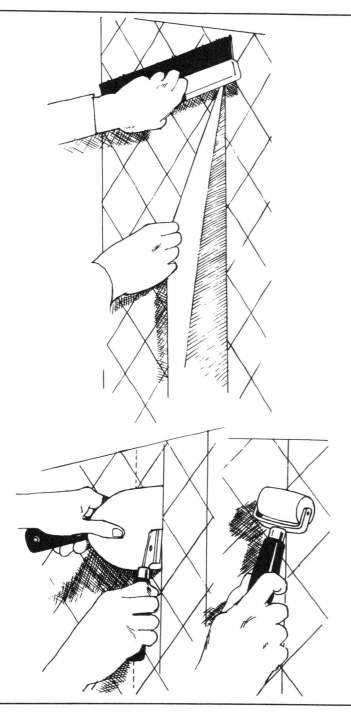

broad knives as illustrated. In the overlap method, hang the second strip so it overlays the first by 1½″ to 2″. Smooth, trim at baseboard and ceiling. Joint cut may be made immediately.

Starting at the top of the baseboard, hold the broad knife flat against the middle of the overlap. Cut through both strips about 5″ to 6″. Insert Vinyl Trimmer so that the shoe is flat against the wall. With the fingers, hold the two end flaps against the top of the shoe. Push the Vinyl Trimmer upward, keeping within the overlap. Straight edge may be used as a guide. Push the Vinyl Trimmer to the ceiling as far as it will go and finish the cut with a broad knife and razor blade. Remove both layers of cut material and thoroughly wash down the joint. This will produce a seam with a slight overlap. Do not roller the seam at this point. Pull back the right hand piece about 6″ from top to bottom. Butt the 6″ peeled piece tightly to the left hand strip. A small ridge will result. Starting at the ceiling, gently smooth straight down with broad knife. The small ridge will disappear leaving the tightly butted seam. Roller the seams and wash off excess paste.

Fig. 5-14. A country casual look is obtained with Mid-State Tile Company's Good Earth 3-inch hex tiles and cabinets by Overton.

great. Any nailing done between joists will hit only the subfloor. Use at least 8-penny cut flooring nails for the job. Do the nailing while standing on the strip being nailed (after you've moved far enough from the wall to make this possible). Stagger butt or end joists, even if the flooring has end matching tongues and grooves (Fig. 5-22).

If you encounter an extremely crooked piece of flooring, you may need help to pull it up tight against the flooring already in place. This can often be done with a helper sitting on the subfloor and pushing with both feet. The longer the crooked strip, the easier it usually is to force into place for nailing. Sometimes flooring must be discarded when you can't close up the cracks. A hydraulic jack laid on its side might help. Use a 2 by 6 to run from the jack, where it is butted against the opposing wall, to the flooring strip. Run the jack out until the cracks close up. Do the nailing.

Lay the final piece of strip flooring so that its tongue is about as far from the last wall as the groove was from the starting wall. You may have to rip the tongue or more of the board off to get a good fit. It is also face-nailed close enough to the wall, so the shoe molding will cover the nailheads.

Wide Board Flooring

Wide board flooring is usually butt-jointed. Otherwise, it is installed about like tongue and groove strip flooring. It will be face-nailed, because nails can not be hidden. You may want to use nails with decorative heads. Eight-penny nails are fine. Nail with a slight lateral slant toward the starter strip. Use two nails per joist for boards up to 3½ inches wide and three nails to each joint for boards up to 6 inches wide (wider boards are not recommended because they tend to warp badly).

Wood Block Flooring

Wood block flooring, often in the form of parquet design blocks, varies from maker to maker. A few brands are made to be nailed in place, but most can be used with adhesives (many come with adhesive already on the backs). Follow the flooring manufacturer's directions for best results (Fig. 5-23).

Resilient Tile

Resilient tile can be classified as the most popular kitchen floor covering. It is relatively simple to lay if you don't get too involved with special patterns for the individual tile layouts.

Too many people go directly from a wood strip or plywood subfloor to resilient tile and then wonder why the tile shows lines, cracks, and ridges after a few months of use. Some plywood subflooring is underlayment grade. You can go straight to the tile finish flooring, but most subfloors require an underlayment.

Fig. 5-15. Almost total tile coverage is possible (courtesy American Olean Tile Company).

Fig. 5-16. American Olean's Primitive tile series (courtesy American Olean Tile Company).

Cutting border tiles for edges around counters and at walls poses the largest problem for most amateur tile layers. For an accurate measurement, place a loose tile over the last full tile laid—close to the wall. Make sure the fit is exact. Take a second tile and butt it against the wall. Draw a line with a pencil or scribe along the loose tile. Cut the tile with scissors, a utility knife, or other tool and fit it in place.

Sheet Flooring

Sheet flooring is commonly constructed in three layers. There is a layer for a wear surface, an inner layer or core of softer foam padding, and a plastic backing. The sheet is installed with as few seams as possible. The edges are secured with staples or cement (adhesive) where needed. Use staples only when the edge will be covered by a base or other molding. Measure and cut the sheet flooring slightly oversize. Change knife blades frequently if there is much trimming to be done. Sheet flooring is generally available in widths of 6, 9, and 12 feet. It need not be installed with anything other than edge fastening.

Ceramic Tile

New adhesives make tile laying easier. Thin-coat adhesives are spread with a notched trowel. The tiles

Use a good grade of particle board or underlayment grade plywood to get a smooth, even surface. Make sure that the plywood is C-plugged or better. When laying underlayment, leave 1/32 inch for edge and end space. Use ring-shanked nails every 6 inches. Use an underlayment with a thickness that brings the finish floor level with floors in adjacent rooms. Sand the underlayment lightly to eliminate any high spots and give the adhesive a better tooth. Make sure the underlayment is free of all dust before laying tile.

Take your chalk line and find the center of each wall. Snap two chalk lines from these points and divide the room into four parts. Spread adhesive along two legs of one square and start laying the tile. Don't spread adhesive too far ahead of yourself, or it will set up and lose its bonding power. Spread adhesive with a brush, roller, or notched trowel. Check the manufacturer's stated set time for the adhesive, so you can figure how far ahead to spread the stuff. Snap tiles in place. After the first row of tiles is laid, place each succeeding tile tight against an already laid tile. Snap the opposite edge into place from an inch or so high.

Fig. 5-17. Ceramic tile from Mid-State Tile Company.

Fig. 5-18. Summitville's Summitstone tile series.

Fig. 5-19. Naples vinyl floorcovering (courtesy Biscayne Decorative Products).

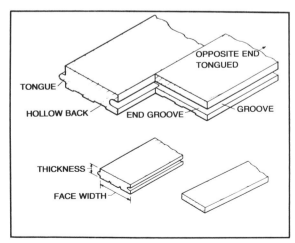
Fig. 5-20. Wood strip flooring.

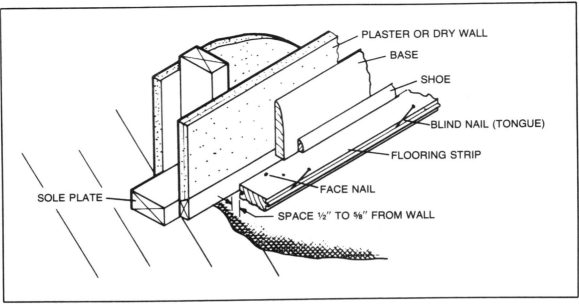

Fig. 5-21. Installation measurements for the first wood strip.

are set in place much like resilient floor tiles. Many ceramic tiles are now available in pregrouted sheets.

Prepare for ceramic tile installation as you did for resilient tile, right up to splitting the room into four sections with chalk lines snapped as required. Determine the joint size for non-pregrouted tiles. Lay one leg of the first square at a time. Use the layover method of determining the proper fit for tiles reaching walls or other edges. Make sure the loose tile is right on the last tile cemented in place. Mark and cut. Use either a rented tile cutter or tile nippers. Ceramic drills and a hole saw tipped for use with ceramic materials are

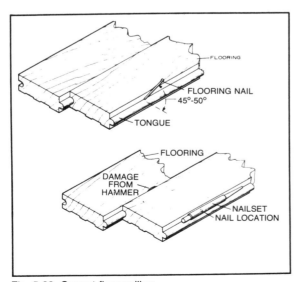

Fig. 5-22. Correct floor nailing.

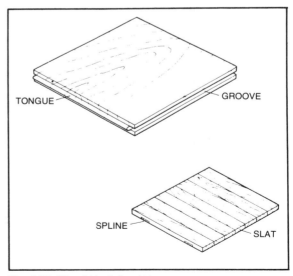

Fig. 5-23. Wood block flooring.

needed to make holes for pipe runs. If you tile a wall, the hole saw is almost essential to get an opening of the correct size for bathtub and shower faucets and outlets.

Epoxy and silicone type grouts are the best to use. Some grouts require water for cleanup while others need alcohol or possibly another solvent. Any ceramic tile floor or wall is ready for use in less than 24 hours.

Carpet

My advice is not to bother with carpet for an entire floor. Use carpet sections at the sink and in front of the stove to help reduce wear. Don't carpet an entire kitchen floor if the room is more then 5 feet by 6 feet. If the carpet is the self-adhesive kind, do not use it.

Self-adhesive carpet squares tend to lose all adhesive qualities whenever they are cleaned, meaning you will probably have to recement them every six or eight months.

Carpet in non-self-adhesive versions can be hard to install. Kick bars are needed so that when the carpet is attached near a baseboard, you can stretch it every couple of feet as you lay the material.

Slate and Brick Flooring

Slate and brick flooring are available in thicknesses approximating those of ceramic tile. They are laid in much the same manner as ceramic tile. The primary difference is the need for good sealant on the brick and slate to keep grime from entering the pores.

Chapter 6

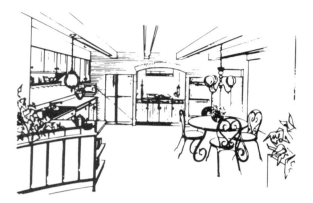

The Shopsmith Mark V

THE MAKING OF CABINETS FOR A KITCHEN IS AN extensive process. You will have to spend a lot of money on tools and plenty of time learning the skills to do a solid, craftsmanlike job.

The tools needed for cabinetmaking are not very portable. Plus, they are expensive.

Buy a device known as the multi-tool shop. There are several on the market, but the oldest and best known is the *Mark V* from Shopsmith. The Mark V includes a 10-inch table saw, a 16½-inch drill press, a 16½ by 34-inch lathe, a 12-inch disc sander, and a horizontal boring machine. Additional blades and accessories to add the shaper to the machine are relatively inexpensive. Its base is the drill press. The jointer is an additional tool, but it uses the same motor as the other listed Shopsmith tools. The jigsaw has its own motor. The band saw also uses the Mark V motor.

You save money by buying a single motor to operate eight separate tools. You save plenty of space by having a base unit that will fit in a 6 by 2-foot space. Conversion from one tool to another takes only a minute or two, even for inexperienced users. The original setup takes longer, but is essential to a good job of cutting, sanding, turning, shaping, and drilling (Figs. 6-1 through 6-5).

I will take a fairly quick look here at the various uses of the Shopsmith Mark V, but for further details you can check *The Complete Handbook of Woodworking Tools and Hardware* (TAB Book No. 1484) or consult Shopsmith Inc., 750 Center Drive, Vandalia, OH 45377. The Shopsmith presently surpasses all similar devices regarding service quality and accessory availability.

TABLE SAW

The table of the Mark V is supported on two steel tubes that pass through holes in the overall carriage and mesh with two gears worked by the table-raising lever. Unlike most other table saws, that of the Mark V changes cut depth by raising and lowering the table, because the saw blade arbor is in a fixed position. Set up the table saw as shown in the manufacturer's instructions. Make sure you also install the saw guard. Do not operate any table saw with the blade guard removed.

The Mark V offers a tilting tabletop for bevel cuts. Most tools of this type offer a tilting arbor, but I feel there is little difference in quality and accuracy of cuts (Figs. 6-6 through 6-8).

When setting up the table saw, check the follow-

Fig. 6-1. Making a dado on a table saw (courtesy Shopsmith Inc.)

ing settings. The table slots for the miter-gauge bar, the rip fence, and the saw blade must be parallel to each other. The rip fence, the saw blade, and the miter-gauge head must be perpendicular to the tabletop. When the miter gauge is set to read 90 degrees, it must be at right angles to the blade and rip fence (Fig. 6-9). Make adjustments according to the owner's manual.

Check the blade type to make sure it will do the work you need done. Combination blades are for moderately rough cuts in all types of wood. The blades can be used to crosscut or to rip, leaving a cut clean enough for most purposes. The crosscut blade is de-signed to make only crosscuts and cannot be used for ripping. The cut is better than with a combination blade. The rip blade is used only for ripsawing and produces a slightly better cut than the combination blade. The hollow ground combination blade is better than a standard combination blade. Other blades, such as paneling and plywood styles, are available and should be used when cut smoothness or accuracy is of great importance. Special blades, such as a dado blade set, can do a number of jobs. The dado blade cuts not only dadoes but also grooves (much wider than standard saw kerfs), hollows, rabbets, notches, tongue and grooves, stud tenons, slots, through-slots,

Fig. 6-2. Horizontal boring (courtesy Shopsmith Inc.).

Fig. 6-3. Disc sanding (courtesy Shopsmith Inc.).

Fig. 6-4. Vertical drilling (courtesy Shopsmith Inc.).

properly in place, the cut itself is easily and accurately done, no matter how complex it sounds.

Crosscuts

Crosscutting is the most usual form of cutting needed with any saw. Simple crosscutting with a table saw is done by placing the work to be cut against the miter gauge and then moving the miter gauge so the blade passes through the work. Miter gauges fit in slots either to the right or left of the blade. I prefer the one to the left of the blade for most cuts. Keep your position almost straight behind the miter gauge. Use the fingers of your left hand to hold the work against the gauge and your right hand to feed the work. Make sure your fingers never get close to the blade. Don't ever force work against the blade; this tends to cause the blade to scorch the work. Make sure the work has completely passed the blade before you start thinking the cut is finished. Don't pick free pieces off the saw table while the blade is still running. Don't wear a tie or loose sleeves.

true tenons, etc. Molding head cutters can produce special cut shapes and styles for virtually all other applications (Figs. 6-10 through 6-13 and Table 6-1).

When you add in the cuts possible with a standard blade, the work possible with a table saw is considerable. There are only four types of basic cuts for circular saws: *crosscut, rip, miter,* and *bevel*. These may be combined to produce all kinds of fancy joints and surfaces. As you go through a list of cuts possible with a standard blade, though, things may seem far more complex. In addition to the first three cuts, you will note cross and rip bevels, compound miters, *chamfers*, two-sided tapers, four-sided tapers, compound rip-bevels, kerfing, and a two-pass narrow rabbet. Some cuts are simple; others are complex. Once the setup is

128

Mounting holes for miter gauge extensions are factory-drilled on most table saws, and the Mark V is no exception. Miter gauge extensions are good accessories and require only a few minutes of work and a few lengths of wood, plus a couple of 1½ by ¼-inch machine bolts with washers and wing nuts. Extensions are extremely useful for supporting short pieces of work. They can also be used as guides to determine cut lines. Simply cut one slot in the extension, then mark the workpiece at the length desired. Place the mark with the slot in the extension, and you will cut at the correct length. Facing an extension with sandpaper will give you a high friction surface handy when you make miter cuts. Use rubber cement to

Fig. 6-5. Shaping (courtesy Shopsmith Inc.).

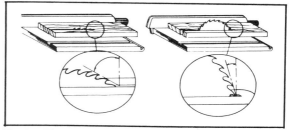

Fig. 6-7. The table saw blade must be adjusted so that it just clears the cut (courtesy Shopsmith Inc.).

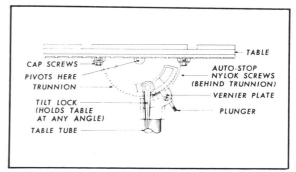

Fig. 6-8. Principal parts of the tilt mechanism (courtesy Shopsmith Inc.).

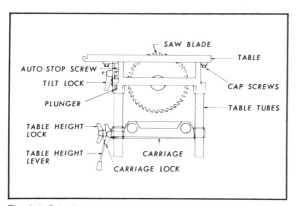

Fig. 6-6. Principal parts of the table saw (courtesy Shopsmith Inc.).

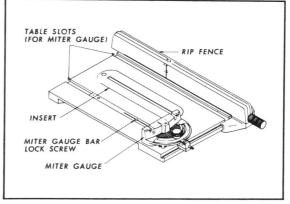

Fig. 6-9. Parts must be accurately set up (courtesy Shopsmith Inc.)

129

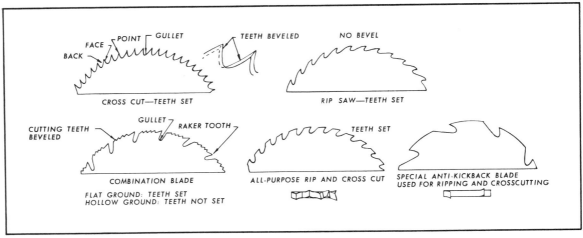

Fig. 6-10. Blade types (courtesy Shopsmith Inc.).

fasten the sandpaper to the extension, so the paper will be easily removed when the time comes (Figs. 6-14 and 6-15).

Crosscutting to length when more than a single piece is needed is done with the miter gauge stop rod. The rod is adjusted to the length of the cut and then held in place as the work is guided through. The guide locks to size and won't slip. For equal-length pieces from a long piece of wood, you can use another method that involves the use of the rip fence. The rip fence cannot safely be used as a stop to guide such cuts, but a stop block fastened to the rip fence will work. Fasten the stop block at a point that allows the back edge of the work to clear the block before the cut

starts. That prevents jamming and kickback problems caused by trying to use the fence as a stop block.

Long work is more easily crosscut if you use the Mark V's table extension mounted on the end away from the saw table to support the longer material. You can construct a long roller for ripping and a roller table for crosscutting if you need these accessories. The long roller will allow you to rip extra-long stock, while the series of rollers will provide needed support for crosscutting stock more than 4 feet long. The stand is set to the same height as the saw table when in use, and the weight of the work simply rides on the rollers. The rollers can be made on the Mark V lathe, or you can buy 1¾-inch round stock from your lumber dealer (Fig. 6-16).

For crosscutting long stock with maximum support, you can increase the table capacity to about 12 inches by reversing the miter gauge in its groove and using it backwards to guide the work through. For even longer crosscuts, start the cut with the roller table supporting the uncut edge of the work. When the cut is nicely started, turnoff the saw and move the roller stand to the cut side of the work.

Rip Cuts

Rip cuts require the use of the rip fence as a guide for the work. Cuts are begun with both hands on the work—when the work is large enough—and the left hand is removed as the work gets closer to the blade. The right hand, with the fingers hooked over the rip fence, is used as the final guide. Once your hand comes within 4 inches of the blade, a push stick is

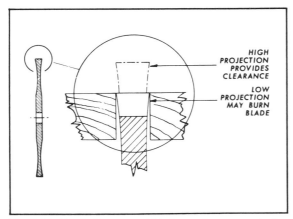

Fig. 6-11. The hollow ground blade needs more projection above the work, because of its shape, to prevent scorching (courtesy Shopsmith Inc.).

130

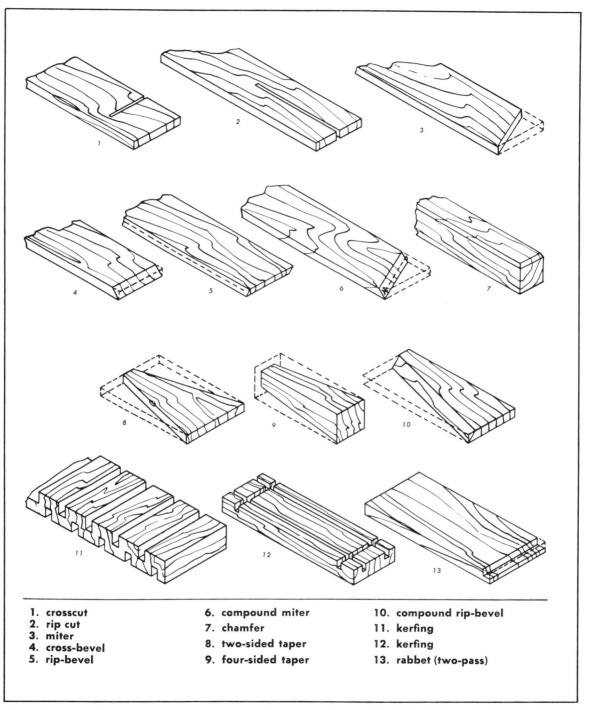

1. crosscut
2. rip cut
3. miter
4. cross-bevel
5. rip-bevel
6. compound miter
7. chamfer
8. two-sided taper
9. four-sided taper
10. compound rip-bevel
11. kerfing
12. kerfing
13. rabbet (two-pass)

Fig. 6-12. Cuts possible with a regular saw blade (courtesy Shopsmith Inc.).

Fig. 6-13. Cuts possible with accessories (courtesy Shopsmith Inc.).

NO.	NAME OF CUT	ACCESSORY
1	dado	dado
2	groove	dado
3	hollowing	dado
4	rabbet	dado
5	rabbet	dado
6	notching	dado
7	tongue-and-groove	dado
8	stud tenon	dado
9	slot	dado
10	through slot	dado
11	true tenon	dado
12	coving	blade
13	coving	blade
14	surface cuts	molding head
15	finger lap	dado
16	dovetail	
17	special groove	dado
18	molded edge	molding head
19	coved edge	molding head
20	molding or edge	molding head

needed. Long work is ripped easily with the rip stand, with its roller allowing a smooth feed (Figs. 6-17 and 6-18).

When work being cut has no straightedge to ride against the rip fence, you will need a squaring board. This secondary table is built to fit on the saw table, with a hardwood bar resting in the table slot. The piece to be squared is then butted against the stop on the squaring board and pushed through the saw. Small pieces may need to be tack-nailed to the board for safety (Fig. 6-19).

Taper Cuts

Taper cuts may be needed for jobs from table legs to decorations. They require that you make up a jig with a straight side for guiding the cut along the rip fence and a slanted side to set up the taper. The ends of the jig must be hinged. The hinges are installed with the two jig pieces clamped together. Use a metal brace with a wing nut to allow different tapers and to secure

each taper setting. It you mark both jig boards 1 foot in from the hinge, you can use those marks to determine the taper-per-foot on each job. For a 2-inch taper per foot, simply set the jig so there is a 2-inch opening at the mark. If you expect to do a lot of tapering work, use machinist's blue layout dye—such as Starrett's Kleenscribe—to coat the cross brace top. Scribe marks at points you expect to use. Coat everything with a clear plastic spray.

Your first taper cut is made with the nontapered board of the jig set against the rip fence. Pass the work through the saw. Double the jig setting for a second taper cut. Turn the work so the tapered side is against the jig. Pass it through the saw, and you will have a second taper cut on the opposite side of your workpiece. Step guides are good for repetition when you have a lot of pieces to cut and don't want to be resetting the guide after each cut. The guide method, using a line on the workpiece, is useful when the work is too long for a jig (Fig. 6-20).

Miter Cuts

Mitering requires you to set the miter gauge at the correct angle and then pass the work on through the saw. You can make various shapes by simply setting the correct angle on your miter gauge and making the cut. With the miter gauge set at 45 degrees, you get four-sided figures. A setting of 67½ degrees will give you twice as many sides—an octagon. To get a hexagon (six sides), set the miter gauge at 60 degrees. Bevel cutting produces different shapes and allows you to make cuts to build planters and window boxes. A bevel of 45 degrees will give you a square or rectangular box. A setting of 22½ degrees will produce an octagon, and a setting of 30 degrees is used to make a hexagon. The bevel angles are set on the table tilt, though, and not the miter gauge, which is kept at its standard setting (Fig. 6-21).

To make sure right and left-hand cuts match up when mitering, you can either use two miter gauges or make the simpler jig illustrated in Fig. 6-22. If the stock has been already cut to length, then the table on the left will do a fine job for you (cut the plywood table top to about 20 by 24 inches). Use either metal or hardwood bars to ride in the miter gauge slots. Place the bars in their slots with the table up far enough to clear the saw blade. Clamp the tabletop material and mark the bars' positions. Remove and fasten the bars in place. Clamp tightly to the saw table. Turn on the saw and slowly lower the table, allowing the saw blade to cut its own

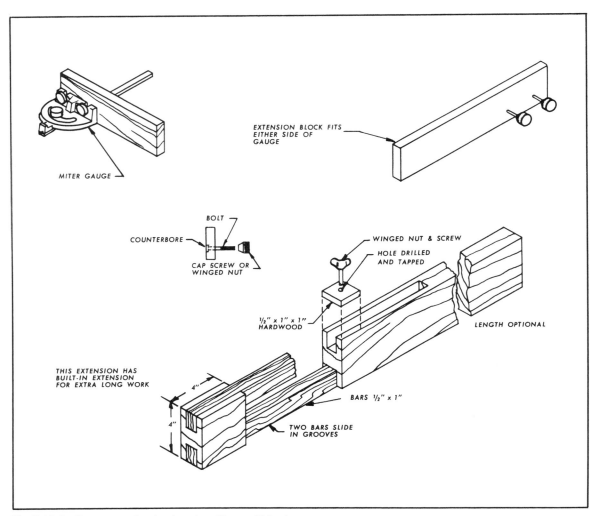

Fig. 6-14. A miter gauge extension (courtesy Shopsmith Inc.).

slot in your jig table. The saw slot will need to be lengthened a bit when you finally remove the platform. Take care when making these jigs, for the accuracy of the final miters depends on your work on the jigs.

For the second type of jig, make the platform about 5 inches longer than the other one. This jig will allow you to cut stock of about any length. The platform slides on the saw table. Both jigs are limited to a single angle cut, but they are fairly easy to build and should last well if cared for properly. Coat with polyurethane. Use something like ZAR Imperial, with a satin finish, for best results. This is after light sanding, with the first coat thinned about one-to-one with mineral spirits.

This is for the ZAR finish. With other brands, check the maker's directions for thinners and solvents to use.

Bevel Cuts

Bevel cuts are made with the miter gauge set at 90 degrees. The work must have good support for cut accuracy and good final fit (Fig. 6-23).

Compound Angle Cuts

Compound angle cuts require both miter gauge settings and table tilt. These operations are probably the hardest to perform with perfection on a table saw. They require accurate settings of the table tilt and the

134

miter gauge and very slow feed speeds. Use the table settings as shown in Fig. 6-23 if you want good, tight fit when making compound cuts.

Dado and Groove Cuts

Dado and groove cuts are basically drawer makers' cuts, and cabinetmakers' cuts. The dado blade assembly consists of two outer blades and a number of inner chipper blades set to a specific width. The outer blades normally each make a kerf of ⅛ inch. Any other dado clearing is done by the chipper blades. Dado blades used to come with interchangeable chipper blades, and you had to essentially reassemble the dado head for each different width. Now you can buy a dado head that dials to width, making it far easier to set up.

In addition to the special head or blade set, dadoing work requires a special blade insert for your table.

The dado head is considerably wider than a standard saw blade. The insert must accommodate this extra width (some dado heads will cut grooves to a width of more than ¾ inch). Dadoes are combination blades, and the blades are always set to cut less than the stock's full thickness. A slow feed is needed to get a smooth cut. More than one pass will provide a better cut when deep grooves are needed.

Grooving cuts are made with the grain of the wood. Both dadoes and grooves can be made wider than the dado head's cut by making several passes.

Woodworking Joints

Common woodworking joints are readily made with the dado head. These include rabbets, dado and groove, splice lap, middle lap, end lap, lapped miter, dado and rabbet, and others shown in Fig. 6-24. When working extensively with a dado head on these joints,

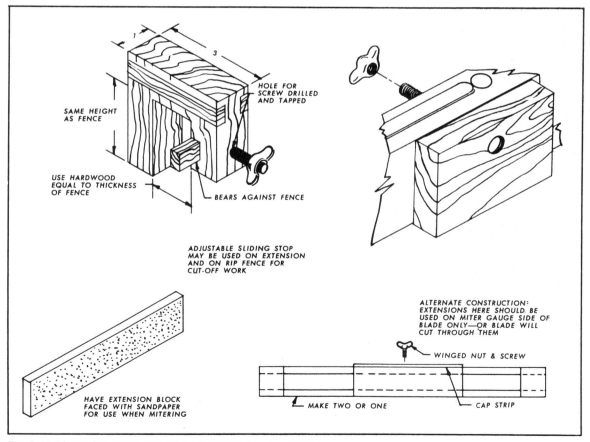

Fig. 6-15. More miter gauge extensions (courtesy Shopsmith Inc.).

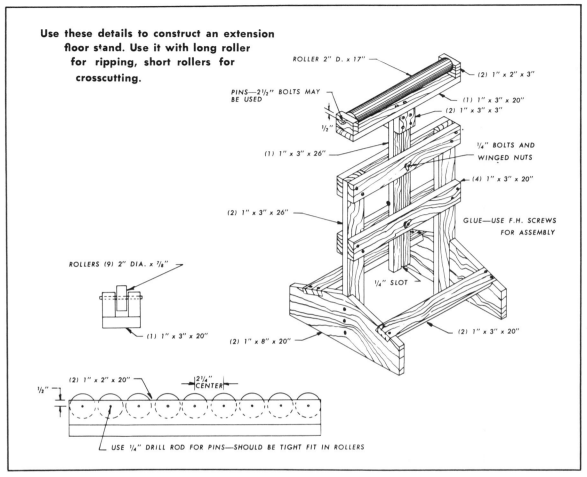

Use these details to construct an extension floor stand. Use it with long roller for ripping, short rollers for crosscutting.

ROLLER 2" D. x 17"

(2) 1" x 2" x 3"

PINS—2½" BOLTS MAY BE USED

½"

(1) 1" x 3" x 20"

(2) 1" x 3" x 3"

(1) 1" x 3" x 26"

¼" BOLTS AND WINGED NUTS

(4) 1" x 3" x 20"

(2) 1" x 3" x 26"

GLUE—USE F.H. SCREWS FOR ASSEMBLY

ROLLERS (9) 2" DIA. x ⅞"

¼" SLOT

(1) 1" x 3" x 20"

(2) 1" x 8" x 20"

(2) 1" x 3" x 20"

(2) 1" x 2" x 20"

2¼" CENTER

½"

USE ¼" DRILL ROD FOR PINS—SHOULD BE TIGHT FIT IN ROLLERS

Fig. 6-16. A roller table for oversized work (courtesy Shopsmith Inc.).

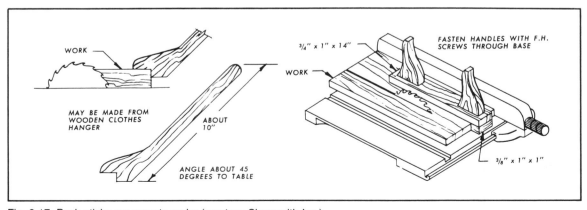

WORK

MAY BE MADE FROM WOODEN CLOTHES HANGER

ABOUT 10"

ANGLE ABOUT 45 DEGREES TO TABLE

FASTEN HANDLES WITH F.H. SCREWS THROUGH BASE

¾" x 1" x 14"

WORK

⅜" x 1" x 1"

Fig. 6-17. Push sticks are easy to make (courtesy Shopsmith Inc.).

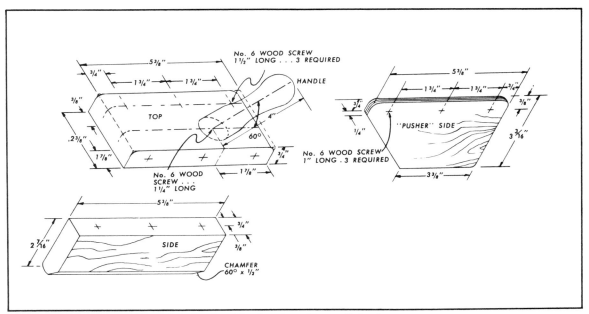

Fig. 6-18. Push sticks can be made in fancier styles (courtesy Shopsmith Inc.).

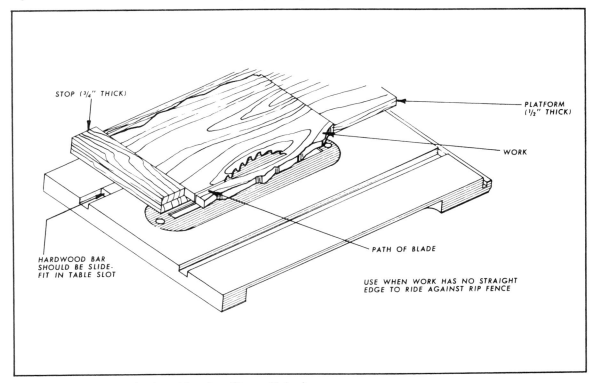

Fig. 6-19. Making a squaring board (courtesy Shopsmith Inc.).

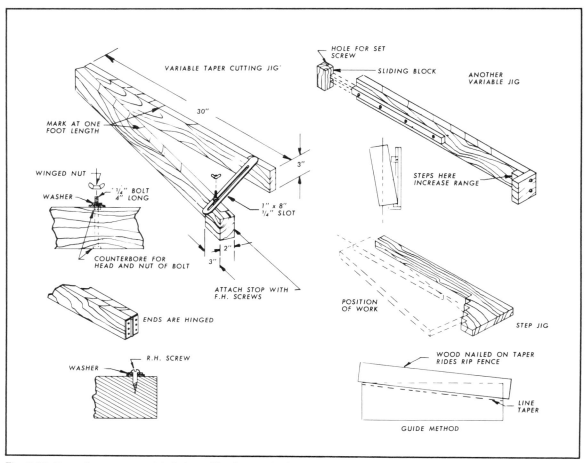

Fig. 6-20. Taper jigs are a great help in making legs and other such appendages (courtesy Shopsmith Inc.).

use some spring sticks to help hold the work against the rip fence (Figs. 6-24 and 6-25).

Spline grooves for frames in cabinets and other projects can be made with the standard saw blade or the dado head (for larger splines). Jigs are helpful for cutting spline grooves in bevels, as well as in mitered frames. Splines are easily made. The grain should run across the narrow width of the spline—not along its length (Figs. 6-26 and 6-27).

Notching cuts are dado cuts across the thickness of the stock and to half its width. The pieces are then fitted together to form a strong joint, as with finger laps in a drawer. Finger laps are easily cut with the illustrated jigs. A distance jig is also handy, especially when the jig can be adjusted to stock of different thicknesses (Figs. 6-28 through 6-31).

Tenons and slots are among the best and strongest joints used to make cabinets. *Tenons* are projections of solid stock that mate with a hole cut into another piece of stock. A tenoning jig uses a regular saw blade to form tenons. It can also be used to cut notches when you install a dado head (Figs. 6-32 through 6-34).

Tongue and groove joints can be useful if you decide to make your own wood countertops. Narrow pieces of wood can be more securely joined to form wide countertop sections. Cut the groove either with a regular saw blade (making two cuts, one at each side of the groove, and then removing the material between the cuts) or a dado blade to make the groove in a single pass. A regular saw blade can also be used to cut the tongue. Make a total of four passes for each tongue.

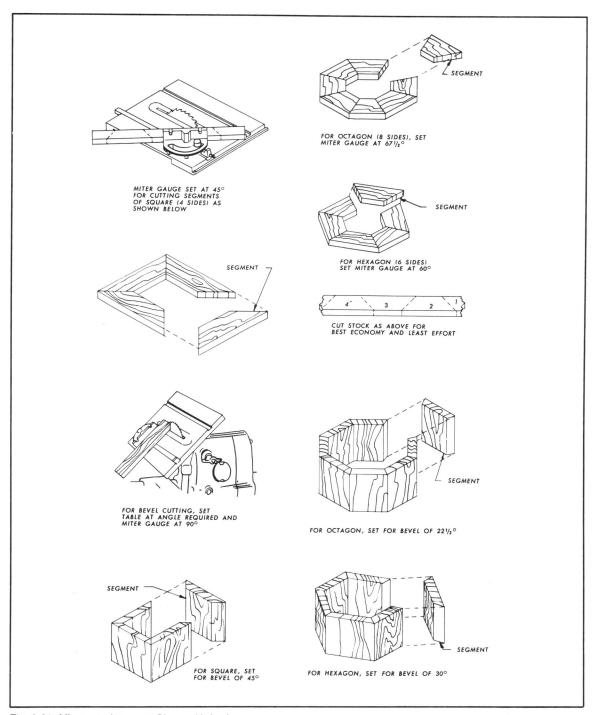

MITER GAUGE SET AT 45°
FOR CUTTING SEGMENTS
OF SQUARE (4 SIDES) AS
SHOWN BELOW

FOR OCTAGON (8 SIDES), SET
MITER GAUGE AT 67½°

SEGMENT

SEGMENT

FOR HEXAGON (6 SIDES)
SET MITER GAUGE AT 60°

SEGMENT

CUT STOCK AS ABOVE FOR
BEST ECONOMY AND LEAST EFFORT

FOR BEVEL CUTTING, SET
TABLE AT ANGLE REQUIRED AND
MITER GAUGE AT 90°

FOR OCTAGON, SET FOR BEVEL OF 22½°

SEGMENT

SEGMENT

FOR SQUARE, SET
FOR BEVEL OF 45°

FOR HEXAGON, SET FOR BEVEL OF 30°

SEGMENT

Fig. 6-21. Miter cuts (courtesy Shopsmith Inc.).

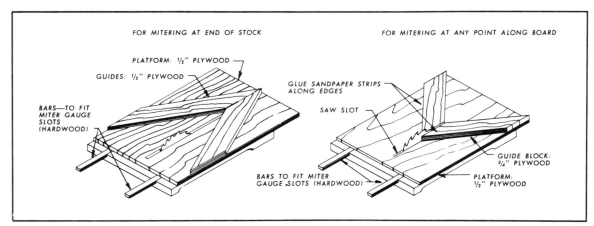

Fig. 6-22. Miter jigs (courtesy Shopsmith Inc.).

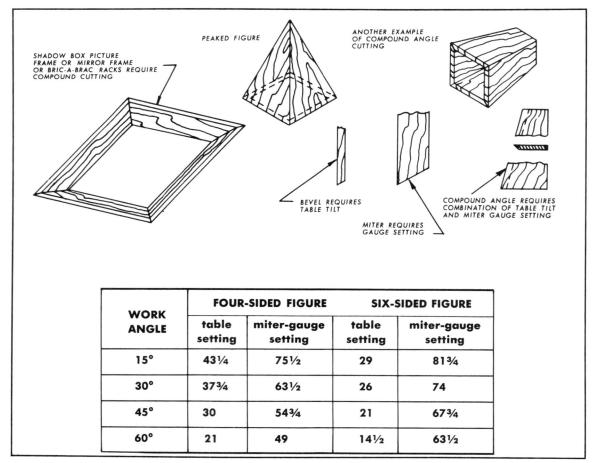

WORK ANGLE	FOUR-SIDED FIGURE		SIX-SIDED FIGURE	
	table setting	miter-gauge setting	table setting	miter-gauge setting
15°	43¼	75½	29	81¾
30°	37¾	63½	26	74
45°	30	54¾	21	67¾
60°	21	49	14½	63½

Fig. 6-23. Bevel cuts (courtesy Shopsmith Inc.).

140

Some of the common woodworking joints that can be cut on the table saw, using a regular saw blade or a dado, are: 1—butt; 2—rabbet; 3—dado and groove; 4—splice lap (end); 5—middle lap; 6—end lap; 7—lapped miter; 8—dado and rabbet (box corners); 9—notch; 10—true tenon; 11—stud tenon; 12—slot (for stud tenon); 13—miter; 14—mitered bevel.

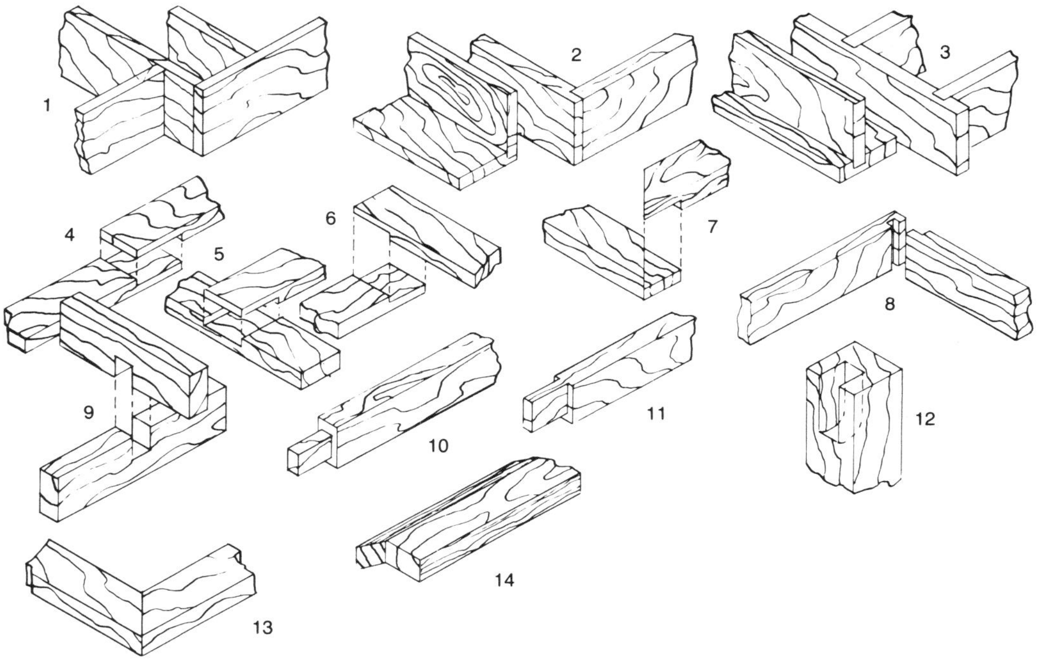

Fig. 6-24. Joints made with the table saw (courtesy Shopsmith Inc.).

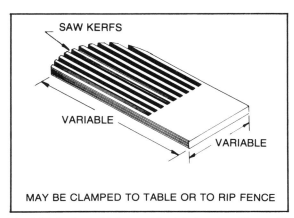

SAW KERFS

VARIABLE

VARIABLE

MAY BE CLAMPED TO TABLE OR TO RIP FENCE

Fig. 6-25. Spring hold-downs aid safety (courtesy Shopsmith Inc.).

Using a dado head requires you to make only two passes to cut a tongue. This will probably result in a tighter, neater joint because fewer adjustments are needed. Make tongues slightly shorter than the depth of the groove to allow for excess glue. You might also want to notch the tongue edge every inch or so to supply room for extra glue. If a countertop is to be totally waterproof at the joints, you must use a resorcinol glue (Figs. 6-35 through 6-39).

Drawers

Decide on one basic design for your own drawers before starting any cabinetmaking. Good drawer construction is imperative if you want a quality cabinet setup. Guides for drawers can be bought from various sources if you don't want to form your own from wood.

141

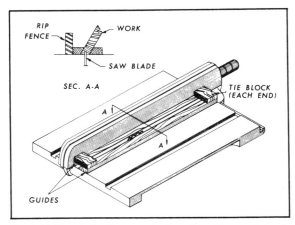

Fig. 6-26. Beveled spline grooving (courtesy Shopsmith Inc.).

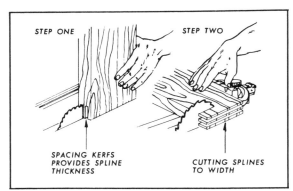

Fig. 6-27. Cutting splines (courtesy Shopsmith Inc.).

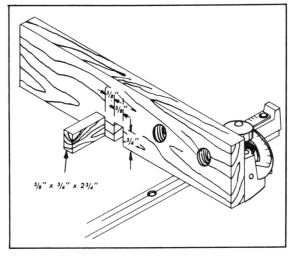

Fig. 6-28. Finger-lap jig (courtesy Shopsmith Inc.).

If you attach any of the illustrated wood drawer rails or guides to your drawers, give them a liberal coating of beeswax at final assembly. This beeswax lubricates and reduces wear (Figs. 6-40 and 6-41).

Avoid butt-jointed and lap-jointed drawers for kitchen cabinets. Use dadoed grooves on the sides (with ends and fronts inserted where possible), finger laps, or dovetailed joints. The fronts of the drawers are more difficult, as you will normally want them to be decorative. Grooves with the sides fitting into them tend to pull apart when the drawer is opened and shut often. Half laps with the drawer fronts intersected by the sides can add greatly to drawer strength, as can screws that are inserted from the front, into the sides, and then covered with cut plugs or dowels.

Molding Heads

Molding heads for the table saw can allow you to make various molding designs for use in cabinets. The

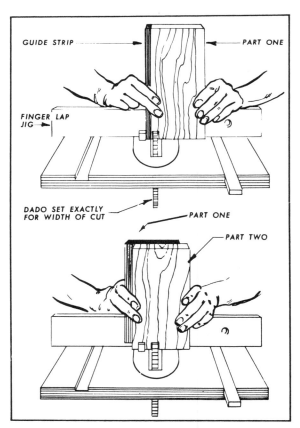

Fig. 6-29. Cutting finger laps (courtesy Shopsmith Inc.).

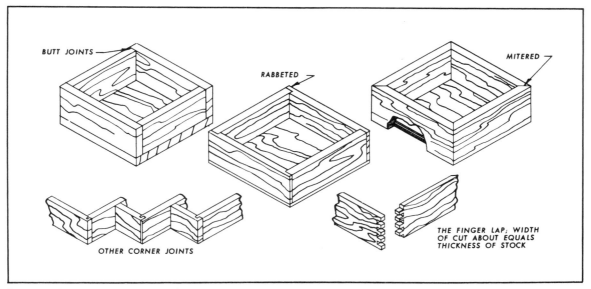

Fig. 6-30. Finger laps compared to butt and rabbet joints (courtesy Shopsmith Inc.).

accessory for doing the work is simply installed and rather easily used. Table edges can be shaped, cabinet door lips can be cut, drawer edges can be trimmed, and so on. The molding head is of steel or aluminum and mounts to the spindle on which the saw blade is normally secured. A dado insert is needed to clear the molding head knives, which are usually about 1 inch wide. If clearance is a problem, make your own plywood insert. Cut the insert to the correct shape. Drill the holes for the hold-down screws (these must also be countersunk). Turn the table up so that the cutters

are below its surface. Mount the insert. Slowly lower the table until the cutters make their own hole. Before starting the saw, make sure that the cutter blades clear the insert to be cut.

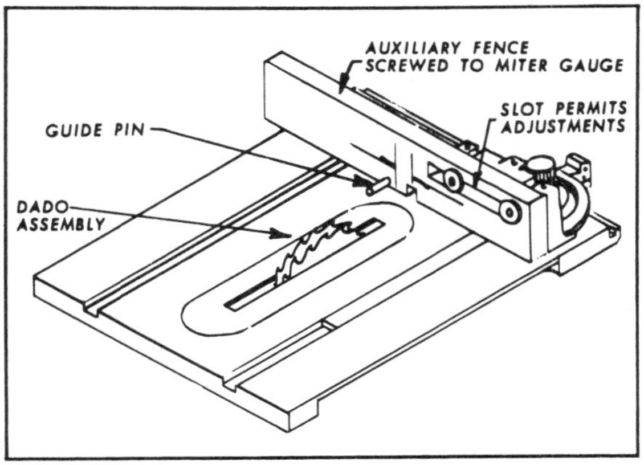

You can use the rip fence with the molding head if you add a wooden auxiliary fence, with a cutout to pass over the blades. Make the insert by bolting it to the rip fence. Mount a blank cutter on the molding head. Slowly lower the table so that the wood fence is over the turning blank cutter blade. Keep cutting until the arc is about 1 inch deep (Figs. 6-42 and 6-43).

Molding head cuts are best made slowly. The feed should be slowed even more when you are cutting across the grain. Cutting with the grain always produces the smoothest finish, but you will sometimes need across-the-grain cuts. Use the miter gauge to advance the work when making cross-grain cuts. Make cross-grain cuts first when you work on adjacent edges or all four edges of a piece (Fig. 6-44).

DRILL PRESS

The drill press used to be considered a shop machine for professionals in metalworking shops. The machine, though, has many uses in the home workshop. The Shopsmith Mark V's drill press can be operated as a boring bar in its horizontal position. With the vertical and horizontal modes available, choose the one most convenient to a particular operation. Capa-

Fig. 6-31. This finger-lap jig is adaptable to stock of varied thicknesses (courtesy Shopsmith Inc.).

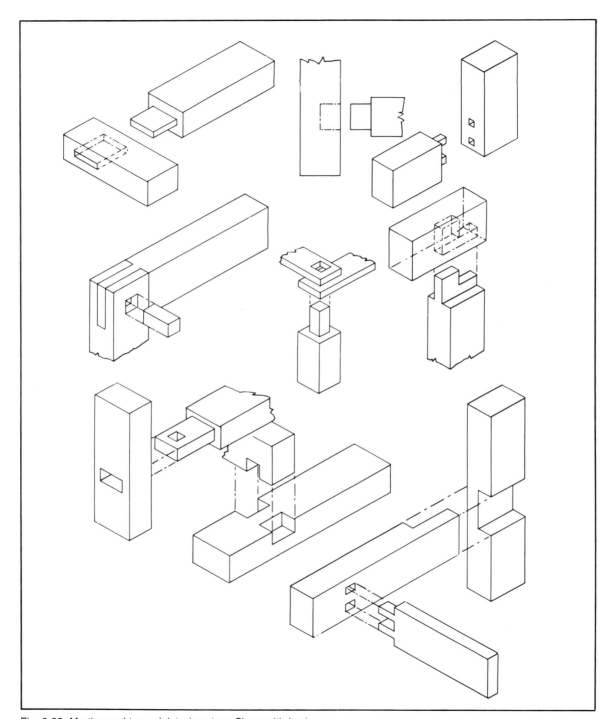

Fig. 6-32. Mortise and tenon joints (courtesy Shopsmith Inc.).

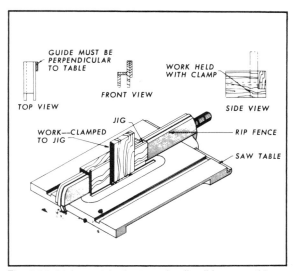

Fig. 6-33. Make certain the tenoning jig slides smoothly on the rip fence (courtesy Shopsmith Inc.).

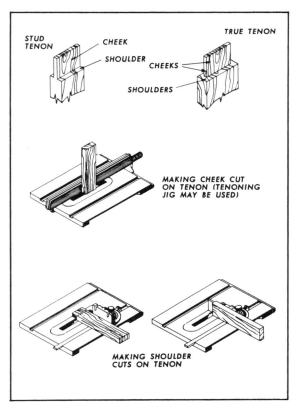

Fig. 6-34. A regular saw blade can be used to make cheek cuts and shoulder cuts (courtesy Shopsmith Inc.).

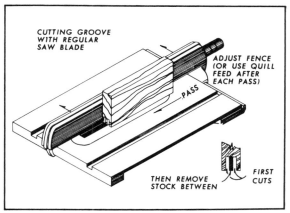

Fig. 6-35. Using a regular saw blade to cut a groove (courtesy Shopsmith Inc.).

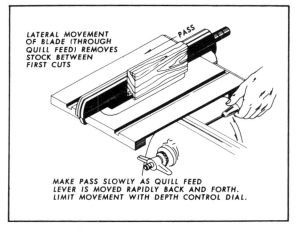

Fig. 6-36. Use the quill feed for lateral movement to take out stock between the kerfs (courtesy Shopsmith Inc.).

city remains the same at 16½ inches, with a feed of 4¼ inches. You can drill through 4 inches of stock at the center of a 16½-inch circle. Vertically, the machine will accept about a 22-inch high workpiece, depending on the length of the installed drill bit or cutter. With the table tilted back, the Mark V, in its vertical position, can drill the top of a piece 4 feet high (Figs. 6-45 and 6-46).

The drill press has evolved into a multiuse tool. You can drill in wood, steel, or plastics; cut plugs; countersink; cut circles; route; dovetail; chisel; buff; wire-brush; grind; and shape (Fig. 6-47).

Some cutting edges are preadjusted (usually the case with table and radial saws), but a drill press needs many speeds. Generally, the larger the cutting opera-

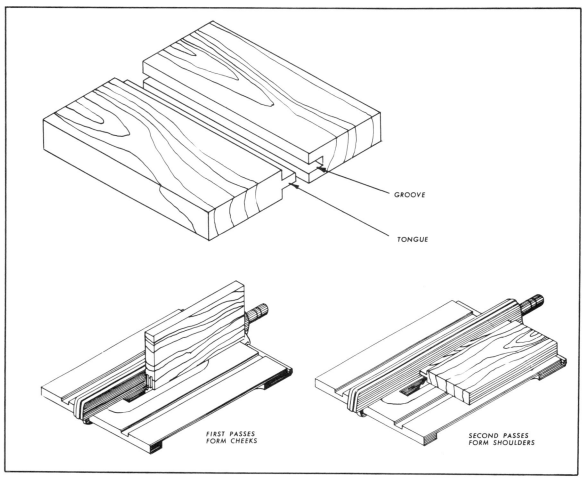

GROOVE

TONGUE

FIRST PASSES
FORM CHEEKS

SECOND PASSES
FORM SHOULDERS

Fig. 6-37. Cutting a tongue with a regular blade (courtesy Shopsmith Inc.).

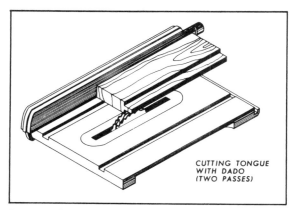

CUTTING TONGUE
WITH DADO
(TWO PASSES)

Fig. 6-38. Dadoing a tongue (courtesy Shopsmith Inc.).

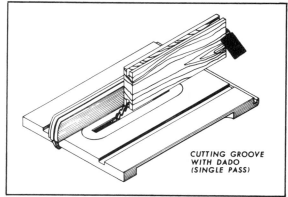

CUTTING GROOVE
WITH DADO
(SINGLE PASS)

Fig. 6-39. Dadoing a groove (courtesy Shopsmith Inc.).

146

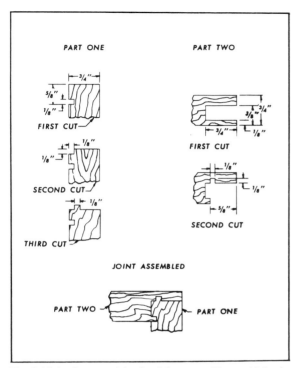

PART ONE

FIRST CUT

SECOND CUT

THIRD CUT

PART TWO

FIRST CUT

SECOND CUT

JOINT ASSEMBLED

PART TWO — PART ONE

Fig. 6-40. Lock-corner joint detail (courtesy Shopsmith Inc.).

tion, the lower the speed will be. The more fragile the item being drilled, the slower the speed. Small holes in wood are spun through at the high speed on the Mark V of about 3,800 revolutions per minute (rpms), while routine and carving are done in the 4,000 to 5,000-rpm range. Table 6-2 shows recommended speeds for some common drill press jobs. Determine feed speed by starting very slowly and increasing speed as the tool and the workpiece allow.

Work Layout and Support

Work layout for drill presses varies little from that required for other tools. Measurement and marking must be accurate. Start by using a hard pencil or a metal-tipped scribe. Keep the pencil sharp. Hole location is most easily marked by drawing two intersecting lines and drilling at the point where they cross. A combination or try square can be invaluable, while a circle square is very useful with round stock to be drilled. Dividers are used to transfer marks from one piece to another, and templates can also be useful if you need more than single pieces of any particular size (Fig. 6-48).

For blind drilling, you can mark the hole locations in one piece. Drive in small headless brads at those locations. Leave about 1/16 to ⅛ inch above the surface and then press the two pieces together. Yank the headless brads with pliers and drill both sets of holes to the correct sizes (Fig. 6-49).

Work support for drilling is important when you want a clean hole. You can either drill in from both sides of the work, or you can place a scrap block under the workpiece to cut down on splintering. If you place a piece of paper between the scrap and the work, or use wood of a different color, you will immediately know when you have penetrated with the bit. Clamping the work to the table is a good idea. This provides great stability and, if your marking is accurate, a very fine hole of exact size. It also keeps the drill from jamming in the hole and yanking the work from your hands. You can often use the rip fence instead of a clamp. The torque or twisting action of the drill bit will force the work against the fence as securely as any clamp might hold it (Fig. 6-50).

Drilling to Exact Depth

Exact depth drilling can be done in two ways with the Mark V. Both methods use the depth control dial, but with the first method you must clamp the work to the table first. Then extend the drill point until it just touches the work surface. Lock the quill in place and turn the dial until it indicates "0." Turn back the dial until it shows the depth of the hole you need. Finally, unlock the quill, put the work in place, and drill your holes. The second method requires that you extend and lock the quill in place, so the drill point lines up with a mark on the edge of the work at the depth you need to drill. Lock the quill in this position, then lock the dial at "0." Unlock the quill and do your drilling.

Screw Holes

Most cabinets are more easily assembled if screw holes are drilled, counterbored, and countersunk ahead of time. The holes needed can be drilled more accurately with a drill press than with a hand drill. As Fig. 6-51 shows, three different sizes are required for the flathead wood screws to be used. The counterbore hole can be run as deep as needed to seat a dowel to cover the screwhead. The lead or pilot hole makes it easier for the screw to penetrate the wood. The body hole is drilled next, and then the hole can be countersunk or counterbored. Sets of countersink/counterbore/pilot hole bits that do the entire job in one pass are readily available (Fig. 6-52 and Table 6-3).

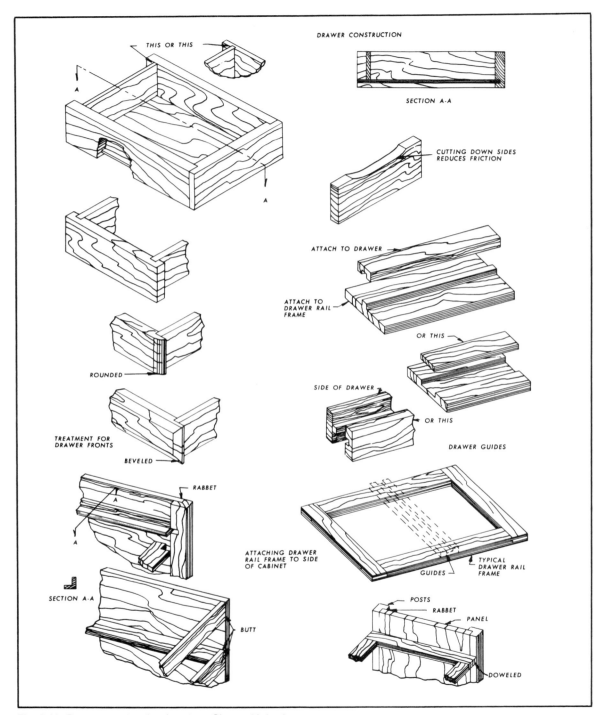

DRAWER CONSTRUCTION

THIS OR THIS

A

SECTION A-A

A

A

CUTTING DOWN SIDES
REDUCES FRICTION

ATTACH TO DRAWER

ATTACH TO
DRAWER RAIL
FRAME

OR THIS

ROUNDED

SIDE OF DRAWER

OR THIS

TREATMENT FOR
DRAWER FRONTS

DRAWER GUIDES

BEVELED

RABBET

A

A

ATTACHING DRAWER
RAIL FRAME TO SIDE
OF CABINET

GUIDES

TYPICAL
DRAWER RAIL
FRAME

SECTION A-A

BUTT

POSTS

RABBET

PANEL

DOWELED

Fig. 6-41. Drawer construction (courtesy Shopsmith Inc.).

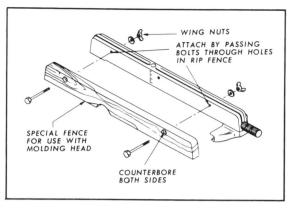

Fig. 6-42. Auxiliary fence for molding head (courtesy Shopsmith Inc.).

If you need to enlarge a hole, seal the original hole with a dowel that fits tightly. Mark the center of the new, larger hole and drill. The same procedure can be followed in metal and plastic, using rod. Enlarging holes without using a plug tends to be very sloppy (Fig. 6-53).

Equally spaced holes are often required when making cabinets or other accessories. Use the jig or guide in Fig. 6-54. Start by clamping an auxiliary fence to the rip fence. Position it to provide the space you need. Make a guide block like that shown in Fig. 6-54. Use the dowel as a guide pin to position the work for each succeeding hole to be drilled.

Angled screw holes are often needed when making cabinets. Screw blocks are used to attach rails or to add strength to cabinet frames. Trying to drill this way causes the side of the bit to touch the work before the center does. This can cause the work to "walk" on you. Use a leveling block to keep the drill on center and the work in place. The leveling block makes sure the center of the bit is engaged before the edge touches (Figs. 6-55 through 6-58).

Mortising

The drill press can also be used for other types of joinery, as well as blind doweling (Fig. 6-59). A mortising bit and chisel can eliminate handwork when making mortise and tenon joints and any other joint requiring a square cavity. The mortising attachment is

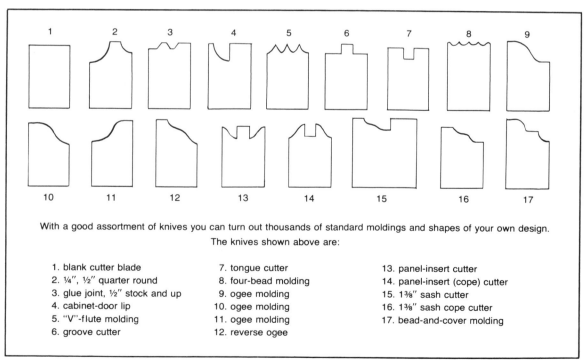

With a good assortment of knives you can turn out thousands of standard moldings and shapes of your own design. The knives shown above are:

1. blank cutter blade
2. ¼", ½" quarter round
3. glue joint, ½" stock and up
4. cabinet-door lip
5. "V"-flute molding
6. groove cutter
7. tongue cutter
8. four-bead molding
9. ogee molding
10. ogee molding
11. ogee molding
12. reverse ogee
13. panel-insert cutter
14. panel-insert (cope) cutter
15. 1⅜" sash cutter
16. 1⅜" sash cope cutter
17. bead-and-cover molding

Fig. 6-43. Molding knives (courtesy Shopsmith Inc.).

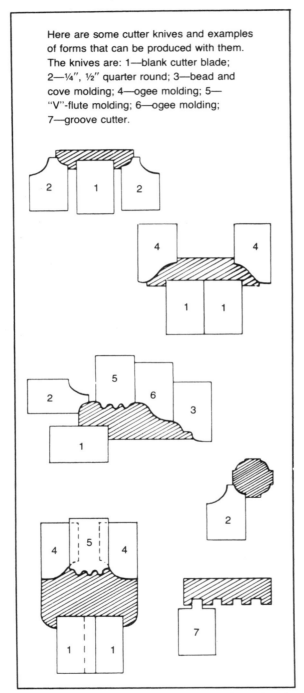

Here are some cutter knives and examples of forms that can be produced with them. The knives are: 1—blank cutter blade; 2—¼″, ½″ quarter round; 3—bead and cove molding; 4—ogee molding; 5—"V"-flute molding; 6—ogee molding; 7—groove cutter.

Fig. 6-44. Shapes that molding knives can easily produce for you (courtesy Shopsmith Inc.).

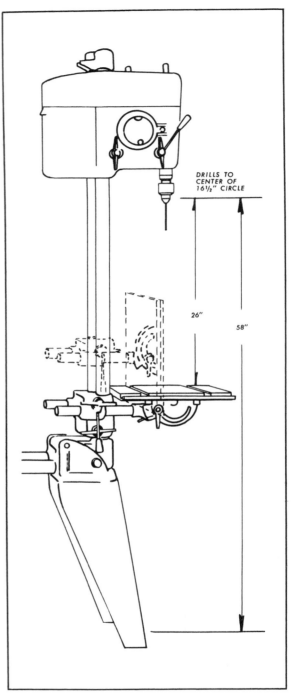

Fig. 6-45. Drill press vertical capacities (courtesy Shopsmith Inc.).

150

slipped over the collar of the quill and secured with the arm of the accessory facing the tubes. The attachment can then be turned to suit the work. The hollow chisel is then put in place. The bit is inserted through it and locked with the chuck key. Leave a gap of no more than 1/16 inch between the cutting edge of the bit and the chisel (Fig. 6-60).

Square the chisel to the fence, because the fence is to be used as a guide for the work. This is done by placing a square against the fence, with the blade against the side of the chisel. Use the adjustable sleeve to make any needed changes and the setscrew to tighten things. Locate the workpiece on the table and depress the chisel to make the cuts. Again, a rapid feed is not a good idea. Hardwoods such as oak and maple cut more slowly than pines and firs. Make the end cuts first and then clean out the center stock.

A drill can also be used to form a mortise, but the ends are going to be round if you don't clear them with a hand chisel. If the tenon is rounded to fit, this is no real problem. Start by drilling two end holes. Drill the intermediate holes, leaving material between each

hole. Come back and drill out the remaining material. Run the mortise back and forth to clear out the slot (Fig. 6-61).

Dovetail Joints

Dovetail joints are often used on drawers in top-of-the-line cabinetry. They can be made with a drill press, using a router bit. A dovetail is considered one of the strongest joints in woodworking. The resistance to pull comes from every direction, except that in which the tenons have been inserted (Fig. 6-62).

The same cutter makes both the key and the tenon, and the cuts are mated by proper positioning of the work as it is cut. The table is placed parallel to the way tubes, and the table is used as a forward feed mechanism (the height lever). Determine spacing dependent on the size of the cutter and the overall joint design with some scrap pieces before starting any serious cutting. You can mark either the work or the table for correct cuts. Again, clamp the work and move the table slowly so that the feed is slow. Sloppy work caused by a too rapid feed is inexcusable. Always

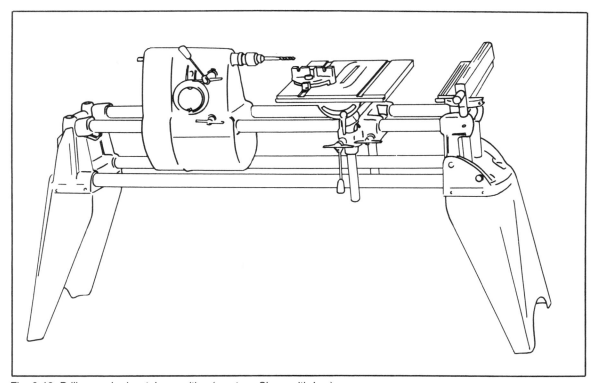

Fig. 6-46. Drill press horizontal capacities (courtesy Shopsmith Inc.).

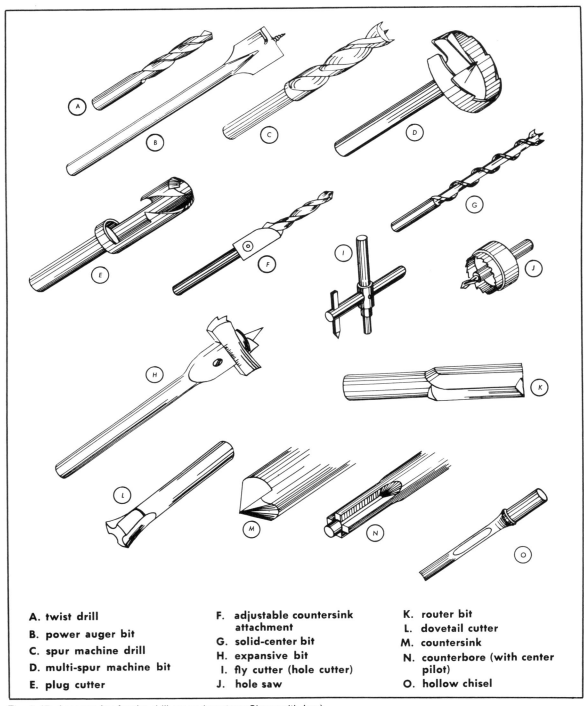

A. twist drill

B. power auger bit

C. spur machine drill

D. multi-spur machine bit

E. plug cutter

F. adjustable countersink attachment

G. solid-center bit

H. expansive bit

I. fly cutter (hole cutter)

J. hole saw

K. router bit

L. dovetail cutter

M. countersink

N. counterbore (with center pilot)

O. hollow chisel

Fig. 6-47. Accessories for the drill press (courtesy Shopsmith Inc.).

152

Table 6-2. Drill Press Speeds (courtesy Shopsmith Inc.).

Material	Operation	Speed (rpm)	Speed-dial Setting
wood	drilling—up to ¼"	3,800	S
wood	drilling—¼" to ½"	3,100	P
wood	drilling—½" to ¾"	2,300	M
wood	drilling—¾" to 1"	2,000	K
wood	drilling—over 1"	700	Slow
wood	using expansion or multi-spur bit	700	Slow
wood	routing	4,000-5,000	Rout-Shape
wood	cutting plugs or short dowels	3,300	Q
wood	carving	4,000-5,000	Rout-Shape
wood	using fly-cutter	700	Slow
wood	using dowel-cutter	1,800	J
hardwood	mortising	2,200	L
softwood	mortising	3,300	Q
metal	fine wire-brushing	3,300	Q
metal	coarse wire-brushing	1,000	D
wood	coarse wire-brushing	2,200	L
soft metals	buffing (cloth wheel)	3,800	S
hard metals	buffing (cloth wheel)	4,700	U
plastics	buffing (cloth wheel)	2,300	M
metal	using fly-cutter	700	Slow
metal	grinding—3"-4" cup wheel	3,100	P
glass	drilling with metal tube	700	Slow

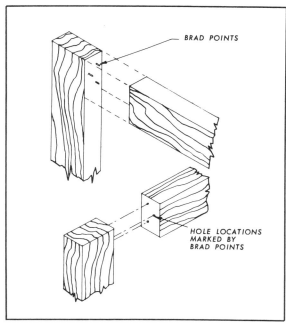

Fig. 6-49. Making use of headless brads for marking (courtesy Shopsmith Inc.).

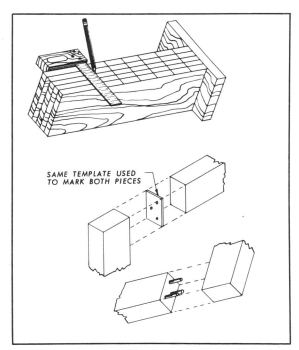

Fig. 6-48. Marking for drilling (courtesy Shopsmith Inc.).

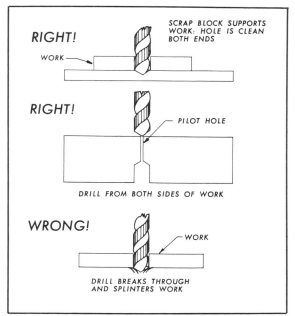

Fig. 6-50. Scrap block protects the drill table and keeps the back of the work being drilled from splintering (courtesy Shopsmith Inc.).

153

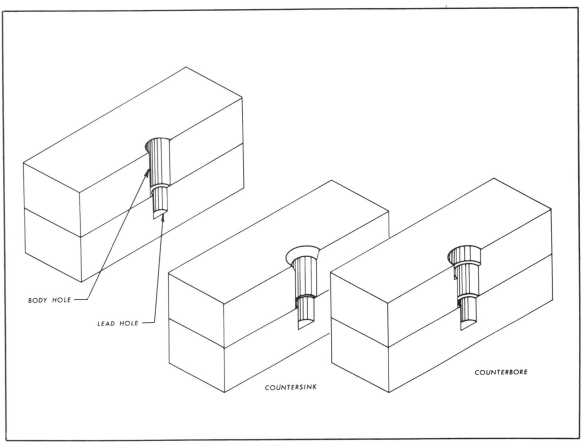

BODY HOLE

LEAD HOLE

COUNTERSINK

COUNTERBORE

Fig. 6-51. Countersink and counterbore holes (courtesy Shopsmith Inc.).

practice joints on scrap material before making any serious cuts (Fig. 6-63).

Mating cuts are formed with the table in the horizontal position, using the rip fence as a guide. Bring the table up as close to the cutting tool as possible. Make any final adjustments by extending the quill. Feed the work forward against the cutting tool. Advance the table—using the table height lever—for cut spacing. The tenon mating cuts require two passes, with one side formed in the first cut. You then turn the work and make the second pass. Always feed slowly and hold the workpiece firmly in place.

A special table will help when very wide stock must be dovetailed. You will need to make two passes for very wide dovetail cuts (Figs. 6-64 and 6-65).

A dovetailing table is most useful when you have a dovetailing jig to make multiple dovetails simultane-ously. Clamp the dovetailing table to the drill press table. You can then use the jig to move the work into the cutters, forming slots and tenons in a single opera-tion.

Doweling

Doweling with a drill press can be simplified by using a jig. The use of dowels to strengthen joints is a good idea when building cabinets. Dowel joints are easier to make than either mortise and tenon or dovetail joints. They can also to be used to join boards edge to edge for wooden countertops. Doweling is made easier with the drill press in its horizontal boring position, particularly when drilling board edges (Fig. 6-66).

Hole spacing for several boards can be equalized by stacking the boards, carefully aligning the edges,

154

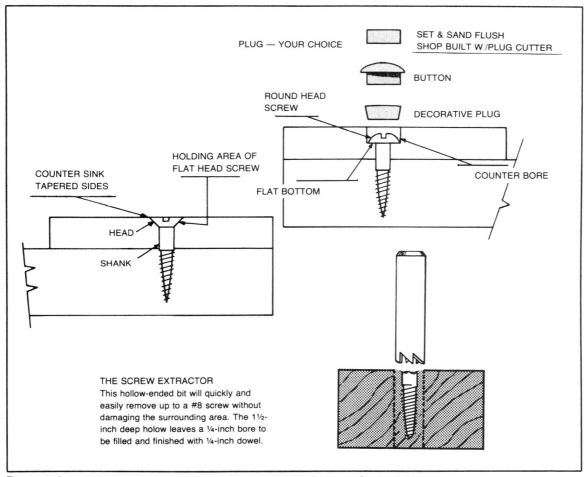

PLUG — YOUR CHOICE

SET & SAND FLUSH
SHOP BUILT W/PLUG CUTTER

BUTTON

ROUND HEAD
SCREW

DECORATIVE PLUG

HOLDING AREA OF
FLAT HEAD SCREW

COUNTER SINK
TAPERED SIDES

COUNTER BORE

FLAT BOTTOM

HEAD

SHANK

THE SCREW EXTRACTOR
This hollow-ended bit will quickly and
easily remove up to a #8 screw without
damaging the surrounding area. The 1½-
inch deep holow leaves a ¼-inch bore to
be filled and finished with ¼-inch dowel.

Fig. 6-52. Countersink, counterbore, plugs, and screw extractor (courtesy Shopsmith Inc.).

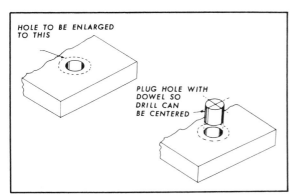

HOLE TO BE ENLARGED
TO THIS

PLUG HOLE WITH
DOWEL SO
DRILL CAN
BE CENTERED

Fig. 6-53. The best method for enlarging drill holes (courtesy Shopsmith Inc.).

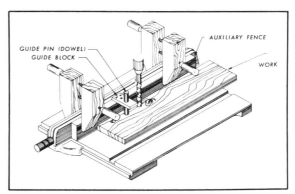

GUIDE PIN (DOWEL)
GUIDE BLOCK

AUXILIARY FENCE

WORK

Fig. 6-54. Screw hole center distance jig (courtesy Shopsmith Inc.).

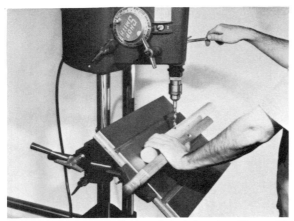

Fig. 6-55. Angle drilling for round stock (courtesy Shopsmith Inc.).

Table 6-3. Wood Screw Hole Sizes (courtesy Shopsmith Inc.)

SCREW GAUGE	BODY HOLE	LEAD HOLE	SCREW GAUGE IN INCHES
0	53	—	.060
1	49	—	.073
2	44	56*	.086
3	40	52*	.099
4	33	51*	.112
5	1/8	49*	.125
6	28	47	.138
7	24	46	.151
8	19	42	.164
9	15	41	.177
10	10	38	.190
11	5	37	.203
12	7/32	36	.216
14	D	31	.242
16	I	28	.268
18	19/64	23	.294

*In hardwoods only.

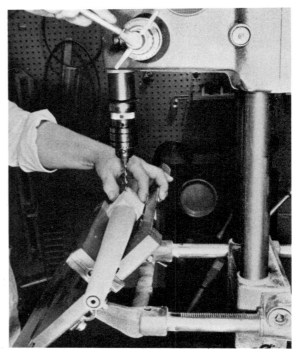

Fig. 6-56. Angle drilling square stock (courtesy Shopsmith Inc.).

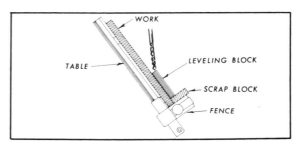

Fig. 6-57. Forming screw hole pockets (courtesy Shopsmith Inc.).

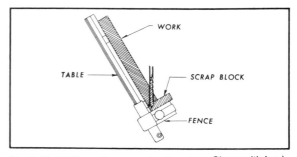

Fig. 6-58. Drilling extreme angles (courtesy Shopsmith Inc.).

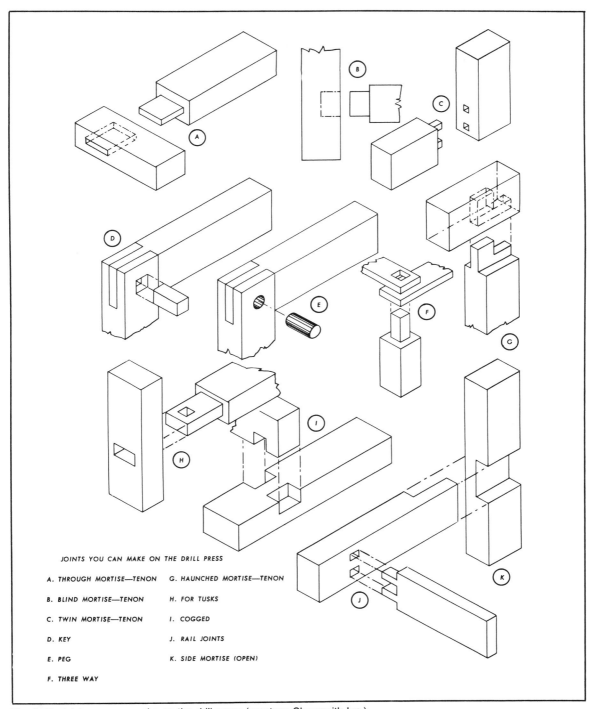

JOINTS YOU CAN MAKE ON THE DRILL PRESS

A. THROUGH MORTISE—TENON G. HAUNCHED MORTISE—TENON

B. BLIND MORTISE—TENON H. FOR TUSKS

C. TWIN MORTISE—TENON I. COGGED

D. KEY J. RAIL JOINTS

E. PEG K. SIDE MORTISE (OPEN)

F. THREE WAY

Fig. 6-59. Joints you can make on the drill press (courtesy Shopsmith Inc.).

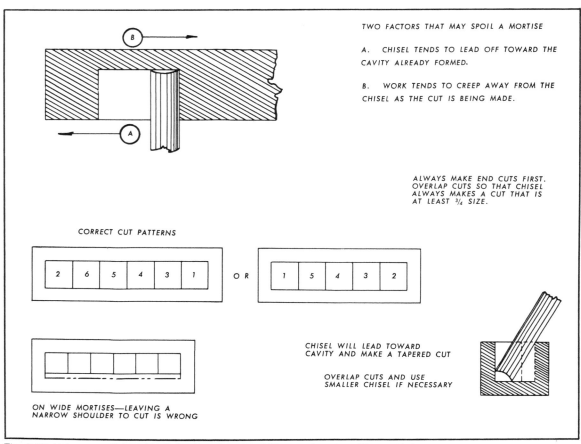

TWO FACTORS THAT MAY SPOIL A MORTISE

A.   CHISEL TENDS TO LEAD OFF TOWARD THE CAVITY ALREADY FORMED.

B.   WORK TENDS TO CREEP AWAY FROM THE CHISEL AS THE CUT IS BEING MADE.

ALWAYS MAKE END CUTS FIRST. OVERLAP CUTS SO THAT CHISEL ALWAYS MAKES A CUT THAT IS AT LEAST ¾ SIZE.

CORRECT CUT PATTERNS

| 2 | 6 | 5 | 4 | 3 | 1 |

OR

| 1 | 5 | 4 | 3 | 2 |

CHISEL WILL LEAD TOWARD CAVITY AND MAKE A TAPERED CUT

OVERLAP CUTS AND USE SMALLER CHISEL IF NECESSARY

ON WIDE MORTISES—LEAVING A NARROW SHOULDER TO CUT IS WRONG

Fig. 6-60. Using a mortising chisel attachment on the drill press (courtesy Shopsmith Inc.).

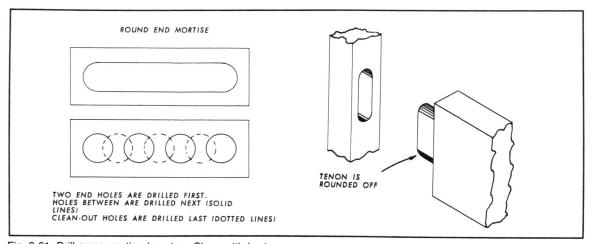

ROUND END MORTISE

TWO END HOLES ARE DRILLED FIRST. HOLES BETWEEN ARE DRILLED NEXT (SOLID LINES) CLEAN-OUT HOLES ARE DRILLED LAST (DOTTED LINES)

TENON IS ROUNDED OFF

Fig. 6-61. Drill press mortise (courtesy Shopsmith Inc.).

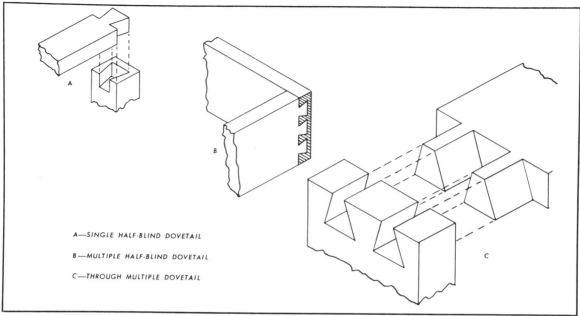

A—SINGLE HALF-BLIND DOVETAIL

B—MULTIPLE HALF-BLIND DOVETAIL

C—THROUGH MULTIPLE DOVETAIL

Fig. 6-62. Dovetail joints (courtesy Shopsmith Inc.).

Fig. 6-63. Routing a dovetail slot (courtesy Shopsmith Inc.).

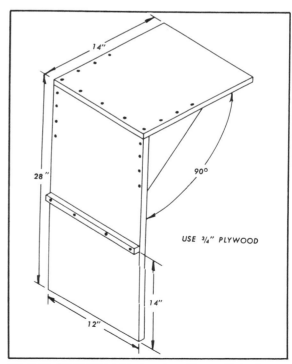

Fig. 6-64. Dovetailing table (courtesy Shopsmith Inc.).

159

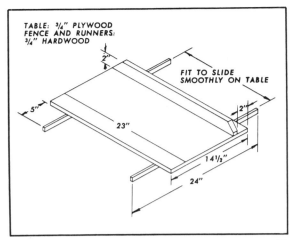

Fig. 6-65. Sliding dovetail slotting table (courtesy Shopsmith Inc.).

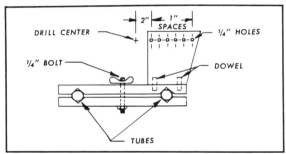

Fig. 6-66. Hole spacing jig for doweling work (courtesy Shopsmith Inc.).

and marking hole locations with a square. A simple jig also allows for equalized hole spacing. Drill the first hole, then insert the dowel on the jig in it. The second hole is automatically located for you. You can make the jig so that it will accept several dowel sizes, allowing you to drill holes of various sizes. Drill the guide for ¼-inch dowels. Attach a short length of larger dowel to one end. The larger dowel can then be used to set distances on larger holes, so a single ¼-inch pin will space holes from, say, ¼ inch to ½ inch in diameter. Additional pins for ⅜, ⅝, ¾, and 1-inch holes can also be done with a ¼-inch base pin.

Pegged Joints

Drawers can be made stronger by pegging the joints. Predetermine the dowel or peg size and the depth of hole you need. Drill the work as required. Hold the front and one side of the drawer together and drill both pieces. When the first hole is drilled, slip a dowel in place to hold things for the rest of the drilling (Figs. 6-67 through 6-69).

Pegged joints add strength to cabinet frames. Dowels need to be a press fit in the holes for maximum strength. Cut glue grooves in the dowel to allow space. Drill a block to fit the required dowel size, then drill a second hole for the router bit (⅛-inch straight bit). Make sure the router bit hole is larger than the bit, so chips clear easily. Rotate the dowel and push it slowly through the block, which must be clamped to the fence. Dowel pins are best made 1/16 inch shorter than the actual hole depth. They should be chamfered on both ends (Fig. 6-70).

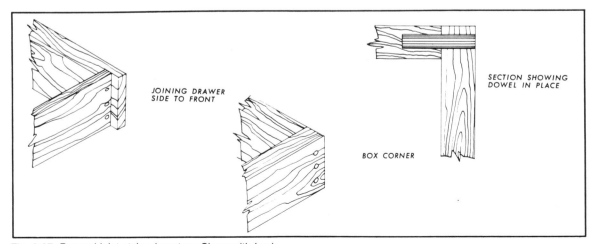

Fig. 6-67. Pegged joint styles (courtesy Shopsmith Inc.).

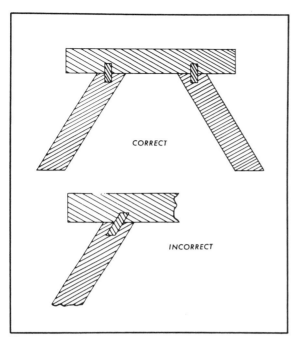

Fig. 6-68. Dowels must enter work at 90-degree angles to surfaces (courtesy Shopsmith Inc.).

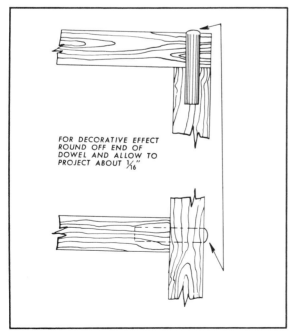

Fig. 6-69. Dowels may be rounded or left projecting. They also may be sanded flush (courtesy Shopsmith Inc.).

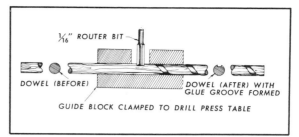

Fig. 6-70. Spiral grooves cut in dowels provide room for glue (courtesy Shopsmith Inc.).

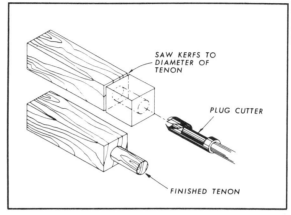

Fig. 6-71. Forming an integrate dowel (courtesy Shopsmith Inc.).

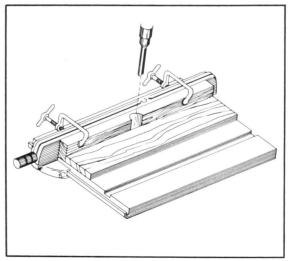

Fig. 6-72. Auxiliary fence for router use (courtesy Shopsmith Inc.).

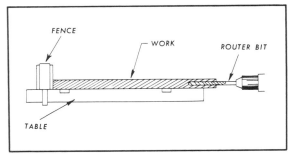

Fig. 6-73. Cutting edge grooves using a router bit (courtesy Shopsmith Inc.).

Form integrate dowels by using the table saw to cut the workpiece to the tenon diameter. A plug cutter is used for the final shaping (Fig. 6-71).

Chuck

The drill press, with a special chuck, can be used as a router and shaper. The special chuck is needed because of the high speed of the spindle, often up to 5,000 rpms. You can cut rabbets, groove edges, or make all sorts of surface designs. All passes are made against the rotation of the routine bit (Figs. 6-72 and 6-73).

ABRASIVE TOOLS

The Mark V offers a 1-foot-diameter *disc sander* as part of its standard package (Fig. 6-74). Abrasive discs for the sander come in many grits and types.

Disc sanding must be done on the downside of the disc's rotation. The work must be placed on the left side of the worktable, unless the disc is being run from

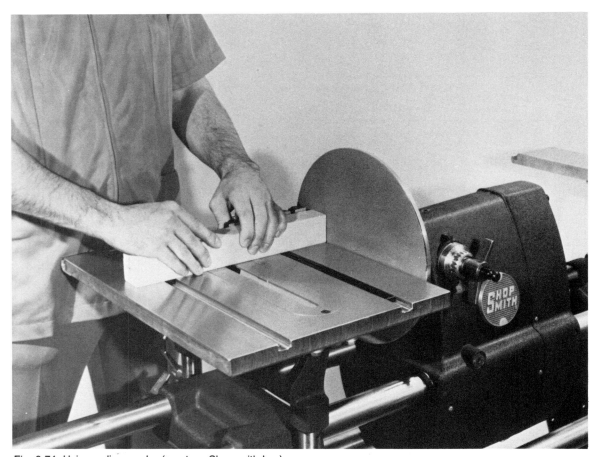

Fig. 6-74. Using a disc sander (courtesy Shopsmith Inc.).

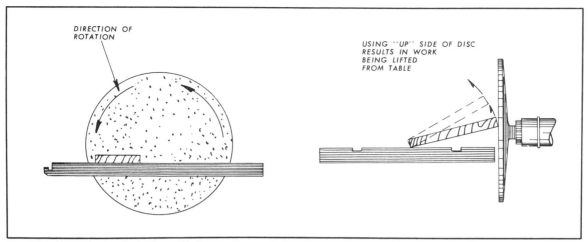

Fig. 6-75. Use only the disc's downside for sanding operations (courtesy Shopsmith Inc.).

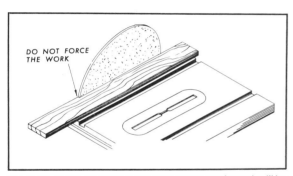

Fig. 6-76. Avoid excessive pressure, or too much stock will be removed. Scorching may also result (courtesy Shopsmith Inc.).

Fig. 6-77. A drum sander (courtesy Shopsmith Inc.).

the upper auxiliary spindle. Then you want to start from the table's right side (Fig. 6-75). Trying to work from the upside of the disc's rotation will mean your work will continue to be lifted from the table. The finish will be marred as a result. Keep the work flat as you feed it into the disc. Fast feeds can cut off too much material from a single spot and leave scorch marks (Fig. 6-76).

Flint is the cheapest abrasive material and wears the most rapidly. Most work is done with *garnet*, unless the material being removed is something that will clog the abrasive paper very rapidly. Flint paper is then ideal. Aluminum oxide is more expensive (Tables 6-4 and 6-5).

Drum sanders to fit on the spindle of the Mark V are easily made (Figs. 6-77 and 6-78). Keep speeds down, and don't look for deep cuts in a single pass (Figs. 6-79 and 6-80).

The *belt sander* for the Mark V uses an endless abrasive belt run between two drums. Belt sanders are great for sanding along the grain because they run in a straight line, leaving very few scratch marks. The Mark V takes a 6-inch-wide, 4-foot-long belt and connects to the Mark V power source, with operating speeds ranging from 915 to 1830 surface feet per minute (Fig. 6-81).

SHAPER

The Mark V *shaper* is an accessory that fits on the drill press in its vertical position. It is an excellent edge-shaping machine. The shaper fence is added, and a special shaper insert is also used for support

163

Table 6-4. Abrasive Selection Chart (courtesy Shopsmith Inc.).

ABRASIVE	USE	GRIT ROUGH	GRIT MEDIUM	GRIT FINE	REMARKS
aluminum oxide	hardwood aluminum copper steel ivory plastic	2½-1½ 40 40-50 24-30 60-80 50-80	1/2-1/0 60-80 80-100 60-80 100-120 120-180	2/0-3/0 100 100-120 100 120-280 240	Manufactured, brown color, bauxite base, more costly than garnet but usually cheaper to use per unit of work
garnet	hardwood softwood composition board plastic horn	2½-1½ 1½-1 1½-1 50-80 1½	1/2-1/0 1/0 1/2 120-180 1/2-1/0	2/0-3/0 2/0 1/0 240 2/0-3/0	Natural mineral, red color, harder and sharper than flint
silicon carbide	glass cast iron	50-60 24-30	100-120 60-80	12-320 100	Manufactured, harder but more brittle than aluminum oxide, very fast cutting
flint	removing paint, old finishes	3-1½	1/2-1/0		Natural hard form of quartz, low cost, use on jobs that clog the paper quickly

around the work while cutting. The unit can be used in the horizontal position, but it is mostly used in the vertical position. Speeds used are from 4,000 to 5,000 rpms. There are many shaping blades. The three-lipped shaper cutter is the safest for home shop use.

Shaping is normally done against the fence, with the workpiece moved in the direction of the cutter's rotation. Again, avoid excessive feed speed. Keep fingers hooked over the work edges and well away from the cutter blades for safety. Shapers not only make special cuts on edges, like those used for drop-leaf table edges, but they can also be used to clean up a board edge. Use spring sticks or other hold-downs when small workpieces are involved (Fig. 6-82).

Table 6-5. Abrasive Classes and Number Equivalents of Various Grit Sizes (courtesy Shopsmith Inc.).

TYPE	VERY FINE	FINE	MEDIUM	COARSE	VERY COARSE
flint	4/0	2/0-3/0	1/0-½	1-2	2½-3½
garnet	6/0-10/0	3/0-5/0	1/0-2/0	1/2-1½	2-3
aluminum oxide and silicon carbide	220-360	120-180	80-100	40-60	24-36
	8/0 = 280 7/0 = 240 6/0 = 220 5/0 = 180 4/0 = 150	3/0 = 120 2/0 = 100 0 = 80 ½ = 60 1 = 50	1½ = 40 2 = 36 2½ = 30 3 = 24		

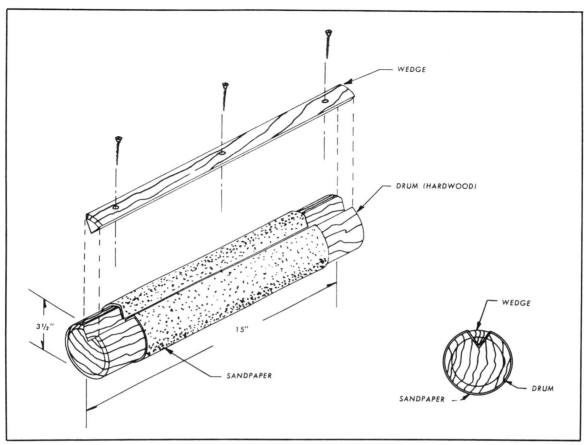

Fig. 6-78. Drum sander details (courtesy Shopsmith Inc.).

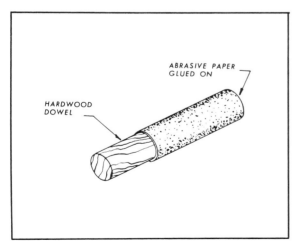

Fig. 6-79. Spindle sander (courtesy Shopsmith Inc.).

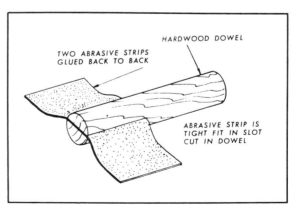

Fig. 6-80. Flexible or flap sander. Greater sanding efficiency in really close areas can be had by slitting each flap, so individual strips are less that ¼ inch wide (courtesy Shopsmith Inc.).

165

Fig. 6-81. The belt sander (courtesy Shopsmith Inc.).   Fig. 6-82. The shaper in use (courtesy Shopsmith Inc.).

Fig. 6-83. The jointer in use (courtesy Shopsmith Inc.).

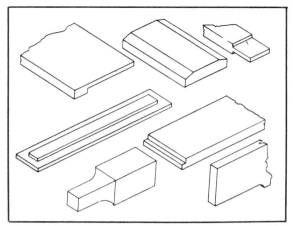

Fig. 6-84. Typical jointer cuts indicate the extra uses to which the Mark V can be put (courtesy Shopsmith Inc.).

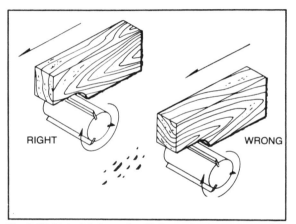

Fig. 6-85. Make jointing cuts wtih the grain whenever possible (courtesy Shopsmith Inc.).

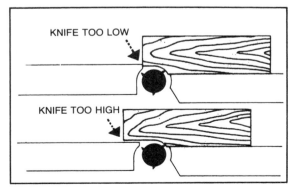

Fig. 6-86. Results of misalignment (courtesy Shopsmith Inc.).

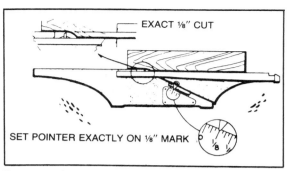

Fig. 6-87. Checking the depth of cutting set (courtesy Shopsmith Inc.).

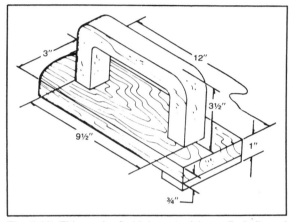

Fig. 6-88. This pusher/hold-down tool is easily built and should be used whenever the jointer is used for facing operations (courtesy Shopsmith Inc.).

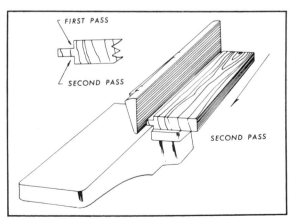

Fig. 6-89. Two rabbet cuts form a tongue (courtesy Shopsmith Inc.).

167

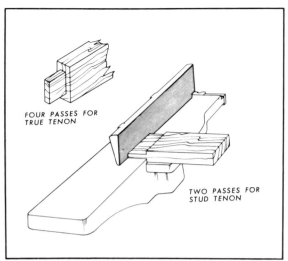

FOUR PASSES FOR TRUE TENON

TWO PASSES FOR STUD TENON

Fig. 6-90. Two and four-pass tenons (courtesy Shopsmith Inc.).

As with many cutting tools, the shaper does a better job with the grain than against it. Cross-grain cuts can be made by taking small cuts, making two or more passes when deep cuts are needed, and by using a very slow feed. Make finish cuts in the direction of the grain to remove any small splinters.

JOINTER

A *jointer* is primarily a rotary cutter for planing edges square and smooth to ready them for gluing and assembly (Fig. 6-83). A jointer is not a planer. The thickness planer is designed to make far heavier cuts, while the jointer is meant for light surfacing cuts. The jointer will form the cuts shown in Fig. 6-84.

Knife settings that are too low will force the work to hit the outfeed table. A too-high setting will keep the work from resting on the outfeed table. Jointer cuts are made with the grain. Cutting across the grain produces plenty of splintering and a generally poor surface (Fig. 6-85). If across or against the grain cuts are essential, make the cuts very slowly. Do not exceed ⅛ inch for cut depth, even with the grain. Expect best results with settings no greater than 1/16 inch (Figs. 6-86 and 6-87).

Surfacing work is done with a pusher/holder (Fig. 6-88). Cuts are never larger than 1/16 inch.

Rabbeting with a jointer, a frequent job for some furniture and cabinetmaking applications, is done with the guard set on the outfeed table rather than on the infeed table. Use more than a single pass for any deep cuts. Feed slowly. Tongues and tenons are forms of rabbets and can be easily made (Figs. 6-89 and 6-90). The jointer will also make bevel cuts and do tapering and chamfering.

Chapter 7

Projects

THE USEFUL PROJECTS IN THIS CHAPTER CAN BE made using basic workshop tools or the Shopsmith Mark V. All kitchen projects but one have been supplied by Shopsmith Inc.

SPICE/PIPE RACK

This versatile *spice rack* will hold large canisters. The addition of a separator turns it into a pipe rack with space for two humidors of tobacco (Figs. 7-1 and 7-2).

Cut all stock to 1/16 inch over dimensions if you have a jointer to finish the edges (they can also be sanded to the requisite size). The board's finished pieces should have widths of 5½ inches, 3¼ inches, and 1 inch. All pieces are then cut to length, with the bottom piece ripped and jointed—or sanded—to a width of 5¼ inches. The shelf pieces are then finished to 3 inches and the shelf rails to ½ inch. Plywood is cut to the exact sizes needed.

With a dado blade or a straight router bit, make a ¼ by ⅜ by 20¾-inch stop rabbet in the back edge of both side pieces. Use a band saw, jigsaw, or coping saw to cut the front contour in the side pieces. Sand all pieces. Make sure you smooth all sawed edges (Figs. 7-3 through 7-6).

Start the assembly by attaching the shelf rails to the shelves using brads and glue. Attach the shelves, and the top and bottom, to the sides. Use the wood screws counterbored in the sides. Glue the dowel buttons in the counterbored holes to hide the screwheads (Figs. 7-7 and 7-8).

The assembled pieces and plywood back are finished separately before you make the final assembly. If you plan to hang the spice rack anywhere around the stove where it might be spattered with grease, use a water-resistant finish such as polyurethane or tung oil. Stain with the same stain you plan to use on your cabinets.

Use brads to attach the back to the assembled portions of the rack. That completes the spice rack.

If you want a pipe rack, dry clamp the two pipe separator pieces together, edge to edge. Use a ¾-inch diameter bit and drill holes centered where the edges meet. Separate the two pieces. They have coves to hold your pipes. Finish the separators. Glue strips of felt inside the coves to protect the pipes. Attach the separators to the front side of the plywood back with wood screws (Fig. 7-9).

KNIFE BLOCK/CUTTING BOARD

This *knife block* design serves also as a *cutting*

Fig. 7-1. Spice/pipe rack (courtesy Shopsmith Inc.).

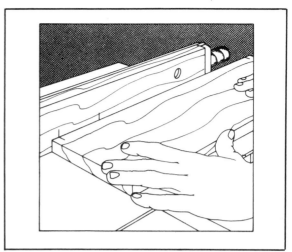

Fig. 7-3. Cutting the stop rabbet in side pieces. Use marks on fence to show the starting and stopping points of the rabbet (courtesy Shopsmith Inc.).

Bill of Materials
(in inches)

A	Top (1)	3/4 x 3-1/4 x 14-1/4
B	Shelf (2)	1/2 x 3 x 14-1/4
C	Shelf rail (2)	1/2 x 1 x 14-1/4
D	Bottom (1)	3/4 x 5-1/4 x 14-1/4
E	Side (2)	3/4 x 5-1/2 x 22
F	Back (1) (plywood)	1/4 x 15 x 20-3/4
(optional)	Pipe separators (2)	3/4 x 1 x 14-1/4
(optional)	Felt (1)	3/4 x 14

Hardware

G	F.H. wood screws (18)	1-1/4 – #8
H	Dowel buttons (18)	3/8 dia.

Fig. 7-2. Materials list for the spice/pipe rack (courtesy Shopsmith Inc.).

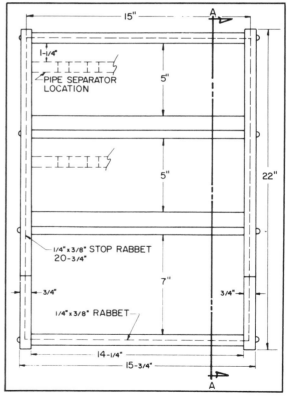

Fig. 7-4. Front view of the spice/pipe rack (courtesy Shopsmith Inc.).

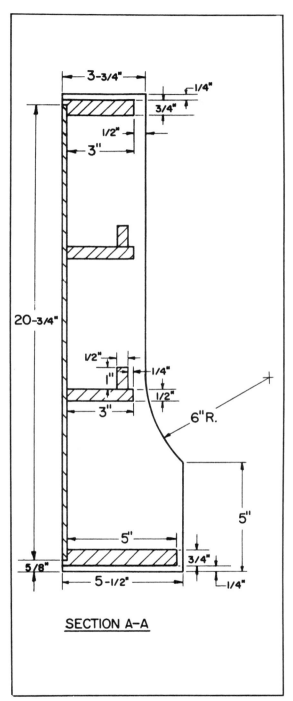

SECTION A-A

Fig. 7-5. Side view of the spice/pipe rack (courtesy Shopsmith Inc.).

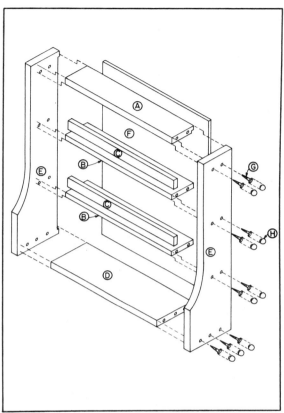

Fig. 7-6. Assembly details for the spice/pipe rack (courtesy Shopsmith Inc.).

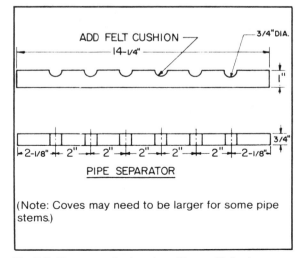

ADD FELT CUSHION
3/4"DIA.
14-1/4"
1"

PIPE SEPARATOR

2-1/8" 2" 2" 2" 2" 2" 2-1/8"
3/4"

(Note: Coves may need to be larger for some pipe stems.)

Fig. 7-7. Pipe separator (courtesy Shopsmith Inc.).

□ **1.** Cut all pieces to size.
□ **2.** Resaw and joint stock for shelves and shelf rails.
□ **3.** Cut stop dado in back edge of sides.
□ **4.** Cut front contour of sides.
□ **5.** Sand all pieces.
□ **6.** Attach shelf rails to shelves.
□ **7.** Assemble top, bottom and shelves to sides. Counterbore screws.
□ **8.** Glue dowel buttons in counterbored holes.
□ **9.** Finish.
□ **10.** Assemble back to rack.

If making pipe rack:

□ **11.** Dry clamp pipe separator pieces edge to edge.
□ **12.** Drill 3/4" diameter holes where edges meet.
□ **13.** Separate pieces and finish, except in coves.
□ **14.** Glue felt in coves.
□ **15.** Attach pipe separators to front side of plywood back.

Fig. 7-8. Spice/pipe rack construction checklist (courtesy Shopsmith Inc.).

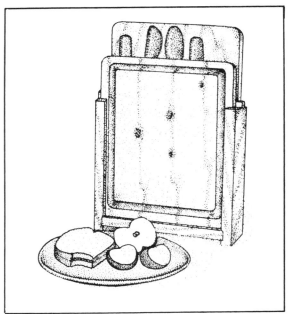

Fig. 7-10. Knife block/cutting board (courtesy Shopsmith Inc.).

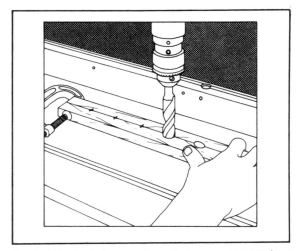

Fig. 7-9. Drilling holes on edges of pipe separators to form coves (courtesy Shopsmith Inc.).

board. The knife block is designed to hold six knives. The cutting board slides in front of the knives for easy access. The finished utensil can be hung on the wall or placed on a countertop (Fig. 7-10).

You need a ¾ by 10 by 14-inch board for the cutting board and a ¾ by 11¼ by 30-inch board for the knife block. Use a close-grained hardwood such as maple or beech. These woods tend to resist the penetration of oils and water. Oily hardwoods such as teak and rosewood are good, but you can't use resorcinol glue with them. Regarding softwoods, both cedar and redwood will do a good job.

Resaw the back, bottom, and knife holder stock to ½ inch on your band saw. Glue the back and cutting board stock edge to edge and face laminate the knife holder stock. Use resorcinol glue. After the glue sets about 10 to 12 hours at 70 degrees Fahrenheit, cut all pieces to size and sand them smooth.

Using a router bit or dado blade, cut the needed joinery in the sides and knife holder. When routing, make three or more passes to get the correct depth. Start with a ½-inch router bit or dado blades to cut ⅜ inch deep and ½ inch wide for the rabbet on the back inside edge of the sides. Use the same setup to cut a dado ⅜ inch deep by ½ inch wide on the sides, so you can attach the bottom. With the ½-inch bit or blade, cut a groove ⅜ inch deep by ¾ inch wide by 10½ inches long in the sides. Also, cut a rabbet ½ inch deep by ¾ inch wide on the ends of the knife holder. If you use a dado blade, do some handwork with a chisel where the groove and dado in the sides meet.

For wall hanging, drill a ¼-inch diameter hole near the top of the back to fit over a nail or dowel. Use a sander to round the corners on the back, sides, and cutting board (Figs. 7-11 through 7-14). Cut knife slots at 30-degree angles in the knife holder, using either a band saw or a handsaw. Use resorcinol glue to assemble the knife block.

Take the cutting board and rout a juice trough using a ½-inch core box bit (Fig. 7-15). An overarm router allows you to taper the groove by tacking or taping a wood strip ⅛ inch thick by 1 inch wide to the bottom side of the cutting board, nearest the edge where you would like the trough to be its deepest. Rout as usual and then remove the wood strip. The trough will be evenly tapered (Figs. 7-16 and 7-17).

Slide the cutting board into the groove in the knife block and check for fit. If it sticks a bit, sand some stock off the edges. Finish the cutting board and knife block with mineral oil or salad bowl finish (Fig. 7-18).

UTENSIL RACK

This *utensil rack* will provide storage space and make the kitchen more attractive. This rack is not difficult to make (Fig. 7-19).

The height for the rack is determined by your reach. Width can be adjusted to fit between cabinets or in other available wall space. The boards in this design have been dadoed to allow cabinets to swing as far open against the rack as possible. Dowels are used.

You need a 1 by 10-inch board 10 feet long, an acrylic sheet ⅛ inch by 2 feet by 3 feet, two dowel rods ¾ inch in diameter by 3 feet long, some 12-gauge wire, and screws. Cut all pieces to the appropriate sizes. Cut 2-inch-wide dadoes in the slats (Fig. 7-20). Also, cut

¾-inch rabbets in the uprights to a depth of half the board's thickness. Mark and drill holes of ¾-inch diameter to join the slats to the uprights. The holes should be centered on the dadoes of the slats and the width of the uprights.

Assemble the slats and uprights and locate the pots and pans in their places on the rack. Tailor the rack to your personal needs. Use dowels of ½-inch diameter for large-handled mugs and for pots and pans. Use wire hooks for lighter utensils such as woks and ladles.

Mark the location for the pegs and drill the holes in the slats. If you are using the Mark V in its vertical position, drill the holes with the table tilted at an 80-degree angle. This gives you a 10-degree upward slant on the pegs. Set the depth so that the drill bit just misses breaking through the slats (Fig. 7-21). Sand all uprights and edges, including the backs of the slats (Fig. 7-22).

Apply glue to the dado cuts on each end of the slats. Set them to line up with the correct holes in the uprights. Apply a small amount of glue to the ¾-inch diameter holes. Use a rubber or plastic-headed mallet

	Bill of Materials (in inches)		
A	Cutting Board (1)	3/4 x 9 x 13-1/4
B	Sides (2)	3/4 x 3-1/4 x 11-1/2
C	Knife holder (1)	1 x 1-3/4 x 9-3/4
D	Back (1)	1/2 x 9 x 17
E	Bottom (1)	1/2 x 2-1/2 x 9

Fig. 7-12. Materials list for the knife block/cutting board (courtesy Shopsmith Inc.).

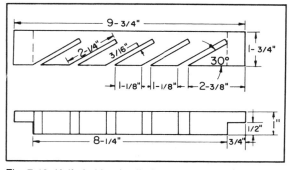

Fig. 7-13. Knife holder details (courtesy Shopsmith Inc.).

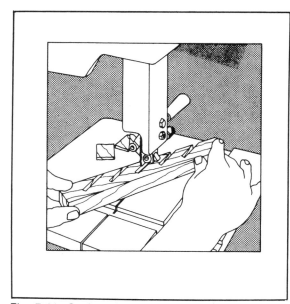

Fig. 7-11. Cutting slots in the knife holder (courtesy Shopsmith Inc.).

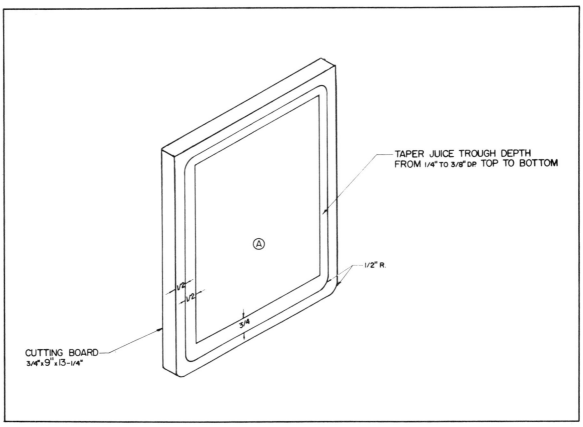

Fig. 7-14. Cutting board details (courtesy Shopsmith Inc.).

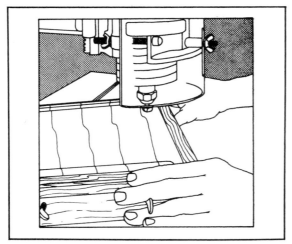

Fig. 7-15. Routing trough in cutting board (courtesy Shopsmith Inc.).

to drive the ¾-inch diameter dowels into the holes, until they are almost flush with the face of the slats. When the glue has set up, you can finish sand the rack's front.

Fasten the wall guard to the rack using four ¾-inch, number 6 flathead wood screws. A spacer is placed between the wall guard and the bottom slat, so the guard is flat against the wall when the rack is hung. Glue or press fit the dowels for the pans and mugs in place. When the glue has set, you can decide whether to coat the rack with stain and lacquer, tung oil, or linseed oil. Linseed oil must be applied every so often to maintain the finish (Fig. 7-23).

To make the wire hooks, use a pair of pliers to bend the upper end of the 12-gauge wire square so it fits over the top of the slats. Bend the lower portion of the wire around a piece of 1-inch pipe, so you have a good-sized hook. Your utensil rack is finished (Fig. 7-24).

174

TRIVETS

Trivets are handy for transferring hot items to the table (Fig. 7-25). The special fixture allows you to adapt almost any reasonable design to the trivets that you will be building (Fig. 7-26). Trivet blanks are held in place by the fixture, so you can go ahead and make accurate cuts. You can change the position of the fixture cradle to either duplicate or alter cut design.

Fixtures can be made to work with either table saws or routers. The table saw requires more material for the fixture. Both types of fixtures are made from ¾-inch stock. Cut all fixture pieces to the appropriate sizes. Use a dovetail router bit to cut the sliding dovetail in the extension bar and the cradle. Make sure the parts can slide smoothly.

Set the cradle and extension bar on the saw table, or the router arm table, and align the center of the cradle V-notch with the cutter. Mark a centerline on the cradle and extension bar. Use a ruler and mark 1-inch increments on both sides of the centerline. Drill holes of ¼-inch diameter for indexing. Make them ⅜ inch deep into the cradle at the marked lines.

With the fixture finished, attach it to the router arm table or the table saw table. Clamp to the router arm table. For the table saw, drill two holes of ¼-inch diameter in the extension bar. Attach the miter gauge with carriage bolts and wing nuts.

Cut your blank stock into 4, 6, and 8-inch squares. Slip a blank into the fixture and start making the cuts to form a trivet (Fig. 7-27). If you are using the table saw, set your dado blade for a ½-inch kerf. If you are using a router arm, a carbide-tipped straight bit or any decorative bit that doesn't need a pilot is fine. Start at one corner of the blank and make your first cut—all cuts are ½ inch deep. Turn the blank 180 degrees and cut the other corner. Remove the stop pin. Slide the cradle and blank in 1 inch. Reinsert the stop pin and cut the next groove. Continue cutting until you reach the middle of the blank, and the top side is done. Turn the

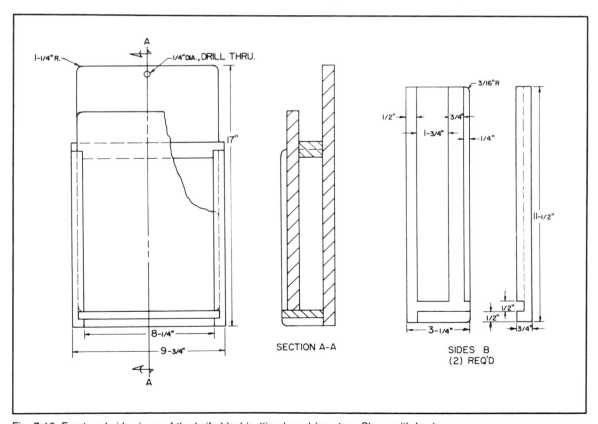

Fig. 7-16. Front and side views of the knife block/cutting board (courtesy Shopsmith Inc.).

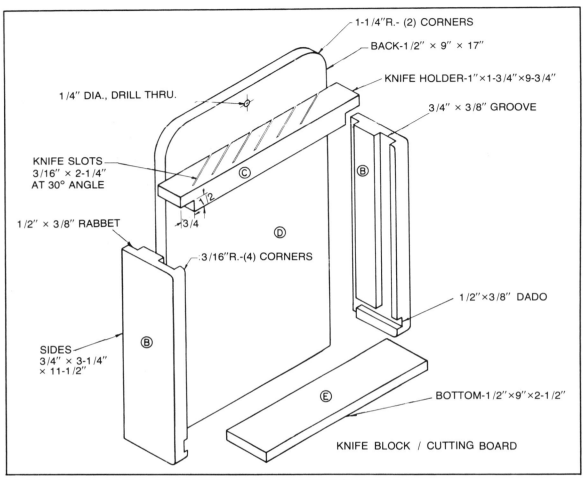

1-1/4"R.- (2) CORNERS

BACK-1/2" × 9" × 17"

KNIFE HOLDER-1"×1-3/4"×9-3/4"

3/4" × 3/8" GROOVE

1/4" DIA., DRILL THRU.

KNIFE SLOTS
3/16" × 2-1/4"
AT 30° ANGLE

Ⓒ

Ⓑ

1/2" × 3/8" RABBET

Ⓓ

3/4

1/2

:3/16"R.-(4) CORNERS

1/2"×3/8" DADO

SIDES
3/4" × 3-1/4"
× 11-1/2"

Ⓑ

Ⓔ

BOTTOM-1/2"×9"×2-1/2"

KNIFE BLOCK / CUTTING BOARD

Fig. 7-17. Assembly details for the knife block/cutting board (courtesy Shopsmith Inc.).

Knife Block/Cutting Board Construction Checklist

- ☐ **1.** Resaw stock for back, bottom and knife holder.
- ☐ **2.** Glue up stock.
- ☐ **3.** Cut all pieces to size.
- ☐ **4.** Cut all joinery in sides and knife holder.
- ☐ **5.** Round corners on back, sides and cutting board by sanding.
- ☐ **6.** Cut knife slots in knife holder.
- ☐ **7.** Drill hole in back for hanging. (optional)
- ☐ **8.** Sand all pieces smooth.
- ☐ **9.** Assemble knife block.
- ☐ **10.** Rout juice trough in cutting board.
- ☐ **11.** Finish.

Fig. 7-18. Construction checklist for the knife block/cutting board (courtesy Shopsmith Inc.).

blank over, rotate it 90 degrees, and start the cutting from corner to middle (Fig. 7-28). Changing bits in a router will give you a totally different trivet pattern (Fig. 7-29). Trivets are sanded on the edges with the disc sander. Use flutter sheets for a good overall sanding before finishing (Fig. 7-30). Select a finish that is heat and water-resistant (Fig. 7-31).

POTS AND PANS ORGANIZER

A file drawer for pots and pans will organize these items (Fig. 7-32). The movable dividers let you change things around as needed, so the addition of a few new pieces of cookware should not cause storage problems.

You may wish to leave this project until you have

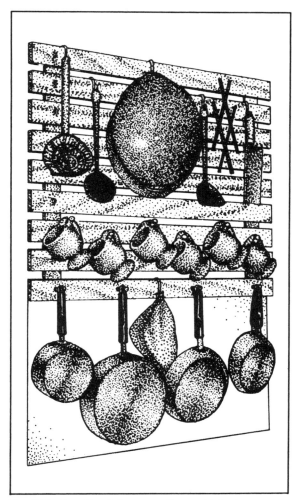

Fig. 7-19. Utensil rack (courtesy Shopsmith Inc.).

Fig. 7-20. Cutting dado in slat (courtesy Shopsmith Inc.).

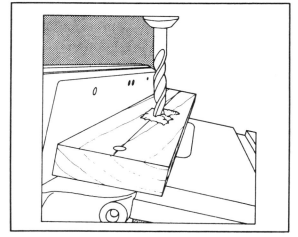

Fig. 7-21. Drilling angled holes for pegs in slats (courtesy Shopsmith Inc.).

finished your cabinet installation. You need accurate interior dimensions to do a good job.

Most under-counter (base) cabinets will allow you room for at least one deep drawer and one pull-out shelf. Drawer depth is determined by the size of your largest pots and pans. This will usually be no more than 10 or 11 inches. The largest solid wood you can normally get at a lumberyard is 11¼ inches wide; you won't have to glue anything up to make wider stock.

The length of the storage drawer should be ⅛ to ¼ inch less than the depth of the cabinet. The same holds true for any pull-out shelves you install. This allows room to close the cabinet doors. Keep the width a bit less than the width of the door opening.

Relatively inexpensive number 2 pine and ¼-inch tempered Masonite hardboard are fine for virtually all parts. Your best bet for drawer guides and runners is sugar or rock maple, for it's a close-grained, extremely hard wood. The finished portions of pine and maple can be stained to match your cabinets, or you can simply rub them down with linseed oil. Tung oil also works well.

You need seven pieces to make each drawer: front, back, bottom, two sides, and two runners. Sim-

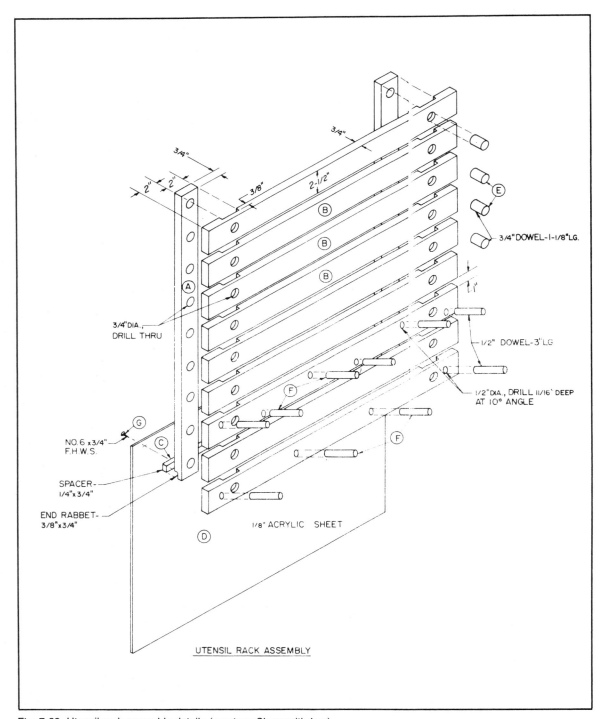

Fig. 7-22. Utensil rack assembly details (courtesy Shopsmith Inc.).

178

Bill of Materials
(in inches)

A	Upright (2)	3/4 x 2 x (length)
B	Slats (x)	3/4 x 2-1/2 x (length)
C	Spacer (1)	1/4 x 3/4 x (length)
D	Wall guard (1)	1/8 x (width) x (length) acrylic sheet
E	Joint peg (2x)	1-1/8 x 3/4 dia. dowel
F	Mug and pan peg(10)	3 x 1/2 dia. dowel

Hardware

G	Wood screws (4)	3/4 – #6 F.H.
H	Wire hooks (x) (Molly anchors or other hanging hardware) (4)	5-3/8 x 12 gauge

Utensil Rack Construction Checklist

□ **1.** Cut all pieces to size.
□ **2.** Cut joinery in pieces.
□ **3.** Drill dowel holes in slats and uprights for assembly.
□ **4.** Drill 10° angled dowel holes in slats for pegs.
□ **5.** Sand all pieces.
□ **6.** Assemble pieces.
□ **7.** Finish.

Fig. 7-23. Materials list and construction checklist for the utensil rack (courtesy Shopsmith Inc.).

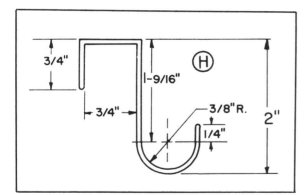

Fig. 7-24. Hook detail (courtesy Shopsmith Inc.).

ple dadoes are used for most of the joinery, except at the sides and front, which need a sliding dovetail.

Using a router or a router accessory for the Mark V, take a 9/16-inch dovetail cutter and rout two vertical slots in the drawer front. The center of each of these slots should be 7/8 inch in from each respective side (Fig. 7-33). The mating dovetails in the sides are made by routing in the horizontal position, with the table height adjusted to allow the dovetail cutter to cut the

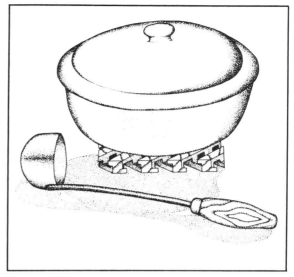

Fig. 7-25. Trivets are useful items (courtesy Shopsmith Inc.).

half dovetail 3/8 inch in from the end. Use the miter gauge and safety grip to pass the sides under the cutter. Flip the board and repeat the procedure. You then have a full dovetail tenon (Fig. 7-34).

The other joinery is cut using either a straight router bit or dado blades. The dado to join the back to the sides is 3/8 inch deep by 3/4 inch wide. The groove to join the bottom to the other drawer parts is 3/8 inch deep by 1/4 inch wide (Fig. 7-35).

Cut additional dadoes 1/4 inch wide by 3/8 inch deep down the insides of the sides. Keep them perpendicular to the length and space them every 2 inches. These will hold spacers needed to organize your utensils.

You can rout a handle in the front of the drawer using a 1/2-inch straight bit. The handle can be a depression 5 inches wide and 1 inch deep in the top edge or a slot, 5 inches wide and 1 1/2 inches deep, 1 1/2 inches below the top edge. The slot usually makes a better handle.

Assemble the front, sides, back, and bottom with glue and wood screws. Yellow glues are best. Use a sander to give a slight crown to the bottom edge of the runners. This will help reduce friction, so the drawer moves in and out easily. Attach the runners to the drawer with glue and wood screws (Figs. 7-36 and 7-37).

The shelf can be made from a single piece of 3/4-inch plywood, but it will need to be faced. Cut four boards 3/4 inch thick by 3 inches wide to make a shelf

Trivets Construction Outline

1. Cut fixture pieces to size.
2. Cut dovetail joint in cradle and extension bar.
3. Align center of cradle V-notch with cutter.
4. Mark inch marks.
5. Drill indexing holes.
6. Attach fixture in place.
7. Cut blanks to size.
8. Cut grooves in blanks.
9. Sand trivets.
10. Finish or stain trivets.

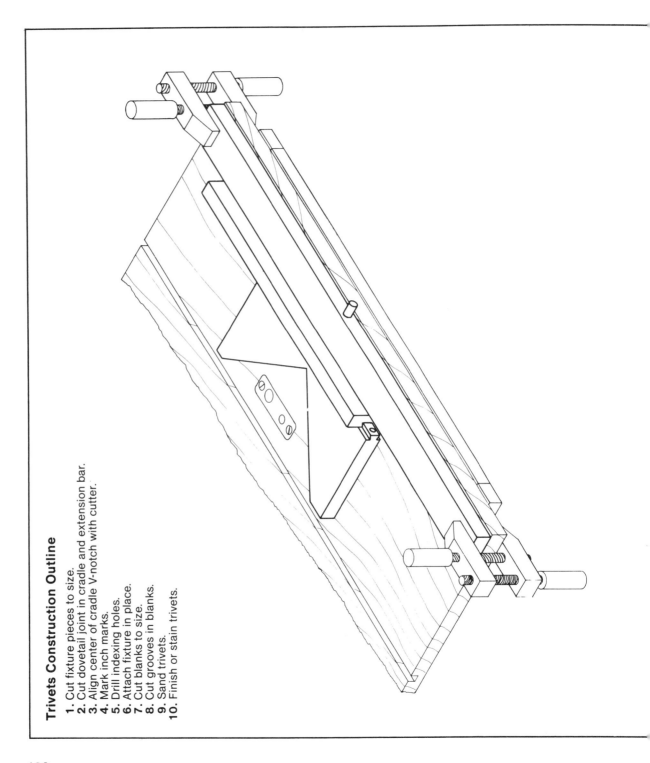

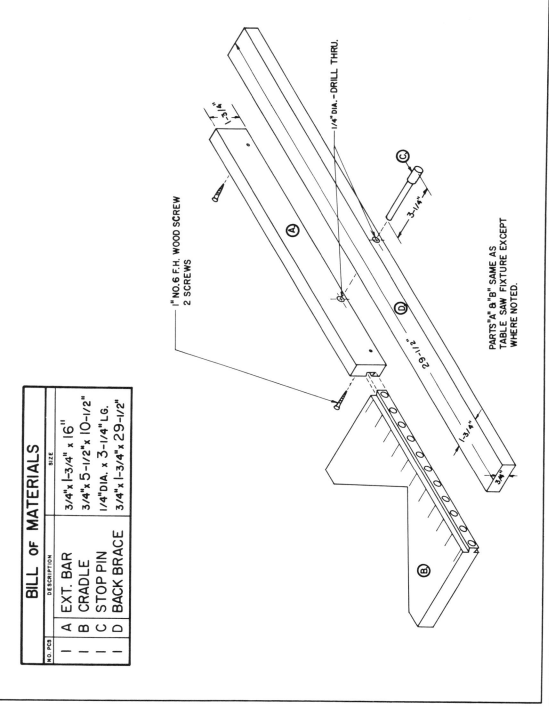

BILL OF MATERIALS

NO. PCS		DESCRIPTION	SIZE
1	A	EXT. BAR	3/4"x 1-3/4" x 16"
1	B	CRADLE	3/4"x 5-1/2"x 10-1/2"
1	C	STOP PIN	1/4"DIA. x 3-1/4" LG.
1	D	BACK BRACE	3/4"x 1-3/4"x 29-1/2"

1" NO.6 F.H. WOOD SCREW
2 SCREWS

1/4" DIA.– DRILL THRU.

PARTS"A"&"B" SAME AS
TABLE SAW FIXTURE EXCEPT
WHERE NOTED.

Fig. 7-26. Trivet fixture construction plans (courtesy Shopsmith Inc.).

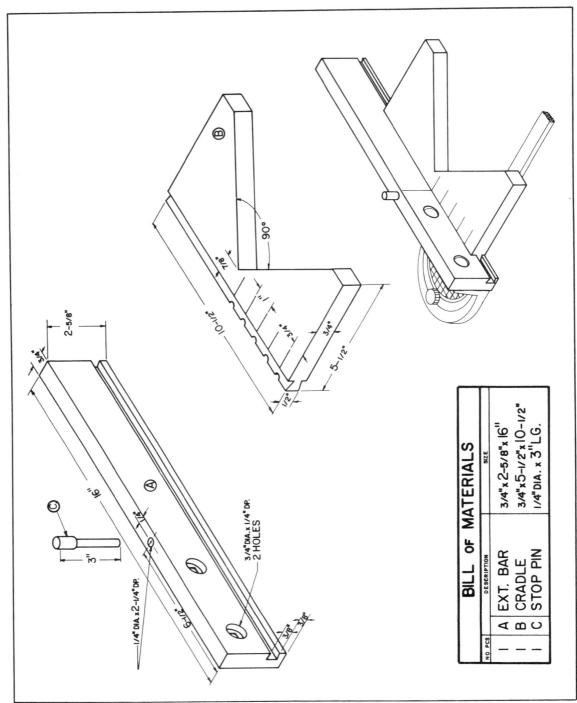

BILL of MATERIALS

NO PCS		DESCRIPTION	SIZE
1	A	EXT. BAR	3/4" x 2-5/8" x 16"
1	B	CRADLE	3/4" x 5-1/2" x 10-1/2"
1	C	STOP PIN	1/4" DIA. x 3" LG.

Fig. 7-26. Continued from page 181.

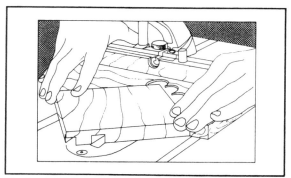

Fig. 7-27. Using the trivet fixtures (courtesy Shopsmith Inc.).

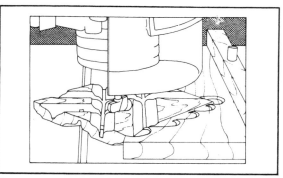

Fig. 7-29. Change bits to vary patterns (courtesy Shopsmith Inc.).

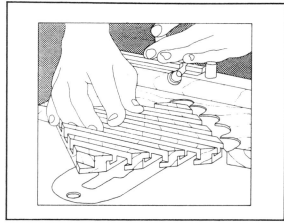

Fig. 7-28. Cutting opposite side grooves in the trivet (courtesy Shopsmith Inc.).

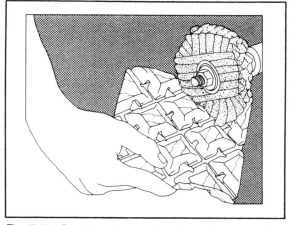

Fig. 7-30. Sand the trivets with flutter sheets (courtesy Shopsmith Inc.).

frame. Cut a dado ¼ inch wide by ⅜ inch deep down the center of the frame members inside edges, using either dado blades or a ¼-inch straight bit. Cut a tenon ¼ inch thick by ⅜ inch long in the ends of the front and back frame members. On the bottom side of the front frame member, rout or dado a 5-inch-long groove ¾ inch wide by ½ inch deep. This groove acts as a pull for the sliding shelf.

Cut a piece of ¼-inch tempered Masonite hardboard to fit inside the frame. Assemble the pieces with glue.

To install the drawer and shelf in the cabinet, make two guides out of a piece of hardwood 1¼ inches thick by 5 inches wide. Cut two dadoes ½ inch deep down the length of the board. Make the shelf dado 13/16 inch wide. The drawer dado is 1½ inches wide, spaced 13/16 inch down from the bottom of the shelf

dado. Cut the board in half to make two guides. These guides will mount a shelf above a drawer. If you want to mount the shelf below the drawer, you will have to make another set of guides.

Using brad points, drill two 1-inch holes, ¾-inch deep, in each of the guides, centered 5/16 inch below the dado for the drawer. Keep these holes positioned 3 inches back from the front edge of the guides and 3 inches back from the center. Mount small shower stall rollers in these recesses. The rollers make excellent glides for heavy drawers.

Purchase four rollers ¾ inch in diameter. Mount them with number 8-by-1¼-inch roundhead screws in the drilled recesses. Ream the roller centers out a bit if the number 8 screws do not go through easily. Do not use smaller screws. Use the pilot hole left by the brad point bit to center the rollers in the recesses, so they

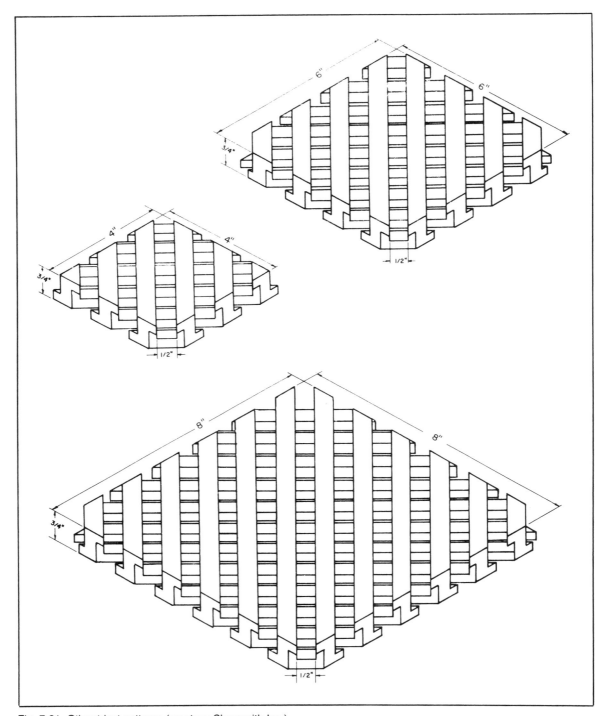

Fig. 7-31. Other trivet patterns (courtesy Shopsmith Inc.).

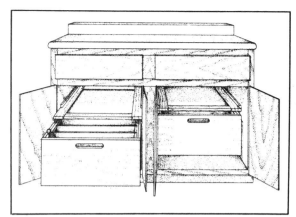

Fig. 7-32. Pots and pans organizer (courtesy Shopsmith Inc.).

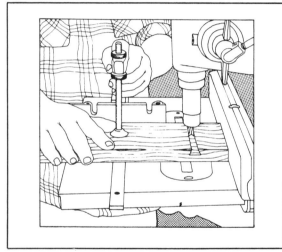

Fig. 7-33. Routing a dovetail groove (courtesy Shopsmith Inc.).

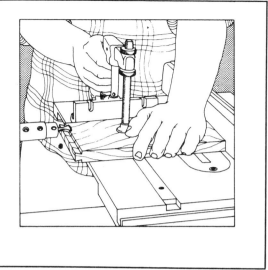

Fig. 7-34. Horizontal routing of a mating dovetail (courtesy Shopsmith Inc.).

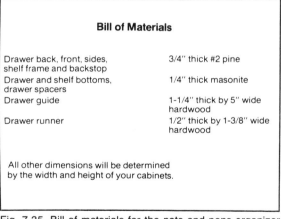

Bill of Materials

Drawer back, front, sides, shelf frame and backstop	3/4″ thick #2 pine
Drawer and shelf bottoms, drawer spacers	1/4″ thick masonite
Drawer guide	1-1/4″ thick by 5″ wide hardwood
Drawer runner	1/2″ thick by 1-3/8″ wide hardwood

All other dimensions will be determined by the width and height of your cabinets.

Fig. 7-35. Bill of materials for the pots and pans organizer (courtesy Shopsmith Inc.).

Hardware

Shower door rollers	3/4″ diameter
Round head wood screws	1-1/4″-#8
Flat head wood screws	1″-#8

Fig. 7-36. Hardware list for the pots and pans organizer (courtesy Shopsmith Inc.).

stick into the dado slot 1/16 inch when they are mounted (Figs. 7-38 through 7-40).

Mount the finished guides to your cabinet frame. Tack or clamp them into place, so you can check to see that the drawer is level and slides easily. You need about 1/16 inch of play in both the drawer and the shelf, and that is what you should get using these measurements. Once the guides are placed correctly, mark the position and attach them permanently to the cabinet frame with glue and wood screws (Fig. 7-41).

Slide the drawers and shelves into place. Cut spacers, two to four per drawer, and put them in place. See Fig. 7-42.

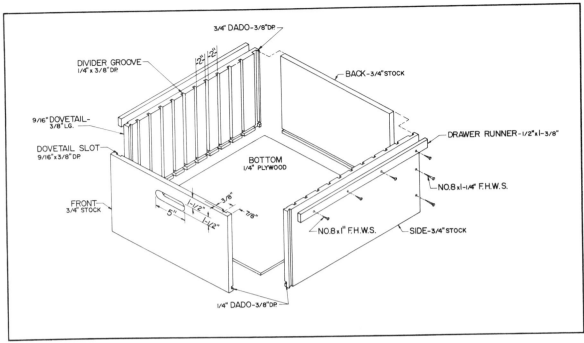

Fig. 7-37. Drawer assembly (courtesy Shopsmith Inc.).

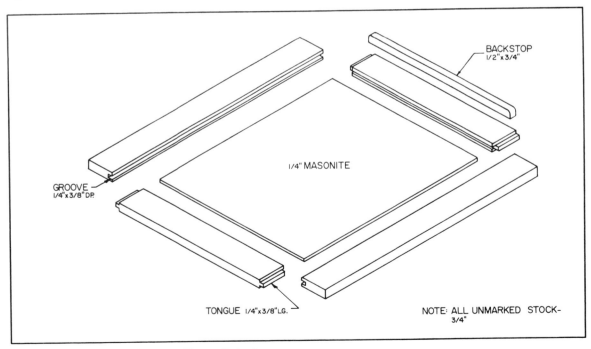

Fig. 7-38. Shelf assembly (courtesy Shopsmith Inc.).

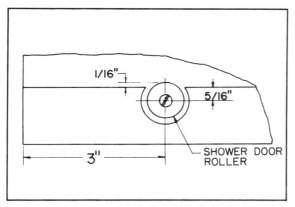

Fig. 7-39. Roller detail (courtesy Shopsmith Inc.).

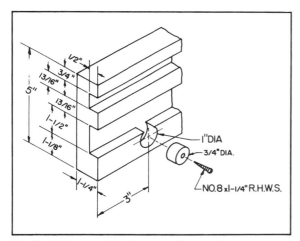

Fig. 7-40. Drawer guide (courtesy Shopsmith Inc.).

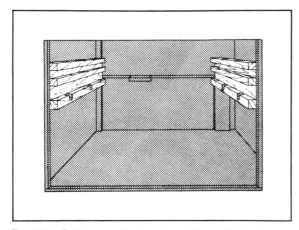

Fig. 7-41. Guide mounting (courtesy Shopsmith Inc.).

Pots and Pans Organizer Construction Checklist

☐ 1. Determine drawer and shelf dimensions.

Making the drawer

☐ 2. Cut drawer pieces to size.
☐ 3. Cut all joinery in drawer pieces.
☐ 4. Cut divider grooves on inside of sides.
☐ 5. Rout handle in drawer front.
☐ 6. Assemble drawer front, sides, back and bottom.
☐ 7. Crown bottom edge of runners by sanding.
☐ 8. Attach runners to drawer.
☐ 9. Cut masonite to size for spacers in drawer.

Making the shelf

☐ 10. Cut shelf pieces to size.
☐ 11. Cut dado in inside edge of frame pieces.
☐ 12. Cut tenon on ends of front and back frame pieces.
☐ 13. Assemble shelf pieces.

Installing the drawer and shelf

☐ 14. Cut drawer and shelf guide stock to size.
☐ 15. Cut two dadoes down length of stock.
☐ 16. Cut stock into two or more guides.
☐ 17. Drill two recesses in each guide.
☐ 18. Install rollers in recesses.
☐ 19. Mount guides to your cabinet frame.
☐ 20. Slide drawer and shelf into place.

Fig. 7-42. Pots and pans organizer construction checklist (courtesy Shopsmith Inc.).

CABINET DOORS

One of the major projects when a kitchen is remodeled is cabinet replacement. A simple remodeling job can often involve merely replacing cabinet doors or just redesigning the doors currently in place (Fig. 7-43)

If you live in the East and Mideast, hardwoods such as walnut, birch, maple, and oak, are readily available and can be used for cabinet doors. Softwoods such as the firs, cedar, hemlock, and pines (also available throughout the East) are easily obtainable in the West and Southwest. Hickory and cherry are seldom used in cabinets.

Cabinet doors can be built in two ways. A solid panel door, made of a single board, is probably the easier to make. Every wide board—especially one as wide as a cabinet door—will warp eventually, and that includes plywood. Using panel and frame construction is the most durable way, though more work is required. Panel and frame door construction gives you a far wider choice of door designs.

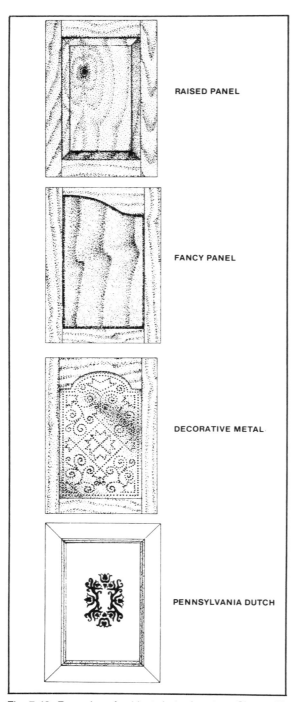

Fig. 7-43. Examples of cabinet doors (courtesy Shopsmith Inc.).

RAISED PANEL

FANCY PANEL

DECORATIVE METAL

PENNSYLVANIA DUTCH

Making the Frame

Door frames are made up of four pieces. Two are vertical stiles, one is a top rail, and the other is a bottom rail. See Fig. 7-44. A rabbet in the inside edge holds the panel in place. The rails and stiles can be joined in several ways, but the strongest and longest-lasting joint for this type of construction is the mortise and tenon (Fig. 7-45).

Start out by determining what size your new cabinet doors must be. The size will depend in large part on the way you want to hang the doors. If the doors are hung inside the cabinet frame, you can cut a lip so they partially overhang the frame, or you can leave them on the outside of the frame. If you want to inset the doors, make them 1/16 inch smaller than the door opening. This is most easily done if you make the doors the same size as the cabinet opening, then use the jointer to cut them down 1/16 inch. If you want them partially inset or overlapping, the door must be ¼ to ⅜ inch larger all around.

Cut the rails and stiles to size. Most of these will be ¾ inch thick and 2 inches wide, except for the top rail, which may be slightly wider. You can cut simple curves in it with a band saw (or jigsaw). Cut a rabbet ¼ inch by 5/16 inch wide on the inside edges of the stiles and rails. Use the shaper accessory to the Mark V (or a router or dado head) with a blank cutter and a 1¼-inch collar.

Make a stub mortise ¾ inch deep, ⅜ inch wide, and 2 inches long in both ends of the stiles, where they must mate with the rails. Use the ⅜-inch mortising chisel and make repeating passes. Where the top rail mates to the stile, the mortise needs to be slightly longer, or shorter, than 2 inches if you are cutting a design in the top rail.

Use either a dado head or molder accessory with a blank cutter to make the tenons in both ends of the

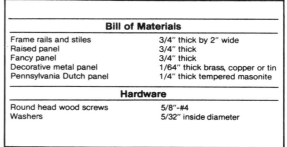

Bill of Materials	
Frame rails and stiles	3/4" thick by 2" wide
Raised panel	3/4" thick
Fancy panel	3/4" thick
Decorative metal panel	1/64" thick brass, copper or tin
Pennsylvania Dutch panel	1/4" thick tempered masonite
Hardware	
Round head wood screws	5/8"-#4
Washers	5/32" inside diameter

Fig. 7-44. Materials list and hardware for cabinet doors (courtesy Shopsmith Inc.).

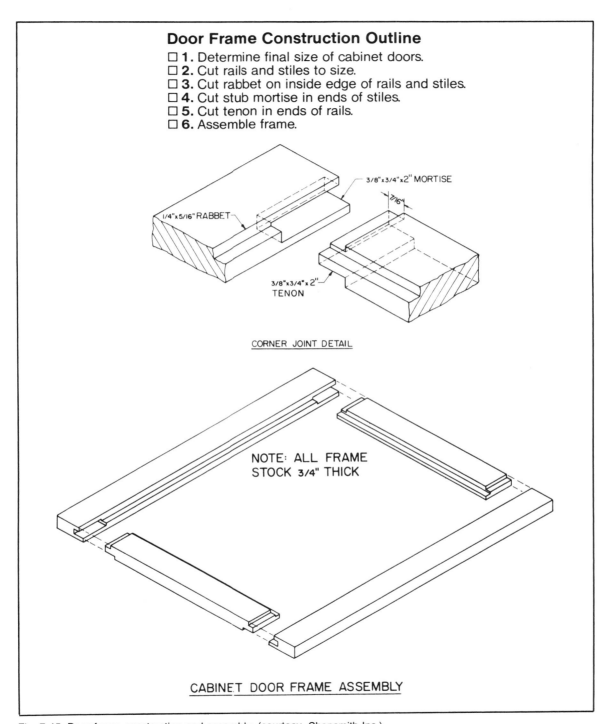

Door Frame Construction Outline
☐ **1.** Determine final size of cabinet doors.
☐ **2.** Cut rails and stiles to size.
☐ **3.** Cut rabbet on inside edge of rails and stiles.
☐ **4.** Cut stub mortise in ends of stiles.
☐ **5.** Cut tenon in ends of rails.
☐ **6.** Assemble frame.

3/8"x3/4"x2" MORTISE

7/16"

1/4"x5/16" RABBET

3/8"x3/4"x2"
TENON

CORNER JOINT DETAIL

NOTE: ALL FRAME
STOCK 3/4" THICK

CABINET DOOR FRAME ASSEMBLY

Fig. 7-45. Door frame construction and assembly (courtesy Shopsmith Inc.).

Raised Panel Construction Checklist

☐ **1.** Glue up stock, edge to edge, if needed.
☐ **2.** Cut panel to size, slightly smaller than actual dimensions.
☐ **3.** Tilt saw table at 15° angle.
☐ **4.** Turn panel on edge and use a hollow-ground planer blade to cut a bevel around outside edges.

GLUE JOINTS MADE WITH SHAPER
OR MOLDER ACCESSORY
TO GLUE UP WIDE PANELS

Fig. 7-46. Raised panel construction (courtesy Shopsmith Inc.).

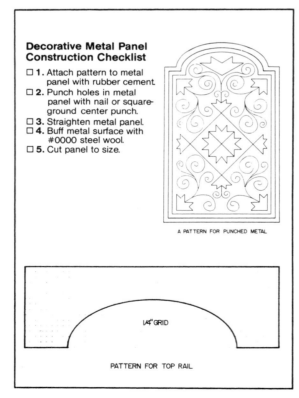

Decorative Metal Panel Construction Checklist

☐ **1.** Attach pattern to metal panel with rubber cement.
☐ **2.** Punch holes in metal panel with nail or square-ground center punch.
☐ **3.** Straighten metal panel.
☐ **4.** Buff metal surface with #0000 steel wool.
☐ **5.** Cut panel to size.

A PATTERN FOR PUNCHED METAL

1/4" GRID

PATTERN FOR TOP RAIL

Fig. 7-47. Decorative metal panel construction (courtesy Shopsmith Inc.).

rails. Make the tenons ⅜ inch wide and ¾ inch long on the front side, and ⅜ inch wide by 7/16 inch long on the back side. Assemble the frames with glue and set them aside to dry.

Raised Panel

Panels can be of many materials and in many designs. Wood and metals such as copper and brass can be used for panels. You can use clear or translucent colored plastics or fiberglass, clear (tempered) glass, or one of Masonite's patterned boards. (Figs. 7-46 through 7-49).

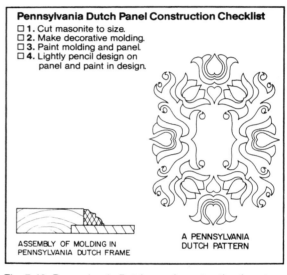

Pennsylvania Dutch Panel Construction Checklist

☐ **1.** Cut masonite to size.
☐ **2.** Make decorative molding.
☐ **3.** Paint molding and panel.
☐ **4.** Lightly pencil design on panel and paint in design.

ASSEMBLY OF MOLDING IN
PENNSYLVANIA DUTCH FRAME

A PENNSYLVANIA
DUTCH PATTERN

Fig. 7-48. Pennsylvania Dutch panel construction (courtesy Shopsmith Inc.).

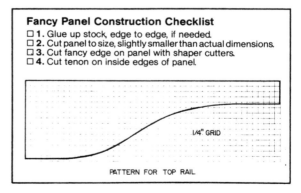

Fancy Panel Construction Checklist

☐ **1.** Glue up stock, edge to edge, if needed.
☐ **2.** Cut panel to size, slightly smaller than actual dimensions.
☐ **3.** Cut fancy edge on panel with shaper cutters.
☐ **4.** Cut tenon on inside edges of panel.

1/4" GRID

PATTERN FOR TOP RAIL

Fig. 7-49. Fancy panel construction (courtesy Shopsmith Inc.).

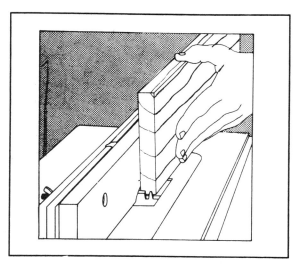

Fig. 7-50. Cutting a glue joint with a molder (courtesy Shopsmith Inc.).

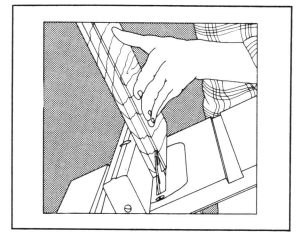

Fig. 7-51. Making a raised panel. This operation must be carried out without an upper saw guard (courtesy Shopsmith Inc.).

For a *raised panel*, consider whether or not you will need to glue up stock, edge to edge, to get a large enough panel. Make sure the end grains cup in the same direction if you do, and don't dowel the stock together. Dowels can eventually split out of the thinner stock. Instead, joint the edges, and then cut a glue joint with a molder or the shaper (Fig. 7-50). The glue joint helps to align the stock and provides more gluing surface.

Always cut the panel slightly smaller than the required dimensions to allow the wood to expand with temperature and humidity changes. Determine the critical dimension, remembering that wood expands ten times more across the grain than with the grain. If the wood grain runs vertically, the critical dimension is the width. If the critical dimension is under foot, allow for ⅛-inch play. If it is over a foot, allow ¼-inch play.

After you have cut the panel to size, tilt the saw table 15 degrees. Turn the panel on edge and use a hollow ground planer blade. Cut a bevel all around the outside of the panel. Adjust the rip fence and table height so the saw leaves a ⅛-inch step between the raised surface and the bevel, and so the bevel tapers down to 3/16 inch from an outside edge (Fig. 7-51).

Fancy Panel

Fancy panels begin the same way as raised panels. Glue up the stock and cut it to size in the same manner. Set up the Mark V for shaping. Select a cutter or combination of cutters that will produce a fancy edge you like. Mount the cutter on the shaper, with a 1¼-inch collar, and make your first pass. Cut all around the edge of the panel. Adjust the depth of cut so that the shaper leaves a ¼-inch-thick tenon on the edge. Change to a ¾-inch collar and make a second pass. By using progressively smaller collars, you reduce the chances of splintering the edges with too large a bite.

After your second pass, the tenon should be about ⅜ inch wide—enough to mount the panel and show off the fancy edging. You can use the shaper or molder to make additional passes for added decoration in the surface area or along the edges of the panel (Fig. 7-52).

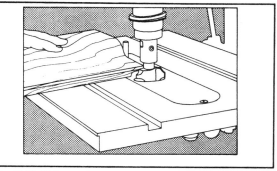

Fig. 7-52. Using a shaper to form a fancy panel edge (courtesy Shopsmith Inc.).

191

To make decorative metal panels, sheets of copper, brass, or tin about 1/64 inch thick are needed. Tin is by far the least expensive material, and it can be rubbed down with gun blueing to take on a blue-brown sheen.

As you begin to make the punched pattern in the sheet metal, don't cut it to size yet. The punching will cause the metal to expand slightly, so you will have to recut it to get a proper fit.

Make a full-sized pattern and attach it to the metal with rubber cement. Punch holes with a nail or center punch that has its end ground to a square point (Fig. 7-53).

Punching will often cause the metal to buckle and curl. When all the punching is done, lay the panel on the flat surface with some give to it (a carpet) and beat it with a dead-blow mallet until it straightens. Be careful not to pound out the design. After the panel is straight, give it a buffing with #0000 steel wool and cut it to size.

Pennsylvania Dutch Panel

Pennsylvania Dutch panels require a piece of ¼-inch tempered Masonite cut to size. Paint the molding and the panel with an enamel. White is traditional for Pennsylvania Dutch designs, but use other colors if you prefer. You might also want to paint the entire assembly—frame and all. After the paint has dried, you can lightly pencil in a design. If you want authentic Pennsylvania Dutch designs, you can probably find a book or two filled with them at your local

Fig. 7-53. Punching metal with a square-ground center punch (courtesy Shopsmith Inc.).

library. Just paint the designs, and the doors are ready to mount.

Mounting the Panel to the Frame

Solid wooden panels are never glued in the door frames. If the panels are glued, the frame may split due to wood expansion. Use four ⅝-inch number 4 round-head screws with washers. Position the screws a few inches to the left and right of center at the end of the panel, so the critical dimension has the greatest freedom of movement.

You can attach Masonite, plastic, metal, or glass panels in the same way. You can also use glazing points or wood strips tacked to the back side of the frame.

Finishing and Installation

Stain the doors. Select a waterproof finish that cleans easily. Tung oil and ZAR polyurethane finishes from United Gilsonite Laboratories are excellent. Tung oil provides a soft, natural look that brings out the grain pattern. When lightly buffed with #0000 steel wool, the look is even softer. Polyurethane provides a deeper, glossier look.

Hardware choice depends on how you intend to hang the doors. Insets, partial insets, and overlaps need different hinges. Clamp the doors in position in the cabinet frames and drill for the hardware. Attach the hinges, latches, and pulls. The job is done, and your kitchen will take on an entirely new look.

FOOD PROCESSOR ISLAND

I developed this island design a few years ago when I needed storage space for a food processor (Fig. 7-54).

The NuTone food processor is a built-in unit. It fits into the countertop and is generally run to an appliance circuit and attached directly. This doesn't solve the problem of accessory storage. It is not easy to trot the processor out on the deck to prepare things for outdoor eating. The rolling island converts the built-in food processor to a more portable form. Check with your local building codes to make sure it is legal.

The cabinet is of simple design, with a Formica laminated plastic top and doors on both sides. Make sure the portable cabinet is of a size that can be used as a worktable with the food processor. It will also serve as a dry bar and counter for use during parties. The Formica laminated plastic top is 2 feet wide and 40 inches long. The cabinet is 32 inches long and 16

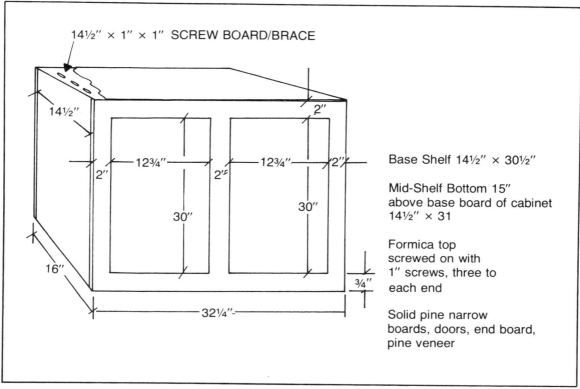

Fig. 7-54. Plan and material sizes for the food processor island.

inches wide, with a reasonable overhang. I used pine veneer plywood with the light blue Formica laminated plastic top. I finished my cabinet with Glidden's number 211 weathered barn stain and ZAR's tung oil.

You may want to build the cabinet alone for general use. Some changes can easily be made. Mine has doors on both sides, but you may want one side closed. My shelf is fixed in place, but you may like a movable shelf. You may want a smaller overhang.

With doors installed on both sides of the rolling island, I used lap joints to join small sections, with a dadoed joint (¾ inch wide and ⅜ inch deep) to hold the ends of the center shelf in place. The shelf is held in the dadoed grooves with brads and glue, but number 6 or number 8 flathead wood screws at least 1½ inches long can be used. Each door is a single piece, 12¾ inches wide by 30 inches high. Overall cabinet height, with round roller wheels at each corner is 36¾ inches. The cabinet itself is 33 inches high.

The only internal bracing needed, other than the shelf, is the hold-down piece at each end for the For-

mica laminated plastic top, which also serves as a brace when it is screwed in place. I used number 10 flathead wood screws 2 inches long to hold the cabinet top in place (Figs. 7-55 through 7-59).

NuTone's instructions for installation of their food processor are excellent. Use the template supplied with the processor for marking the hole for the base unit. You will have to determine hole location, but I opted for an off-center arrangement to allow more work space to one side of the processor.

My base unit is located 9¾ inches from the edge of the countertop. There is a 9-inch distance from the top's edge to the cover plate's edge after installation is complete. When locating the unit, make sure the hole is cut far enough in to allow things to clear the cabinet sides. If you use my measurements, you must cut in at least 5 inches.

I drilled four pilot holes to outline the hole. The saber saw adapts well to cutting curves, so only a single hole is really essential. I don't like using scrolling blades for anything more than cutting curves. They are

Fig. 7-55. Cutting trim pieces. Use a guard.

very narrow and are harder to hold straight and true on the vertical cuts. This series of holes allowed me to use a scrolling blade to cut the curves. I made a single blade change to cut the straights and drop out the waste wood neatly.

The cord used is 14 gauge, with ground. Strip the wire ends back ¾ inch. Slip the cable through the hole drilled close to the final position of the base unit. The cord I used slipped easily through a ⅜-inch hole, but a larger hole can take a plastic grommet to reduce wear. I checked the height of the hole by holding the base unit in place and marking the hole at about the same height as the bottom of the unit (Figs. 7-60 and 7-61).

Wire nuts secure black wire to black and white wire to white as in all residential wiring. The ground lead runs to the green screw-nut inside the connection box. The wire must be fed through a junction box cable clamp. Tie a knot in the cord about 18 inches from its end (between the base unit and the interior of the cabinet) to make sure the connections get no stress.

After you wire and install the cover plate, the power unit is set into its hole. The adjuster nut is turned

to bring up a pair of wing grips that clamp solidly to the underside of the countertop (Figs. 7-62 through 7-66).

The cover plate for the base unit mounts by means of spring clips that drop through slots in the power unit's top. When the cover plate is in place, clean up any sawdust and fasten the control dial and cover (Figs. 7-67 and 7-68).

The result is an easy-to-push cabinet of moderate size. There is plenty of storage space for accessories (Fig. 7-69).

SALT BOX

Cooks used to keep a box of coarse salt near the stove to season soups and stews. The boxes used are antiques now. They are generally used now to hold coupons rather than salt. This project provides a shelf for some spice jars and a couple of small drawers for other items (Fig. 7-70).

Fig. 7-56. Center shelf dadoed.

Fig. 7-57. Fit trim pieces.

Fig. 7-58. Make sure solid trim pieces fit accurately over particle core plywood edges.

To make the projected salt box, start with 7 board feet of lumber and some hardware. Begin by cutting all stock to size. For the bowl, you need three boards—¾ by 11½ by 11½ inches, ¾ by 10½ by 10½ inches, and ¾ by 9½ by 9½ inches. These form laminated rings. Use a compass to mark circles on the boards. On the first board (the largest), mark circles of 5½ inches, 8½ inches, and 11½ inches in diameter. On the second board, mark circles of 4½ inches, 7½ inches, and 10½ inches in diameters. The third board is marked at 6½ inches and 9½ inches. Cut the circles out with a jigsaw or band saw tilted to give a 30-degree cut angle. With the jigsaw, drill a ⅛-inch-diameter pilot hole to start the cuts. Make the hole at the same 30-degree angle. Slip the jigsaw blade through the pilot hole and cut, repeating until all the rings are cut (Fig. 7-71). If you are using a band saw, cut the board down the middle and then cut out each half-ring. Glue the rings back together with resorcinol glue.

Stack the rings one on top of the other and glue them together, again with resorcinol glue. Make sure all the grains run in the same direction, so splitting won't be a problem later. Set the glued-up stock aside to dry.

Glue up the ¾-inch stock for the back edge-to-edge. Resaw remaining ¾-inch stock (except that for the drawer fronts) to the thicknesses for the various salt box pieces. The drawer bottoms are ¼ inch thick. Cut all pieces to final dimensions.

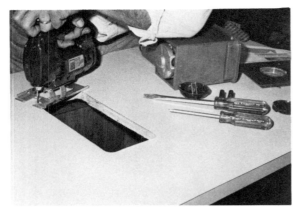

Fig. 7-59. Jigsawing is the simplest and fastest way to make the cutout for the NuTone food processor.

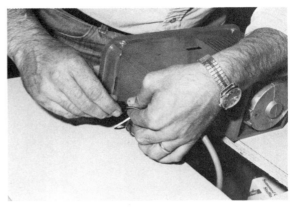

Fig. 7-62. Wire nuts are used to make connections.

Fig. 7-60. Stripping wire.

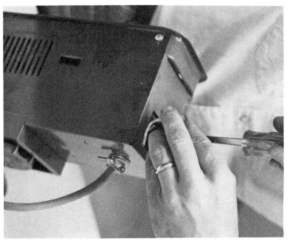

Fig. 7-63. The ground wire runs to a screw inside the box on the food processor.

Fig. 7-61. Use a locknut for the receptacle box.

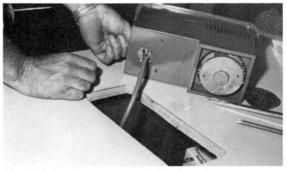

Fig. 7-64. The box cover must clear the wires.

196

Fig. 7-65. Secure the box cover.

Fig. 7-66. Bring up the clamping wing nuts using the screw.

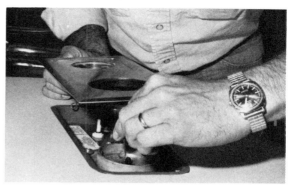

Fig. 7-67. Install the cover.

Fig. 7-68. The cover is in place.

Cut the joinery in the drawer and frame pieces. Use a ½-inch router bit or dado blade to cut rabbets ¼ inch deep by ½ inch wide in the ends and dadoes ¼ inch deep by ½ inch wide in the middle of the drawer frame's top and bottom. Use a ⅜-inch router bit or dado blade to cut a top groove ⅛-inch deep by ⅜ inch wide in the door frame's top piece. Cut rabbets ⅜ inch deep by ⅜ inch wide in both ends of the drawer fronts and rabbets 3/16 inch deep by ⅜ inch wide in the edge of the drawer sides. For drawer bottom assembly to the other drawer pieces, make a groove 3/16 inch deep by ¼ inch wide in the drawer sides, front, and back. Assemble the drawers and drawer frames with carpenter's glue and set aside for final assembly.

Fig. 7-69. The NuTone food processor—island-mounted and ready for use.

Turn the wooden bowl and the drawer knobs (Fig. 7-72). Using a piece of masking tape as a guide, mark a straight line down the center of the bowl. Saw the bowl in half with your band saw (Fig. 7-73).

Glue the bowl and door frame to the back. Reinforce the butt joints with 1¼-inch-by-number-8 flathead wood screws. Hinge the lid pieces together and glue the rear piece to the lip of the bowl. Drill drawer fronts for knobs, glue the knobs, and slide the drawers in place (Figs. 7-74 through 7-80).

The edges of the lid, drawers, and drawer frame can be rounded with a rasp or Surform tool to provide an antique look. Use a nontoxic finish like salad bowl oil or mineral oil.

KITCHEN ORGANIZER

This kitchen organizer is compact. It provides storage space for 12 spice jars, a box of tissues, a roll of paper towels, and other small items (Fig. 7-81).

Start with a pine board 1 inch by 12 inches by 8 feet, some scrap pieces of oak, and a quarter sheet of ¼-inch plywood. You also need a quarter sheet of ⅛-inch Masonite, a square foot of cork, and hardware (two hinges, two short aluminum bars, a wood knob, magnetic catch, four foot-long hacksaw blades, and some wood screws) (Fig. 7-82).

Begin the work by cutting all pieces to size. Add an extra ½ inch to the box top width. Cut all joinery needed for later assembly. Most of the joints are common and quite simple, but the corners of the door and the spice shelves are assembled with two uncommon joints.

Door corners are fitted together with spline and miter joints. To make these joints, you cut the ends of

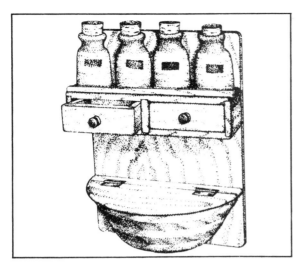

Fig. 7-70. Salt box (courtesy Shopsmith Inc.).

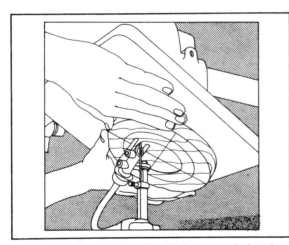

Fig. 7-71. Cutting the rings at a 35-degree angle (courtesy Shopsmith Inc.).

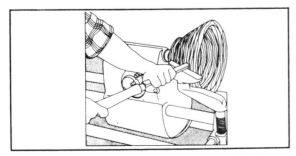

Fig. 7-72. Turning the bowl (courtesy Shopsmith Inc.).

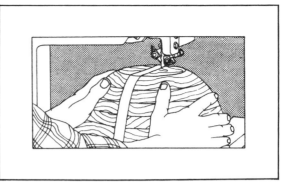

Fig. 7-73. Cutting the bowl in two (courtesy Shopsmith Inc.).

Bill of Materials
(final dimensions in inches)

A	Back (1)	3/4 x 12 x 16-5/8
B	Drawer frame top and bottom (2)	1/2 x 3-1/2 x 12
C	Drawer frame sides and partition (3)	1/2 x 2-1/2 x 3-1/2
D	Shelf bar (1)	3/8 x 1/2 x 12
E	Drawer front (2)	3/4 x 2 x 5-3/16
F	Drawer back (2)	3/8 x 2 x 4-13/16
G	Drawer side (4)	3/8 x 2 x 3-1/8
H	Drawer bottom (2)	1/4 x 2-5/8 x 4-13/16
J	Lid (rear) (1)	1/2 x 1-1/2 x 12
K	Lid (front) (1)	1/2 x 4-1/2 x 11-1/2
L	Bowl (1/2)	4-1/2 x 11 dia.

Hardware

Small brass hinges and mounting screws (2 sets)
F.H. wood screws (9) (if needed)   1-1/4 – #8

Salt Box Construction Checklist

☐ **1.** Cut stock to size.
☐ **2.** Use the method of laminating rings to make bowl.
    a. Mark circles on the bowl stock.
    b. Cut rings out at a 30° angle.
    c. Stack rings and glue together.
☐ **3.** Glue up back.
☐ **4.** Resaw stock to thicknesses needed for other pieces.
☐ **5.** Cut all pieces to width and length.
☐ **6.** Cut joinery in drawer and drawer frame pieces.
☐ **7.** Assemble drawer and drawer frame pieces.
☐ **8.** Turn bowl and drawer knobs.
☐ **9.** Saw bowl in half.
☐ **10.** Attach bowl and drawer frame to back.
☐ **11.** Hinge lid pieces and attach lid to bowl.
☐ **12.** Drill for drawer knobs and attach knobs.
☐ **13.** Slide in drawers.
☐ **14.** Finish with non-toxic finish.

Fig. 7-74. Materials list for the salt box (courtesy Shopsmith Inc.).

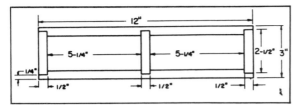

Fig. 7-75. Drawer frame—front view (courtesy Shopsmith Inc.).

the boards off at 45-degree angles, as if you were going to make a standard butt mortise joint. Set the rip fence of your dado saw and the dado blade, so you can cut a kerf ¼ inch wide by ½ inch deep down the middle of the ends of the board. Set the board with the outside face against the fence and the mitered end against the saw table. Run the board through the saw to make the kerf. Repeat the procedures for the opposite end of the board.

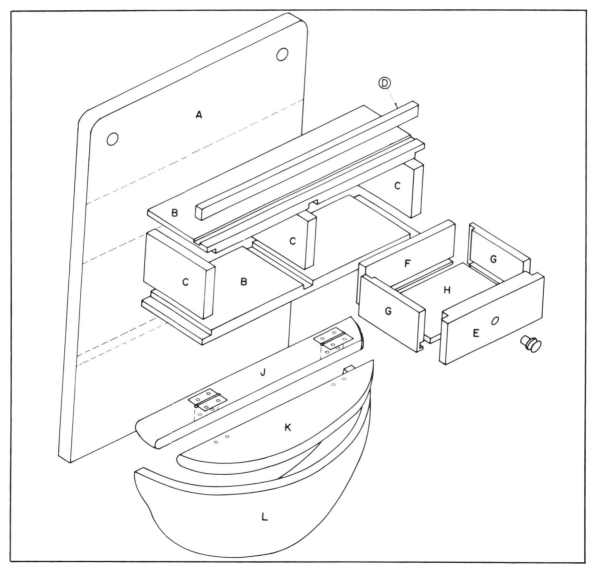

Fig. 7-76. Salt box assembly (courtesy Shopsmith Inc.).

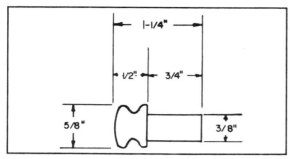

Fig. 7-77. Knob detail (courtesy Shopsmith Inc.).

Cut the splines to fit the kerf using plywood ¼ inch thick. Hardwoods cut so the grain runs the short way on the spline also work well.

The spice shelves attach to the sides with stop dado joints. Stop dadoes are not completely cut across the width of the stock. Use a ¾-inch dado setting and clamp a stop block to the saw table to control the cut length (Fig. 7-83). Cut the stop dado to the dimension given in the plans, then turn the saw off and wait for the blade to stop turning before removing the workpiece. Round off the end of the adjoining board to fit the stop dado, or chisel out the stop dado for square ends.

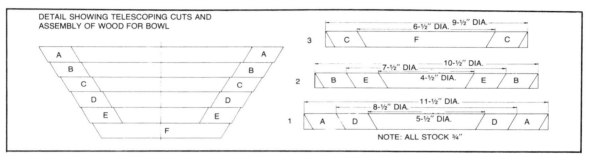

Fig. 7-78. Detail of cuts and assembly for bowl (courtesy Shopsmith Inc.).

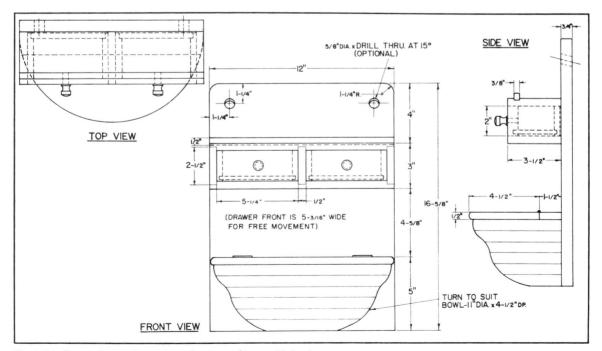

Fig. 7-79. Front, side, and top views (courtesy Shopsmith Inc.).

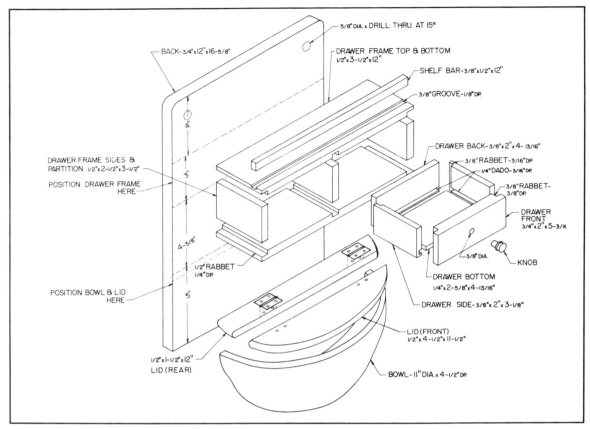

5/8" DIA. x DRILL THRU. AT 15°

BACK-3/4"x12"x16-5/8"

DRAWER FRAME TOP & BOTTOM
1/2"x3-1/2"x12"

SHELF BAR-3/8"x1/2"x12"

3/8"GROOVE-1/8"DP

DRAWER BACK-3/8"x2"x4-13/16"

3/8"RABBET-3/16"DP

1/4"DADO-3/16"DP

3/8"RABBET-3/8"DP

DRAWER FRAME SIDES &
PARTITION 1/2"x 2-1/2"x3-1/2"

POSITION DRAWER FRAME
HERE

DRAWER
FRONT
3/4"x2"x5-3/16

3/8" DIA.

KNOB

1/2"RABBET
1/4"DP

DRAWER BOTTOM
1/4"x2-5/8"x4-13/16"

POSITION BOWL & LID
HERE

DRAWER SIDE-3/8"x 2"x 3-1/8"

LID (FRONT)
1/2"x 4-1/2"x 11-1/2"

1/2"x1-1/2"x12"
LID (REAR)

BOWL-11"DIA.x 4-1/2"DP.

Fig. 7-80. Assembly instructions for the salt box (courtesy Shopsmith Inc.).

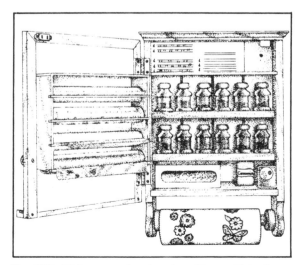

Fig. 7-81. Kitchen organizer (courtesy Shopsmith Inc.).

After cutting all the joinery, cut out the lower contour of the sides with a band saw or jigsaw. Use a multispur bit or another flat-bottomed bit to drill the recesses for the spice jars. Drill a pilot hole in the box top to start the piercing cut for the tissue dispenser. Cut the dispenser hole with a jigsaw or saber saw and sand the inside edge (Fig. 7-84). Use a router or shaper to edge around the box top and round the inside of the dispenser. Rip the box top to its final width.

For the long towel roller, turn a cylinder 1¼ inches in diameter and 12⅞ inches long on the lathe. Cut out and machine the towel roller holders to the proper dimensions. Use a ¼-inch router bit and rout recesses 5/32 inch deep into the towel roller holders for the aluminum bars. Chisel out the corners square for the aluminum bars to fit 1/32 inch below the surface. Drill ¾-inch holes in the center of the towel roller holders for the towel roller to pivot. Attach the bars to the towel roller holders.

202

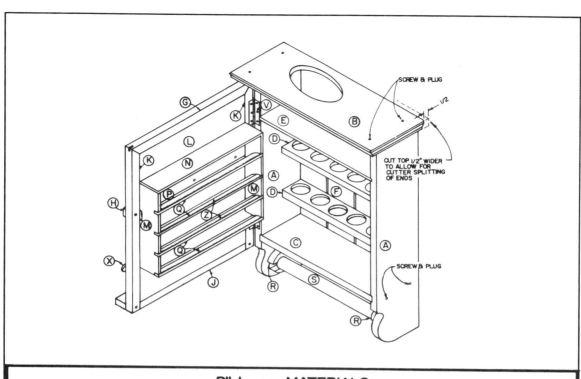

BILL of MATERIALS

NO. PCS		DESCRIPTION	SIZE				DESCRIPTION	SIZE
2	A	SIDES	3/4" x 5" x 22"		1	L	BACK	1/8" x 12-3/4" x 16-5/16"
1	B	TOP	3/4" x 7" x 16-1/4"		2	M	SIDES	1/4" x 2-1/4" x 9"
1	C	SHELF	3/4" x 5" x 13-3/4"		1	N	TOP	1/4" x 2-1/4" x 12-3/4"
2	D	SHELF	3/4" x 2-1/4" x 13-3/4"		1	P	HANGER BAR	1/4" x 1-1/4" x 12-1/4"
1	E	SHELF	1/4" x 4-3/4" x 13-3/4"		4	Q	TEAR BAR	1/4" x 3/4" x 12-3/4"
1	F	BACK	1/4" x 13-3/4" x 17-1/8"		2	R	ROLLER HOLDER	3/4" x 2-1/2" x 2-1/2"
1	G	TOP RAIL	3/4" x 1-1/4" x 12-3/4"		1	S	TOWEL ROLLER	1-1/4" DIA. x 12-7/8"
1	H	MIDDLE RAIL	3/4" x 3/4" x 14-3/4"		1	T	CORK BOARD	1/16" x 6-1/8" x 12-3/4"
1	J	MARKER LEDGE	3/4" x 2" x 14-3/4"		1	U	WRITING BOARD	1/8" x 10-3/16" x 12-3/4"
2	K	STILES	3/4" x 1-1/4" x 17-13/16"					

HARDWARE

2	V	BUTT HINGES	2-1/2" x 1-5/8"		1	GREASE PENCIL	
2	W	ALUM. BARS	1/8" x 3/4" x 2"		3	WOOD SCREWS	3/4" - No. 6 F.H.
1	X	WOOD KNOB	3/4" DIA.		13	WOOD SCREWS	1-1/4" - No. 8 F.H.
1	Y	MAGNETIC CATCH			6	WOOD SCREWS	1/2" - No. 6 F.H.
4	Z	HACKSAW BLADE	12" LONG		2	WOOD SCREWS	1" - NO. 8 F.H.

Fig. 7-82. Assembly detail and materials list for the kitchen organizer (courtesy Shopsmith Inc.).

Fig. 7-83. Cutting the stop dado for spice shelves (courtesy Shopsmith Inc.).

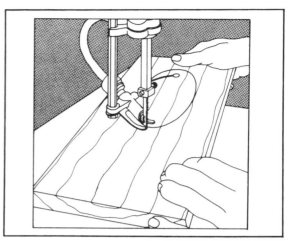

Fig. 7-84. Making the piercing cut for the tissue dispenser (courtesy Shopsmith Inc.).

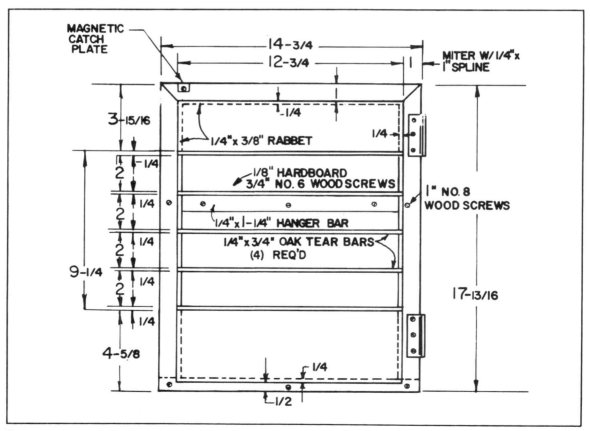

Fig. 7-85. Door—rear view (courtesy Shopsmith Inc.).

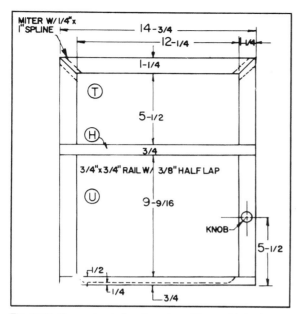

Fig. 7-86. Door—front view (courtesy Shopsmith Inc.).

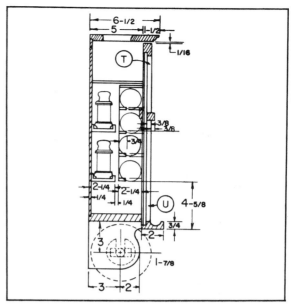

Fig. 7-88. Side view (courtesy Shopsmith Inc.).

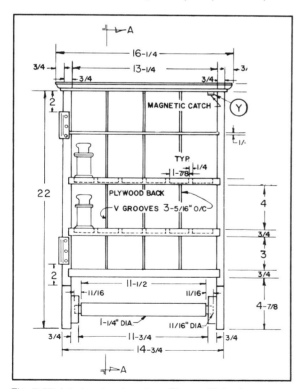

Fig. 7-87. Interior view (courtesy Shopsmith Inc.).

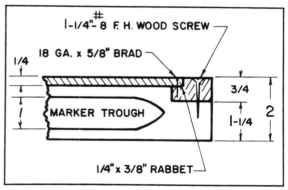

Fig. 7-89. Marker ledge, stile, and writing board assembly (courtesy Shopsmith Inc.).

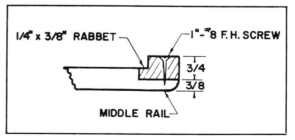

Fig. 7-90. Middle rail and stile assembly (courtesy Shopsmith Inc.).

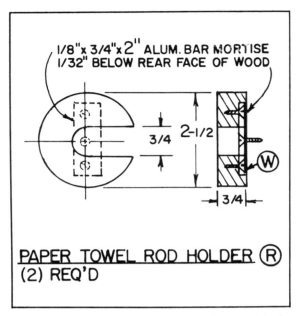

Fig. 7-91. Paper towel rod holder (courtesy Shopsmith Inc.).

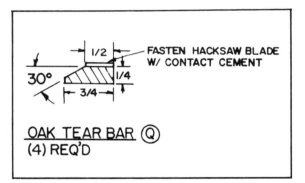

Fig. 7-92. Oak tear bar (courtesy Shopsmith Inc.).

Use a 1-inch flute molding cutter or core box router bit to cut the trough for the wax pencil in the marker ledge. Switch to a V-groove cutter and make decorative grooves in the plywood back for the box. With a chisel or ¼-inch straight router bit, make recesses in the door stile and box side for the hinges (the stile is the upright piece of the door frame). Drill a hole for the doorknob.

Kitchen Organizer Construction Checklist

- ☐ **1.** Cut all pieces to size.
- ☐ **2.** Cut all joinery.
- ☐ **3.** Cut lower contour of sides.
- ☐ **4.** Drill recesses in shelves.
- ☐ **5.** Cut out dispenser hole.
- ☐ **6.** Edge box top and dispenser hole.
- ☐ **7.** Rip box top to width.
- ☐ **8.** Turn towel roller cylinder.
- ☐ **9.** Make towel roller holder.
- ☐ **10.** Cut trough in marker ledge.
- ☐ **11.** Make decorative grooves in box plywood back.
- ☐ **12.** Make hinge recesses in door stile and box side.
- ☐ **13.** Drill door knob hole.
- ☐ **14.** Sand all pieces.
- ☐ **15.** Assemble roll holder.
- ☐ **16.** Assemble shelves and top to box sides.
- ☐ **17.** Assemble top rail, middle rail and marker ledge to door stiles.
- ☐ **18.** Finish all subcomponents.
- ☐ **19.** Complete assembly of box.
- ☐ **20.** Complete assembly of door.
- ☐ **21.** Hinge door to box.
- ☐ **22.** Add hardware.

Fig. 7-93. Construction checklist for the kitchen organizer (courtesy Shopsmith Inc.).

Sand all pieces smooth before assembling anything. Attach the hacksaw blades to the tear bars (make the tear bars of oak for strength). Complete the assembly of the roll holder. Attach the shelves and the box top to the box sides. Fasten the top rail, the middle rail, and the marker ledge to the door stiles.

Finish all subcomponents before doing the final assembly. Use a tough finish such as tung oil or polyurethane after you stain or paint the wood to match your kitchen. It's probably best to paint the Masonite or plywood panels, but you can use stain (Figs. 7-85 through 7-93).

After finishing, attach the plywood back and towel roller holders to the box. Assemble the door by attaching the Masonite panel and roll holder with its hanger bar. Screws go through the hanger bar and Masonite panel and attach to the middle rail to hold the cork board and writing board in place. Assemble the door to the box with hinges. Add the doorknob and magnetic latch, and you can hang the organizer on the wall.

Chapter 8

Wood, Cabinets, and Countertops

Y OU SHOULD KNOW SOMETHING ABOUT THE DIF-
ferent woods available for use in kitchen building and remodeling work. The appearance, strength,
durability, and workability of woods are important considerations.

Knowing how to assemble cabinets and attach
them to kitchen walls is essential. An attractive cabinet
isn't worth much if it becomes dislodged from a wall
and crashes.

Ceramic tile, formica, laminated plastic, or wood
butcher block styles are suitable countertop materials.
Find a style that will fit your overall kitchen decor.

WOOD

If you examine a piece of wood under a micro-
scope, you will notice that it is comprised of several
small cells. The size and arrangement of the cells
determine the wood's grain and many of its other
characteristics. These cells are arranged in a circular
pattern, as you can see by examining any freshly cut
tree stump, with the pith in the center.

Sapwood is the outer section of a tree. Heartwood, which is darker in color than the sapwood, is the
inner section. The bark covers everything. Sapwood
darkens as it ages and takes, depending on tree type,
from 10 to 40 years to become the same color as
heartwood.

A wood with tightly packed cells will have a fine,
tight grain that is easily finished. Open-grain woods
have loosely packed cells and tend to be porous, so a
grain filler is needed before finishing is done. Maple
and birch are fine or close-grained woods, while oak,
walnut, and hickory are coarse or open-grained
woods. Weak woods—cedar, spruce, basswood, and
others—should be used only in nonstructural applications.

Hickory is not really suitable for cabinet frames,
because it is very hard to work. Ash accepts finishes
well. It is hard, strong, durable, and easy to work. Ash
is hard to find in large quantities.

Kiln drying brings moisture content of wood down
under 10 percent. Wood with 7 or 8 percent moisture
content is best for kitchen cabinets, but wood dried to
10 to 15 percent moisture content should be suitable.

In most work lumber defects that affect durability
are more important than those that affect appearance,

but in cabinetmaking both are critical. A huge knothole on the front of a cabinet door or in an exposed section of the frame affects durability and also looks bad.

Bark pockets are patches of bark enclosed in the wood. A *check* is a crack in the wood structure, most often running along the grain. *Pecks* are channeled or pitted areas that affect appearance but have little effect on durability. *Decay* is the disintegration of a wood fiber. A *shake* is a crack between the parallel growth rings. *Heart pith* is a soft inner growth that may appear on the surface of lumber. *Stain* means that the wood is discolored, with penetration into the wood fiber. Very light stains are hard to see, but plenty of lumber has heavy staining. Stain has no effect on cabinet portions that are not visible.

Knots are found where a portion of a branch or limb has joined the tree. *Branch knots* have been sawed nearly parallel to the direction of limb growth, while *spike knots* run to the edge of the piece of lumber. They grow larger as they get close to the edge. Spike knots tend to be quite long. Knots may be sound and not sound, depending on whether they are loose, tight, decayed, or not decayed.

Pitch is a buildup of resin and may form *pockets* in varying sizes. *Wane* is the presence of bark or missing wood on corners of lumber. *Warping, bowing, cupping,* and *crooking* are all obvious on individual boards and must be avoided in any wood intended for cabinets.

Cabinet woods need to be reasonably free of warping, excessive shrinkage, and swelling. Wood used on doors, backsplashes, and other areas should resist denting. These features apply to some pines and most hardwoods, but softer woods can readily be used for cabinet framing. Table 8-1 gives uses and characteristics of common woods.

PLYWOOD

Plywood is used almost exclusively in building cabinets and other furniture pieces. Plywood's strength is equalized along and across the panels, because the grain runs two ways. Solid wood is strongest along its grain and far weaker across the grain, but in plywood the grain direction of adjoining plies is set at right angles to provide strength in both directions.

The dimensional stability of the wood is high, for the thinner plies are less affected by moisture buildup than are thicker sections of wood. Glues are affected little by small amounts of moisture. Decreasing thickness in plies and alternating the grain directions also reduce the chances of warping and splitting. The range of wood sizes is increased. The increase is partly due to the increase in directional stability, and partly because the plies are unwound from the circumference of the tree and not sliced across like solid lumber.

Plywood is far cheaper than solid wood, because forest products are not wasted. Also, only a thin ply of the finish wood, if it is an expensive species, is required. Working with large panels of plywood usually saves construction time.

Plywood is made by gluing together three, five, seven, nine, or some other odd number of plies. This is the veneer core method. Lumber-core plywood is sometimes found. It is made by gluing in a core of narrow, sawed lumber strips. Crossbands are also used with face veneers on both sides.

Hardwood plywoods generally have only the face plies made of hardwoods, though a few types may be found with interior plies of hardwood. Hardwood plywood has the most attractive grain patterns.

Appearance Grades

Premium grade plywoods offer a specific kind of hardwood face ply. The face must be made of smooth, tightly cut veneers that are carefully matched for color and grain patterns.

Good grade plywoods are made to take a natural finish and are close to premium in appearance. They do not have as closely matched face colors and grains.

Sound grade plywoods offer a smooth painting base with a face free of open defects but not color matched, and often having stains and streaks. No grain matching is done.

Utility grade plywoods will have some discoloration and knotholes to ¾ inch in diameter, minor open joints, and some areas of rough grain. No shakes or similar defects are allowed.

Backing grade plywoods have no color or grain match. They may have limited knotholes and splits, but no defects that would detract from panel strength are allowed.

Specialty grade plywoods are matched grain panels for specific architectural uses. They offer special veneer selections.

Adhesives

Different adhesives are used to bond plies together, and the plywood is thus also classified as to adhesive types used. Of the four generally available types, three are of interest to the kitchen cabinetmaker. Exterior, or type I, will withstand weather exposure and is water-resistant. Exterior glue interior plywood is resistant to heavy moisture and will stand up to repeated wetting and drying cycles. Standard interior plywood adhesives are moisture-resistant, but not waterproof. If interior plywood grades occasionally get fairly wet, that is fine. Continued exposure to water will soon ruin the bond, and the plies will begin to separate.

Plywood is generally found in 4 by 8-foot sheets, but it can be bought as narrow as 2 feet and in 12-foot lengths. Check with your local distributor for sizes. Plan to work with standard panel sizes to reduce costs.

Virtually all projects can be built with plywood thicknesses ranging from ¼ to ¾ inch. The number of plies varies with the thickness, in many cases, with three-ply panels being ¼ inch or thinner, five-ply panels ranging from 5/16 inch to ⅝ inch, and seven-ply panels in ⅝ and ¾-inch thicknesses. Nine-ply panels are available in ¾ inch and thicker. Lumber core and pressed or particle board core plywoods of ¾-inch thickness are generally five-ply panels.

All *softwood plywood* is of the veneer ply type, and standards have been developed by the American Plywood Association. Grade veneer may have neatly made repairs, but it is completely free of open defects and has a smooth surface for finishing. Grade B veneers can have solid, 1-inch knots, plugs, and patches. Grades C and D allow large, solid knots and certain sizes of knotholes. Exterior panels use phenolic resin waterproof glues. For most kitchen cabinetry, select A-B grades. Backing can be made of B-C grades if you plan to paint (as can doors and other exposed panels), and shelves are more cheaply made from B-C grades.

Working with Plywood

Plywood sheets must be laid flat if possible, but storing them on edge for a few days will not harm them if the panels are supported. Don't tilt plywood against a wall, though, as this damages the panels and is especially bad for the thinner ones. Keep the panels dry, including those with exterior ratings. Exterior panels can be stored outside and covered well, so they are not exposed to water. Interior panels should be stored as close as possible to the area in which they are to be used.

When cutting plywood panels, always use at least two sawhorses for support. For thinner panels, you can lay at least two 2 by 4s at 90-degree angles across the sawhorses for even better support. If you use a handsaw to cut plywood, lay the panel with the good face up. Use a saw with 10 points or more per inch to get a smooth cut. When using a circular saw, make your cuts with the face of the panel down. Use a special plywood blade, preferably hollow ground, for the cutting. Adjust the circular saw blade so the teeth clear the panel by no more than ¼ inch or so. Table saws should also have fine-toothed plywood blades installed. The panel should be cut with the good face up. Most saber saws and jigsaws require the good face of the plywood to be down, because the blade cuts on the upstroke. Special blades are made to cut on the downstroke. When they are used, the panel face should be up.

When working with plywood edges, remember that nails, screws, and glues do not hold as well on the edges as they do on the faces. It is much like working with end grain on solid woods. If possible, always work through the face for fastening plywood or for fastening other materials to plywood. Nail holes are best predrilled to reduce the chances of splitting. Screws also need predrilled holes and must be adjusted to the thickness of the plywood, with ⅝-inch and ¾-inch plywood best fastened with screws at least number 8 in size and, respectively, 1½ and 1¼ inches long. When nailing, glue will increase the joint strength significantly.

Butt joints are seldom useful in plywood cabinetry, as the plies will then show. Such edges can be filled and painted. For natural finish cabinetry, though, you must use a joint that doesn't show the ply, unless you want to add a wood laminate edging. You can use miter joints in most cabinets to avoid the edging problems.

Always protect the face veneer when working with cabinet plywoods. Once you cut corners and are getting ready for installation, consider covering the cuts with masking tape. Marking for holes can be done on the tape, and drilling can be done through it. If you think a panel is likely to be knocked during cutting, tape a kraft paper facing to it. This will reduce the possibility of scratching. Always use scrap wood at the backs of drilling spots if the back side of the plywood has any chance of being exposed to view.

Sanding furniture grade plywood veneers is a sensitive process. The finish on these plywoods is already very fine. The veneer is very thin, so power

Table 8-1. Common Woods.

Type	Sources	Uses	Characteristics
Ash	East of Rockies	Oars, boat thwarts, benches, gratings, hammer handles, cabinets, ball bats, wagon construction farm implements.	Strong, heavy, hard, tough, elastic, close straight grain, shrinks very little, takes excellent finish, lasts well.
Balsa	Ecuador	Rafts, food boxes, linings of refrigerators, life preservers, loud speakers, sound-proofing, air-conditioning devices, model airplane construction.	Lightest of all woods, very soft, strong for its weight, good heat insulating qualities, odorless.
Basswood	Eastern half of U.S. with exception of coastal regions.	Low-grade furniture, cheaply constructed buildings, interior finish, shelving, drawers, boxes, drainboards, woodenware, novelties, excelsior, general millwork.	Soft, very light, weak, brittle, not durable, shrinks considerably, inferior to popular, but very uniform, works easily, takes screws and nails well and does not twist or warp.
Beech	East of Mississippi, Southeastern Canada.	Cabinetwork, imitation mahogany furniture, wood dowels, capping, boat trim, interior finish, tool handles, turnery, shoe lasts, carving, flooring.	Similar to birch but not so durable when exposed to weather, shrinks and checks considerably, close grain, light or dark red color.
Birch	East of Mississippi River and North of Gulf Coast States, Southeast Canada, Newfoundland.	Cabinetwork, imitation mahogany furniture, wood dowels, capping, boat trim, interior finish, tool handles, turnery, carving.	Hard, durable, fine grain, even texture, heavy, stiff, strong, tough, takes high polish, works easily, forms excellent base for white enamel finish, but not durable when exposed. Heartwood is light to dark reddish brown in color.
Butternut	Southern Canada, Minnesota, Eastern U.S. as far south as Alabama and Florida.	Toys, altars, woodenware, millwork, interior trim, furniture, boats, scientific instruments.	Very much like walnut in color but softer, not so soft as white pine and basswood, easy to work, coarse grained, fairly strong.
Cypress	Maryland to Texas, along Mississippi valley to Illinois.	Small boat planking, siding, shingles, sash, doors, tanks, silos, railway ties.	Many characteristics similar to white cedar. Water resistant qualities make it excellent for use as boat planking.
Douglas Fir	Pacific Coast, British Columbia.	Deck planking on large ships, shores, strongbacks, plugs, filling pieces and bulkheads of small boats, building construction, dimension timber, plywood.	Excellent structural lumber, strong, easy to work, clear straight grained, soft, but brittle. Heartwood is durable in contact with ground, best structural timber of northwest.

210

Type	Sources	Uses	Characteristics
Elm	States east of Colorado.	Agricultural implements, wheel-stock, boats, furniture, crossties, posts, poles.	Slippery, heavy, hard, tough, durable, difficult to split, not resistant to decay.
Hickory	Arkansas, Tennessee, Ohio, Kentucky.	Tools, handles, wagon stock, hoops, baskets, vehicles, wagon spokes.	Very heavy, hard, stronger and tougher than other native woods, but checks, shrinks, difficult to work, subject to decay and insect attack.
Lignum Vitae	Central America.	Block sheaves and pulleys, waterexposed shaft bearings of small boats and ships, tools handles, small turned articles, and mallet heads.	Dark greenish brown, unusually hard, close grained, very heavy, resinous, difficult to split and work, has soapy feeling.
Live Oak	Southern Atlantic and Gulf Coasts of U.S., Oregon, California.	Implements, wagons, ship building.	Very heavy, hard, tough, strong, durable, difficult to work, light brown or yellow sap wood nearly white.
Mahogany	Honduras, Mexico, Central America, Florida, West Indies, Central Africa, other tropical sections.	Furniture, boats, decks, fixtures, interior trim in expensive homes, musical instruments.	Brown to red color, one of most useful of cabinet woods, hard, durable, does not split badly, open grained, takes beautiful finish when grain is filled but checks, swells, shrinks, warps slightly.
Maple	All states east of Colorado, Southern Canada.	Excellent furniture, high-grade floors, tool handles, ship construction crossties, counter tops, bowling pins.	Fine grained, grain often curly or "Bird's Eyes." heavy, tough, hard, strong, rather easy to work, but not durable. Heartwood is light brown, sap wood is nearly white.
Norway Pine	States bordering Great Lakes.	Dimension timber, masts, spars, piling, interior trim.	Light, fairly hard, strong, not durable in contact with ground.
Philippine Mahogany	Philippine Islands	Pleasure boats, medium-grade furniture, interior trim.	Not a true mahogany, shrinks, expands, splits, warps, but available in long, wide, clear boards.
	Virginias, Tennessee, Kentucky, Mississippi Valley.	Low-grade furniture cheaply constructed buildings, interior finish, shelving, drawers, boxes.	Soft, cheap, obtainable in wide boards, warps, shrinks, rots easily, light, brittle, weak, but works easily and holds nails well, fine-textured.
Red Cedar	East of Colorado and north of Florida.	Mothproof chests, lining for linen closets, sills, and other uses similar to white cedar.	Very light, soft, weak, brittle, low shrinkage, great durability, fragrant scent, generally knotty, beautiful when finished in natural color, easily worked.

Table 8-1. Common Woods. (Continued from page 211.)

Type	Sources	Uses	Characteristics
Red Oak	Virginias, Tennessee, Arkansas, Kentucky, Ohio, Missouri, Maryland.	Interior finish, furniture, cabinets, millwork, crossties when preserved.	Tends to warp, coarse grain, does not last well when exposed to weather, porous, easily impregnated with preservative, heavy, tough, strong.
Redwood	California.	General construction, tanks, paneling.	inferior to yellow pine and fir in strength, shrinks and splits little, extremely soft, light, straight grained, very durable, exceptionally decay resistant.
Spruce	New York, New England, West Virginia, Central Canada, Great Lakes States, Idaho, Washington, Oregon.	Railway ties, resonance wood, piles, airplanes, oars, masts, spars, baskets.	Light, soft, low strength, fair durability, close grain, yellowish, sap wood indistinct.
Sugar Pine	California, Oregon.	Same as white pine.	Very light, soft, resembles white pine.
Teak	India, Burma, Siam, Java.	Deck planking, shaft logs for small boats.	Light brown color, strong, easily worked, durable, resistant to damage by moisture.
Walnut	Eastern half of U.S. except Southern Atlantic and Gulf Coasts, some in New Mexico, Arizona, California.	Expensive furniture, cabinets, interior woodwork, gun stocks, tool handles, airplane propellers, fine boats, musical instruments.	Fine cabinet wood, coarse grained but takes beautiful finish when pores closed with woodfiller, medium weight, hard, strong, easily worked, dark chocolate color, does not warp or check, brittle.
White Cedar	Eastern Coast of U.S., and around Great Lakes.	Boat planking, railroad ties, singles, siding, posts, poles.	Soft, light weight, close grained, exceptionally durable when exposed to water, not strong enough for building construction, brittle, low shrinkage, fragment, generally knotty.
White Oak	Virginias, Tennessee, Arkansas, Kentucky, Ohio, Missouri, Maryland, Indiana.	Boat and ship stems, sternposts, knees, sheer strakes, fenders, capping, transoms, shaft logs, framing for buildings, strong furniture, tool handles, crossties, agricultural implements, fence posts.	Heavy, hard, strong, medium coarse grain, tough, dense, most durable of hardwoods, elastic, rather easy to work, but shrinks and likely to check. Light brownish grey in color with reddish tinge, medullary rays are large and outstanding and present beautiful figures when quarter sawed, receives high polish.

sanding can carry you on through to the next ply too quickly. The last or finish ply on furniture grade hardwood plywood is usually only about 1/28 inch thick. A good belt sander will cut through that in seconds. Sand such veneers by hand.

HARDBOARDS

The most common brand name for hardboards today is Masonite, but other companies do make similar materials. This glue-impregnated wood product has many uses. Hardboard is made from wood fibers chipped into pieces about ⅝ inch by 1 inch long. The chips are then reduced to fibers mechanically or by using steam. Some wood fibers are refined further, depending on the process. Some types of hardboard will have other chemicals added to produce specific properties. The boards are then glued and pressed to size. Finally, moisture is added to stabilize the boards to prevailing atmospheric conditions.

The chemicals added and treatment after the original pressing determine the grading of the hardboard after it is made. *Standard* hardboard gets no extra treatment after pressing, but it is water-resistant and strong. Standard hardboard finishes well, with a good sheen, and is fine for cabinetry. *Tempered* hardboard is standard board to which chemical and heat-treating processes have been applied to improve stiffness and finish properties. *Service* hardboard is lower in strength than standard; it is low in weight and doesn't have as good finishing characteristics.

Hardboard may be made with one or both sides smoothed. It is available in thicknesses from 1/16 through ¾ inch. Most common are the ¼, 3/16, and ⅛-inch thicknesses. Panel size is standard at 4 by 8 feet, but special panels up to 16 feet are also available.

Perforated hardboard, more commonly known as *pegboard*, has punched or drilled holes closely spaced over its surface. The holes can be fitted with metal hooks or other materials. Embossed patterns in leather and wood grains, are also available.

Stand hardboard on edge for at least 24 hours, so it can adjust to the surrounding humidity. Tempered hardboards should be stood on edge for 48 hours. Cut hardboard as you would plywood, but work with carbide blades and bits. Use normal wood sanding procedures on cut edges. Sanding is not normally needed on other areas. Always follow the glue manufacturer's directions when gluing hardboard. Nailing should be done with ring-shanked nails, and any stapling should be done with narrow point and crown staples.

Particle board and hardboard differ in some ways, but their uses in making cabinets are virtually identical, as are the methods of working with the materials. Wood scraps — sawdust, splinters, chips, and shavings — are used to make the wood.

FINISHES

Stains are used to give a tone that might not exist in the natural wood and to bring out grain details not easily visible when the wood is left totally natural. The sap is generally given a first coat of thinned stain. The stain is brushed or wiped on. It is applied in continued coats until the lighter sapwood approaches the darker color of the heartwood. If you want to have the color variation, you would ignore this procedure. Standard staining procedures are followed after the sapwood color is adjusted.

Stains

Stains are made of two materials — the *coloring agent* and the *vehicle* or carrying agent. Soluble dye or pigment makes up the coloring agent and goes into the wood's pores upon application. Dyes are usually derived from coal tar or other chemical bases. Pigments are finely ground particles that disperse in the carrying agent, but do not dissolve. When staining is done, the colors remain on the surface of the wood, providing a uniform color.

Water-based stains are available in common colors. The stains are easily applied and relatively cheap. They darken with the application of successive coats and dry rapidly. The major disadvantage of water stains is that they tend to raise the grain of the wood and can affect glued joints if waterproof glues are not used.

Oil stains may be either pigment or penetrating. For pigment stains, the pigment is added to boiled linseed oil and turpentine. Many colors are available. The stains are easily mixed and applied. They don't raise the wood grain and can be mixed with wood fillers to match patches to the rest of the surface. Pigment stains are more costly, do not penetrate the wood deeply and are slow-drying. Pigment stains are best used on close-grained wood and on unevenly colored surfaces.

Penetrating oil stains have the soluble dyes mixed in oil. These stains are usually bought ready-mixed. They are easy to apply and don't show streaks easily.

The stains can be mixed with wood filler for patching and covering nailheads. Penetrating oil stains are not normally used with lacquer finishes. They tend to bleed through the lacquer and fade in strong sunlight.

Spirit stains use soluble dyes in alcohol. These do not penetrate deeply because of the rapid drying of the carrying agent. Second coats are almost always needed to produce dark shades. These stains tend to bleed through some finishes.

Non-grain-raising stains offer a slightly different solution to staining problems. Using soluble dyes in an alcohol and glycol (much like automobile antifreeze) base, these stains offer all the advantages of water stains. They do not fade or bleed and must be sprayed on.

Sealer stains are generally best avoided. These stains are synthetic sealers with coloring added and will cover up grain detail badly.

Fillers

Wood fillers are needed to get smooth finishes on woods such as oak, walnut, mahogany, hickory, and ash. A paste filler is most often used with those woods. The fillers are about 75 percent pigment and 25 percent liquid. The pigment material is basically ground silica and coloring, while the liquid is usually oil.

Liquid fillers are often used on birch, cherry, and beech. Liquid fillers are made by adding turpentine to paste fillers.

When filler is applied to the wood, it is best to apply a sealer coat before putting on the finish coats. Of the three basic sealers, shellac (white) is probably the most commonly used. Make a shellac sealer by mixing 1 part of 4-pound cut white shellac with 7 parts of alcohol. A penetrating resin sealer will also do the job.

Lacquers

After sanding, filling, and sealing, the last finish step is the application of the protective coat. *Nitrocellulose lacquer* is one common protective coat. Follow the manufacturer's directions carefully. Lacquer thinner must be made by the same manufacturer. Lacquers dry very quickly. The coat is very thin and very clear. Damage is easy to repair, while the finish itself has good durability. The finish is easily damaged, though, by substances like nail polish. Excessive moisture will cause the finish to peel, or water spots may form. Lacquers dry so quickly that brush application is very difficult.

Varnishes

Varnishes are slow-drying, so the place of application must be dust-free. These finishes are *oleoresinous*, which simply means they are made from compounds of oils and resins. Examples are tung oil and linseed oil. Tung oil finishes have their own synthetic resins applied, and the application is very easy. Varnishes contain 40 to 50 percent solids. The coverage is good. The varnishes are very tough and durable.

Always apply varnish at temperatures of 65 degrees Fahrenheit or more. Use either a clean, lint-free cloth (for wipe-on finishes such as ZAR tung oil) or a top-quality, clean brush. Stir the varnish before use, but never shake it. Brush or wipe the finish on evenly and liberally, stroking with the grain. Don't touch up partially-dried spots. With ZAR tung oil, United Gilsonite Laboratories recommends a drying time of 6 to 12 hours. If you want more than a single coat, first rub down the dried coat with #0000 steel wool. All surfaces to be varnished should first be wiped with a rag dampened with paint thinner or turpentine before application of the finish.

Synthetic Finishes

Synthetic finishes are the *epoxies, polyurethanes,* and *polyesters*. Follow the manufacturer's directions regarding uses and application. Polyurethanes cannot be used over shellacs or lacquers. The surface must be clean and free of all wax and oil deposits. Wipe bare wood surfaces with a cloth dampened in mineral spirits. Then brush on the polyurethane finish—ZAR's Imperial is the one I have used most recently—with a clean, good-quality brush. Make sure the temperature is more than 50 degrees Fahrenheit. The first coat should be thinned slightly (no more than ½ pint of mineral spirits per gallon) to make brushing easier. Time between coats should approach 24 hours. A gloss finish polyurethane should be sanded lightly between coats.

CABINET ASSEMBLY

The method of assembling various partially-assembled kitchen cabinets vary (Fig. 8-1). Some cabinets require no more than a screwdriver. Others involve use of hammer, nails, and glue.

You need only a screwdriver to install cabinets from Paragon Wood Products (Figs. 8-2 through 8-4). The quality of these partially assembled cabinets is

Fig. 8-1. An attractive looking kitchen (courtesy Yorktowne Cabinets).

high. Save on assembly and shipping costs to help keep overall costs down (Fig. 8-5). You can get a high quality-kitchen for some work and a bit less money than you would find possible by purchasing fully assembled cabinetry. The Paragon line is available in a variety of finishes: pecan, with recessed panel doors and solid oak frames; wheat-colored with solid oak raised panel doors; and oak in a pecan finish, with knotty oak veneer doors and drawer fronts. Other drawer fronts and front frames are solid oak. Hinges are heavy-duty, self-closing styles, and drawers glide on metal ball bearing runners. Doors and drawers are reverse beveled to make opening easy. The doors are also prehung. There are four styles in the Paragon Connect-Ables line (the Yorktowne lines come from the same factories, but are fully assembled and come in at least five different styles). The cabinet assortment includes an island, corner and microwave oven

cabinets, base cabinets, a combination corner/island cabinet, revolving corner cabinets, specialty drawer units, tall cabinets, a universal oven cabinet, and broom cabinets. Accessories for later installation include food storage units with swing-out shelves, revolving corner wall kits, and various fillers and valances.

To assemble a Paragon Connect-Able cabinet, simply join the pieces and lock them together with a screwdriver. The hardest part is determining what goes where. Even the drawer glide runners slip into place with no fuss. Further information, check with any building supply dealer, many large department stores, or write to: Paragon Wood Products, P.O. Box 231, Red Lion, PA 17356 (Figs. 8-6 through 8-11).

Sears, Roebuck and Company also sells partially assembled kitchen cabinetry, and it is not much more difficult to put together than the Paragon products. You

Fig. 8-2. Connect-Able method of joining cabinet parts (courtesy Paragon Wood Products).

Fig. 8-3. Use a screwdriver to assemble the cabinet (courtesy Paragon Wood Products).

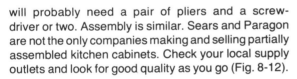

Fig. 8-4. It is not difficult to assemble a Connect-Able cabinet (courtesy Paragon Wood Products).

Fig. 8-5. A Connect-Able kitchen (courtesy Paragon Wood Products).

will probably need a pair of pliers and a screwdriver or two. Assembly is similar. Sears and Paragon are not the only companies making and selling partially assembled kitchen cabinets. Check your local supply outlets and look for good quality as you go (Fig. 8-12).

CABINET INSTALLATION

Cabinet installation actually begins back in the planning stages. If you have not made careful measurements at that time, nothing is going to work very well later. Measurement accuracy both before and during construction stages is your job. Measure everything at least twice before recording the measurements or transferring them to a cabinet.

If your kitchen installation is a remodeling job, remove all old countertops and cabinets. Get the appliances out of your way so you have room to work. Make sure any electrical and plumbing work is already completed. Baseboards and shoe moldings can be removed and set aside if they are being saved. Make any patches needed in walls that will be exposed. Use a level to drop a plumb line—you can also use a chalk

line in a case as a plumb bob and marker—down the wall from any screw holes where cabinets were properly attached to studs (Figs. 8-13 through 8-16).

Mark all stud locations wherever possible with plumb lines from floor to ceiling. Cabinets must be installed with screws running into the studs, so you must know where the studs are. If the studs are not already located, take a drill or nail after old wall cabinets are removed and measure out 16 inches from the corner. Start driving the nail partway in until you locate a stud. Move about ½ inch at a time until the first stud is located, then move back into the corner to make sure you have a nailing stud there. If you keep all nail holes from this work at a point where the wall cabinets will cover them, you save a lot of later patching work. Measure 16 inches from the first located stud and try again (Figs. 8-17 and 8-18).

Mark the bottom line for your wall cabinets at the height recommended by the cabinetmaker, or at the height you determined was best for your family if you have built your own cabinets (Figs. 8-19 and 8-20). Lay out the entire kitchen; mark every cabinet's spot and

217

Fig. 8-6. Corner saver (courtesy Yorktowne Cabinets).

appliance positions. All marking is done to exact sizes. When this is done, take a wall cabinet and support it with the top or bottom of the cabinet on the marked line. Wall cabinets always go up first (Fig. 8-21). Each cabinet will have hanging strips, and you will drill through these and into the studs. Use wood screws to secure the cabinet to the studs. Before you tighten the screws — leave about half a turn — check that the cabinet is plumb and level. If not, you will need some shim stock. Shim stock is usually made of cedar shingles. When the cabinet is plumb and level, tighten the screws. Work away from corners. Cabinets are also attached to each other as you go along, so the load is spread throughout the entire wall of cabinets. Drill through one cabinet wall into the frame of the adjacent cabinet (Figs. 8-22 through 8-29).

Fillers are used where manufactured cabinet sizes are not exact enough for the space you must fill. The filler is simply cut to the size required and fastened to a cabinet, which is then installed in the normal manner.

Even the smallest cabinet should have a minimum of four screws holding it in place. Larger cabinets

Fig. 8-7. Tall cabinet storage (courtesy Yorktowne Cabinets).

Fig. 8-8. Pull-out shelves (courtesy Yorktowne Cabinets).

Fig. 8-9. Drawer dividers (courtesy Yorktowne Cabinets).

will take proportionately more screws to do the job. Screws are countersunk and should be no less than 2 inches long, with longer screws preferred unless they are hitting pipe or wiring runs. If you are installing partially or fully assembled manufactured cabinets, the cabinets should come with wood screws of the correct size. If you are installing cabinets you have built yourself, you will need to determine the correct size for the screws used in relation to the expected cabinet weight over the years.

Plan to use number 16 flathead wood screws no shorter than 2½ inches. This will give you about 1½ inches of thread holding in the stud, which should support about 150 pounds per screw. Six screws will hold a fairly large cabinet and its load. You want to use a 3-inch-long number 20 screw, assuming you hit the center of the stud. This should give you a full 2 inches

or a bit more in the stud, for a holding power in white pine approaching 250 pounds.

Base cabinets are installed after wall cabinets. It's far easier to work under the wall cabinets than to work over the base cabinets.

Base cabinets are lined up from the corners out as are wall cabinets, and the shim stock is used to get them plumb and level. Carefully check the space left for appliances. Don't forget to drill and countersink all screw holes. You won't need such large screws with base cabinets. Base cabinets, like wall cabinets, must be joined to each other (Figs. 8-30 through 8-36).

PLASTIC LAMINATED COUNTERTOPS

Plastic laminated countertops are ideal. The materials used as top laminates are virtually impervious to all common kitchen chemicals. They are not harmed by large amounts of heat for short periods of time. The laminates are less likely to be harmed by long exposure to moderately high temperatures than are the contact cements with which they are attached to the top. Setting a hot pan down on one for a few minutes should do no harm. Most knives won't cut the laminates well, so that the worst effect from slicing things on the counter is usually a few scratch marks. It is still more sensible to use a cutting board. Laminated countertops are available in many styles and colors.

The countertops are available with and without backsplashes. End splash units can be added or just end caps. Most of the instructions for laminated countertops, apply to non-laminated countertops too. If you are installing an Exterior plywood base so that you can place ceramic tile in thin set cement, begin just as if you were installing a laminated countertop already made up. You would finish differently, naturally, but all cutouts and basic installation operations would be the same until tile-laying time.

Make sure you have the correct amount of countertop in the proper styles and that all the colors are

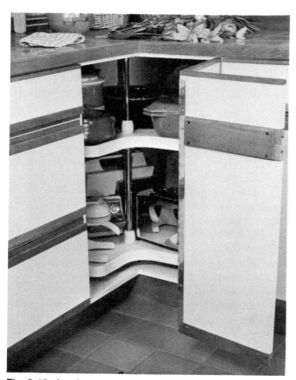

Fig. 8-10. Another corner space saver (courtesy Yorktowne Cabinets).

matches. Get the proper number of straight sections to fill long counter spaces. Obtain any needed support blocks. If you are buying mitered sections of countertop, make sure the miters fit properly and that you have the needed number of pieces, along with extra contact cement, end splashes, and end caps (Fig. 8-37). You need either a fine-toothed handsaw or a circular saw with a plywood blade, a claw hammer, a level at least 2 feet long, a keyhole or saber saw, a rafter square, a tape measure or folding rule, a mill file, a drill and several bits, a countersink for some installations, a screwdriver, a block plane, and a scriber. For mitered tops, a box or open-end wrench is handy.

If there is old countertop in place, remove it. All plumbing and wiring connections, along with sinks and built-in cooking units, must be removed for installation of new countertops. If old tops are in place and are of laminates, they will most often be installed from underneath using screws. Removing drawers will usually give access to the screws. After the screws are removed, the countertops can be slipped off. Ceramic tile countertops will need to be broken apart with a hammer and crowbar. Wear safety glasses or goggles when doing the job. Cover the floor with a drop cloth to reduce cleanup time.

Once the old tops are removed, make sure all measurements for the new tops are accurate. Allow ¾ inch for overhang. Deduct ¾ inch for the end splash where it will be used. This will be in spots where the countertop butts against a wall or cabinet.

If you use a handsaw to make cuts through the top material, first lay a strip of masking tape along the line being cut. This helps to stop splintering of the laminate and the top material immediately under it. Make certain that you apply pressure to the saw only on the downstroke. Never use a saw with fewer than 10 teeth to the inch. If the cuts are to be made with a circular saw, turn the countertop over. Do the marking and cutting from the back side.

Miters, End Caps, and End Splashes

Do not try to make your own miter cuts. Most brands of countertop with laminate in place can be bought with miters already cut.

On precut miters, you will find several fasteners underneath the cuts. First, coat the two edges being brought together with contact cement and allow for drying. Align the edges at the front of the countertop. Work back to align the entire miter joint. The next step, working from front to rear, is the tightening of fasteners.

This unique connecting mechanism makes cabinet assembly fast and easy. To match connectors, simply make sure the lock is open (A), slide the lock over the post (B), then tighten the screw ½ turn. That's it.

1. Place cabinet front frame with door(s) face down on a flat protective surface such as carpeting. Attach side panels to front frame by matching connectors (notched ends toward front frame and below door(s), grooved sides facing each other). Tighten screw ½ turn.

2. Slide bottom panel into grooves of side panels (notched ends toward front frame, finished side facing cabinet interior). Slide shelf into grooves of side panels, finished edge facing front frame and door(s).

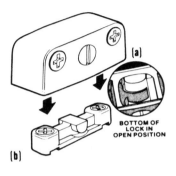

BOTTOM OF LOCK IN OPEN POSITION

(a)

(b)

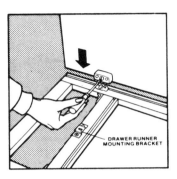

DRAWER RUNNER MOUNTING BRACKET

3. Attach toe board to notched ends of side panels by matching connectors. Tighten screw ½ turn.

4. Glide groove of wood hanging strip onto bottom panel, matching connectors on side panels. Tighten screw ½ turn.

5. Attach remaining wood hanging strip to the top of the cabinet back by matching connectors on side panels. Make sure strip is flush with the top of side panels. Tighten screw ½ turn.

CONNECTOR HERE

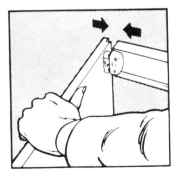

* It may be necessary to change placement of cabinet door depending upon right hand or left hand corner placement of cabinet. Be sure to install drawer on correct side of cabinet BCB cabinet includes a filler. See installation instructions.
** These cabinets have louvers in place of drawers and no shelf.

Fig. 8-11. Connect-Able cabinet assembly details (courtesy Paragon Wood Products).

6. To assemble drawers, match connectors on drawer front and drawer sides (grooved sides facing each other). Tighten screw ½ turn. Slide drawer bottom panel (finished side toward inside of drawer) into grooves of drawer sides and front. Attach drawer back by matching connectors. Attach with screws.

7. Separate drawer runner and slide pointed tab of shorter runner part into center of groove under drawer bottom. Slide remaining tab into mounting bracket on drawer back. Attach with screws.

8. After standing cabinet upright, slide short tab of remaining runner part into mounting bracket on front frame. Rest rear tab against back wood hanging strip.

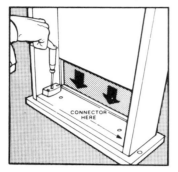

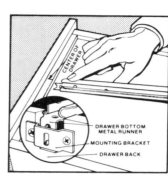

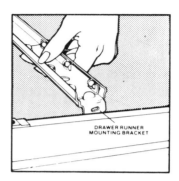

9. Slide drawer box bottom runner onto cabinet mounted runner. To assure correct attachment of rear tab, test drawer for easy open-close and check drawer front for level positioning. (A) With drawer closed, mark placement of rear tab. (B) Attach with screws.

10. To attach cabinet back, remove protective covering from tape on the wood hanging strips. Place finished side of back panel over tape. For a tighter fit, use the enclosed metal tabs to hold cabinet back to side panels.

A

B

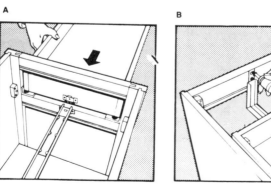

NOTES: Base cabinets greater than 24 in. wide have bottom supports. Be sure to join bottom support pieces and place under cabinet(s) before installing. All single door base cabinets are hinged on the right-hand side. Cabinet front frames are spotted for hinge placement on the left, should you desire to change door opening direction.

Fig. 8-11. Connect-Able cabinet assembly details (courtesy Paragon Wood Products) (continued from page 221).

Fig. 8-12. A completed Yorktowne kitchen (courtesy Yorktowne Cabinets).

When the miter joints are made, add end caps and end splashes where they are needed. End caps go on exposed ends of the countertops, while the end splashes will generally go on where the top fits against a cabinet, and sometimes where it fits against a wall. End cabs require that you nail a support block at the end of the countertop. Most brands will need a support to bring the exposed edge to a thickness of about 1½ inches. A filler block is attached at the rear of the backsplash, if any. The end cap can be cemented in place.

After the cement has set, smooth off any irregularities using a file. Always file in the direction of the countertop. File carefully to prevent chipping.

End splashes are also easy to install. Attach an end support pad, then the end splash is nailed and cemented to it. Just make sure the front and top edges align perfectly, and use a clear sealer on the seam to prevent leakage.

Placing the Countertop Against the Wall

As you get ready to place the assembled countertop against the wall, allow for irregularities along the wall surfaces. Trimming the back of the countertop, or the backsplash, is needed for a tight fit along most walls. Place the countertop on the top of the base cabinets with the line formed by the front of the countertop parallel with the front of the cabinets. The back of the countertop is set a small distance in front of the highest spot on the wall. Measure that distance from the high spot to the back of the countertop, and open the scribe/compass up to match it. Take the scribe and run it along the wall and the countertop. Remove any material to the rear of the scribed line using a block plane, file, or Surform tool. You have a flush fit along the wall.

Attaching the Countertop to Base Cabinets

Once the fitting is finished, attach the countertop to the base cabinets. Check the level of the base cabinets before starting. Glue and nail any needed support blocks into their appropriate positions. These blocks are placed so that they rest on the front and rear main support members of the base cabinets. When two or more sections make up base cabinets, place the support blocks so they bridge the assembled joints. Do the same if you are using more than a single piece of countertop. Make sure the screws are the proper length. Drive in the screws after drilling pilot holes.

Cutting Openings for Appliances

Cut openings for sinks and any other appliances that fit through the countertops. Most sinks and other appliances are supplied with a template that will provide you with an accurate measurement for the opening to be cut. Make sure the cutout will allow adequate clearance. Cut the opening with a compass saw, keyhole saw, or electric saber saw. The cuts must be accurate and neatly done.

For sinks or other appliances that do not have templates, or if you are reinstalling an old sink, turn the sink over and take rim-to-rim measurements. Subtract an inch from these measurements and mark the cut lines. Make the cuts. Check the sink for fit. The hole may still be too small, so you may have to widen it. If an inch subtracted from lip-to-lip measurements seems too little, make it 1½ or even 2 inches.

Most laminated countertops will resist heat of up to 275 degrees Fahrenheit. Temperatures greater than 275 Fahrenheit may cause separation of laminate and backing.

Fig. 8-13. Remove all old cabinets (courtesy Yorktowne Cabinets).

CERAMIC TILE COUNTERTOPS

Ceramic tile makes an ideal countertop and a wall covering (Figs. 8-38 through 8-40). It is easy to clean, a fast wipe with a soapy rag will usually do the job. Modern grouts do not come out as easily or leak as much as older ones. Quick-set and thin-set adhesives make the installation well within the range of most do-it-yourselfers. Special trim pieces make edge finishing easy (Fig. 8-41).

The Tile Council of America has made the job easier with its quality controls. Member companies must submit random samples for testing. Certain tiles are not made for use on floors. For wall use, almost any tiles made today will last far beyond reasonable expectations. A floor tile can be used on a wall, but a wall tile can not be used on a floor.

Measure the area to be tiled carefully. Buy enough tiles to do the job in one purchase, so that the tile comes from the same production run. Try to have at least 2 square feet of tile left over to store for possible repairs later.

The Tile Council of America says the average kitchen countertop arrangement can be tiled for under 100 dollars. The job may be cheaper than installing new laminated countertops (Figs. 8-42 and 8-43).

Fig. 8-14. Remove all wall cabinets (courtesy Yorktowne Cabinets).

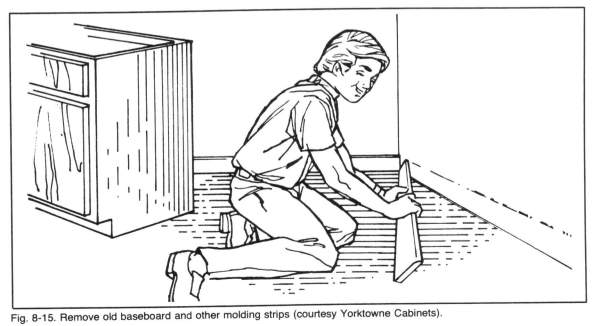

Fig. 8-15. Remove old baseboard and other molding strips (courtesy Yorktowne Cabinets).

TOOL CHECKLIST

GOOD CRAFTSMAN TOOLS MAKE ANY JOB EASIER. BELOW IS A SUGGESTED LIST OF TOOLS
THAT WILL BE REQUIRED TO DO A PROFESSIONAL QUALITY CABINET INSTALLATION.

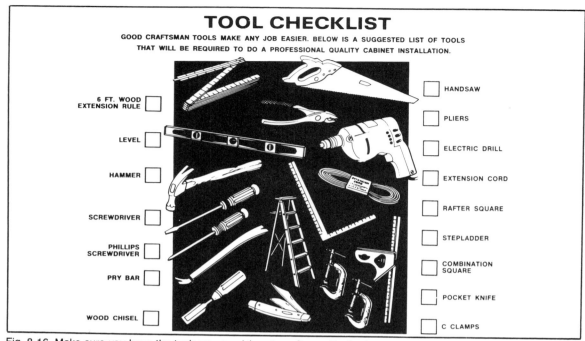

6 FT. WOOD EXTENSION RULE ☐

LEVEL ☐

HAMMER ☐

SCREWDRIVER ☐

PHILLIPS SCREWDRIVER ☐

PRY BAR ☐

WOOD CHISEL ☐

☐ HANDSAW

☐ PLIERS

☐ ELECTRIC DRILL

☐ EXTENSION CORD

☐ RAFTER SQUARE

☐ STEPLADDER

☐ COMBINATION SQUARE

☐ POCKET KNIFE

☐ C CLAMPS

Fig. 8-16. Make sure you have the tools you need (courtesy Sears, Roebuck and Company).

MATERIALS

THESE ITEMS ARE GENERALLY REQUIRED TO DO A
GOOD JOB OF INSTALLING CABINETS

☐ **CEDAR SHINGLES**

1 per cabinet approximate. Use as shims (wedges) to align cabinets on floor and walls.

☐ **WOOD SCREWS AND WASHERS**

4 per cabinet approximate. For fastening cabinets to plastered or dry-wall type construction. Be sure screws are long enough to fasten securely to studs.

NOTE:

If fastening cabinets to BRICK or MASONRY WALLS use special plugs to accommodate metal screws. A MASONRY DRILL will be required to make holes.

☐ **PLASTER** (or patching compound)

For wall repair after tear out of old cabinets.

NOTE:

If you are closing in the area from the top of the wall cabinets to the ceiling (this is called the soffit), you will need framing material. 1" x 2" FUR STRIPS are commonly used. The frame can be covered with DRY WALL which will have to be painted, papered or you may prefer to use finished wood paneling which is available in matching finishes for most SEARS cabinets.

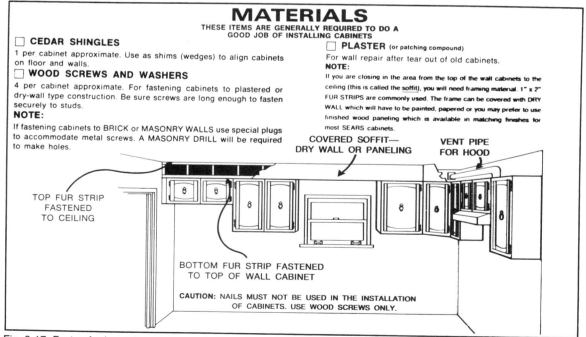

COVERED SOFFIT—
DRY WALL OR PANELING

VENT PIPE
FOR HOOD

TOP FUR STRIP
FASTENED
TO CEILING

BOTTOM FUR STRIP FASTENED
TO TOP OF WALL CABINET

CAUTION: NAILS MUST NOT BE USED IN THE INSTALLATION
OF CABINETS. USE WOOD SCREWS ONLY.

Fig. 8-17. Fasten furring strips where needed (courtesy Sears, Roebuck and Company).

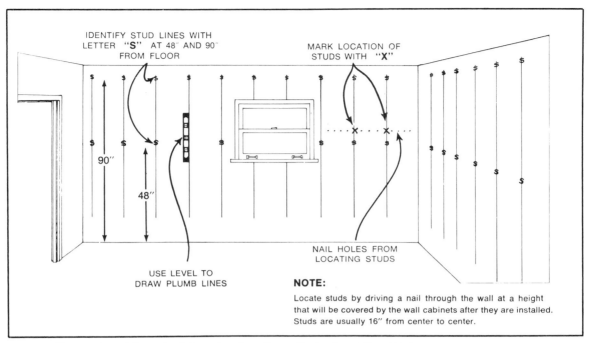

Fig. 8-18. Find studs and draw plumb lines (courtesy Sears, Roebuck and Company).

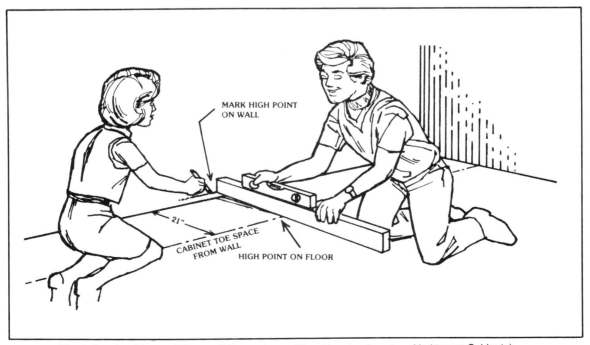

Fig. 8-19. Check floor level to see if there will be much need for shimming (courtesy Yorktowne Cabinets).

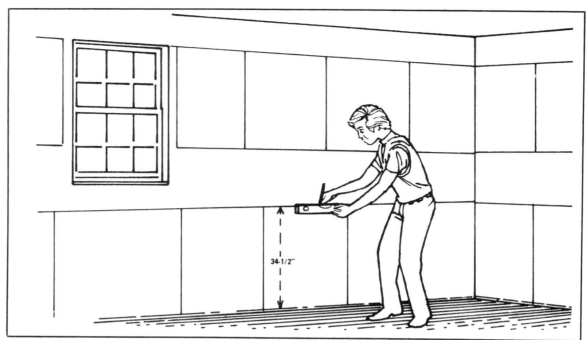

Fig. 8-20. Mark the walls (courtesy Yorktowne Cabinets).

Build a simple prop box or T-brace to support the wall cabinets at the desired height until they are secured to the wall studs.

Fig. 8-21. Use temporary supports where needed (courtesy Yorktowne Cabinets).

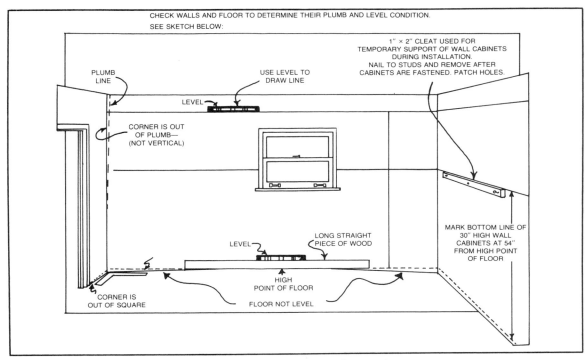

Fig. 8-22. Check walls one more time (courtesy Sears, Roebuck and Company).

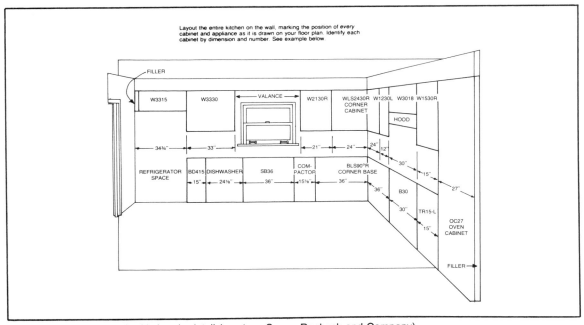

Fig. 8-23. Lay out the entire kitchen in detail (courtesy Sears, Roebuck and Company).

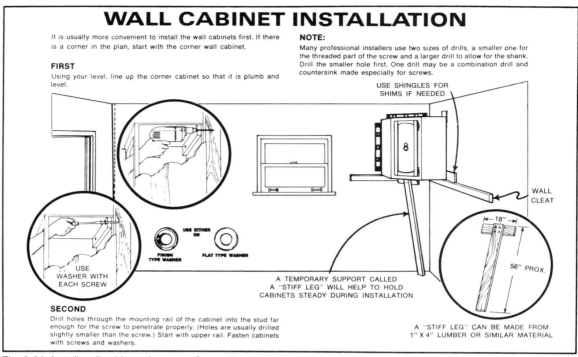

WALL CABINET INSTALLATION

It is usually more convenient to install the wall cabinets first. If there is a corner in the plan, start with the corner wall cabinet.

FIRST

Using your level, line up the corner cabinet so that it is plumb and level.

NOTE:

Many professional installers use two sizes of drills, a smaller one for the threaded part of the screw and a larger drill to allow for the shank. Drill the smaller hole first. One drill may be a combination drill and countersink made especially for screws.

USE SHINGLES FOR SHIMS IF NEEDED

WALL CLEAT

USE WASHER WITH EACH SCREW

USE EITHER OR

FINISH TYPE WASHER   FLAT TYPE WASHER

A TEMPORARY SUPPORT CALLED A "STIFF LEG" WILL HELP TO HOLD CABINETS STEADY DURING INSTALLATION

18"

56" PROX.

SECOND

Drill holes through the mounting rail of the cabinet into the stud far enough for the screw to penetrate properly. (Holes are usually drilled slightly smaller than the screw.) Start with upper rail. Fasten cabinets with screws and washers.

A "STIFF LEG" CAN BE MADE FROM 1" X 4" LUMBER OR SIMILAR MATERIAL

Fig. 8-24. Install wall cabinets (courtesy Sears, Roebuck and Company).

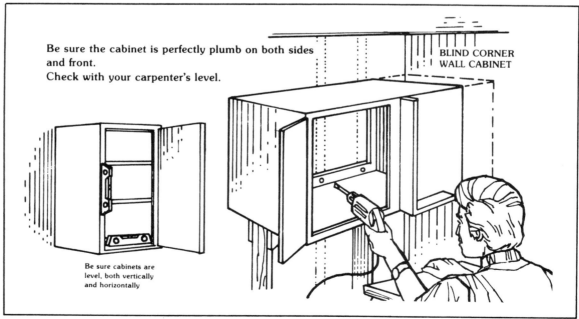

Be sure the cabinet is perfectly plumb on both sides and front.
Check with your carpenter's level.

BLIND CORNER WALL CABINET

Be sure cabinets are level, both vertically and horizontally

Fig. 8-25. Start wall cabinet installation at a corner (courtesy Yorktowne Cabinets).

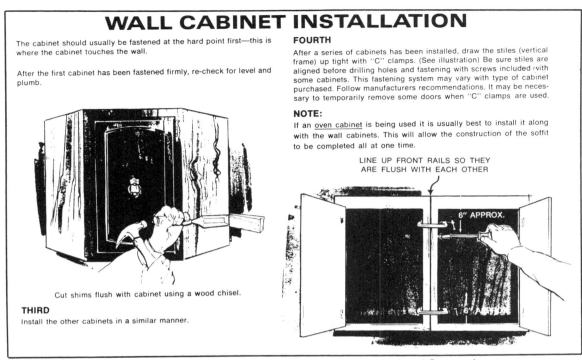

WALL CABINET INSTALLATION

The cabinet should usually be fastened at the hard point first—this is where the cabinet touches the wall.

After the first cabinet has been fastened firmly, re-check for level and plumb.

Cut shims flush with cabinet using a wood chisel.

THIRD

Install the other cabinets in a similar manner.

FOURTH

After a series of cabinets has been installed, draw the stiles (vertical frame) up tight with "C" clamps. (See illustration) Be sure stiles are aligned before drilling holes and fastening with screws included (with some cabinets. This fastening system may vary with type of cabinet purchased. Follow manufacturers recommendations. It may be necessary to temporarily remove some doors when "C" clamps are used.

NOTE:

If an <u>oven cabinet</u> is being used it is usually best to install it along with the wall cabinets. This will allow the construction of the soffit to be completed all at one time.

LINE UP FRONT RAILS SO THEY ARE FLUSH WITH EACH OTHER

6" APPROX.

Fig. 8-26. Shim carefully and screw all cabinets together (courtesy Sears, Roebuck and Company).

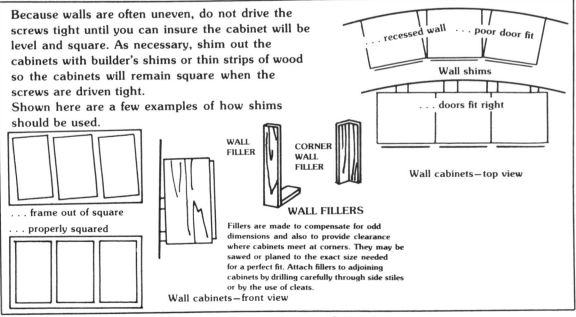

Because walls are often uneven, do not drive the screws tight until you can insure the cabinet will be level and square. As necessary, shim out the cabinets with builder's shims or thin strips of wood so the cabinets will remain square when the screws are driven tight.

Shown here are a few examples of how shims should be used.

. . . recessed wall   . . . poor door fit

Wall shims

. . . doors fit right

Wall cabinets—top view

. . . frame out of square

. . . properly squared

WALL FILLER

CORNER WALL FILLER

WALL FILLERS

Fillers are made to compensate for odd dimensions and also to provide clearance where cabinets meet at corners. They may be sawed or planed to the exact size needed for a perfect fit. Attach fillers to adjoining cabinets by drilling carefully through side stiles or by the use of cleats.

Wall cabinets—front view

Fig. 8-27. Use fillers and shim stock as needed (courtesy Yorktowne Cabinets).

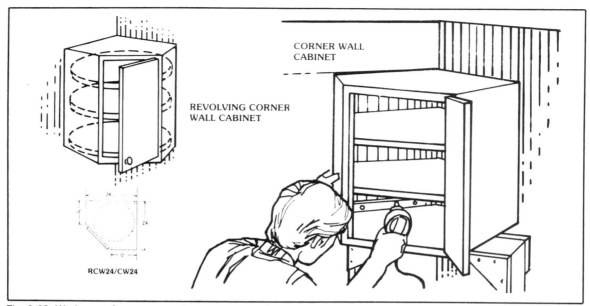

Fig. 8-28. Work away from corner units (courtesy Yorktowne Cabinets).

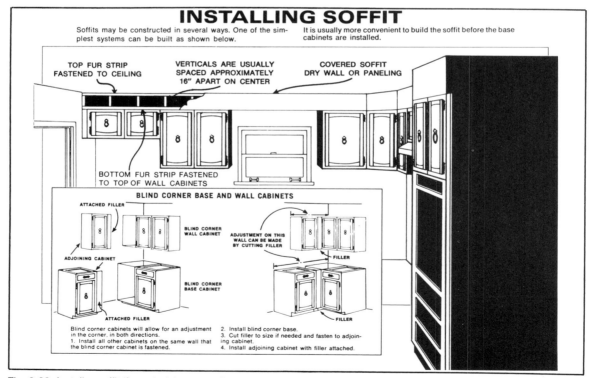

Fig. 8-29. Install a soffit if needed (courtesy Sears, Roebuck and Company).

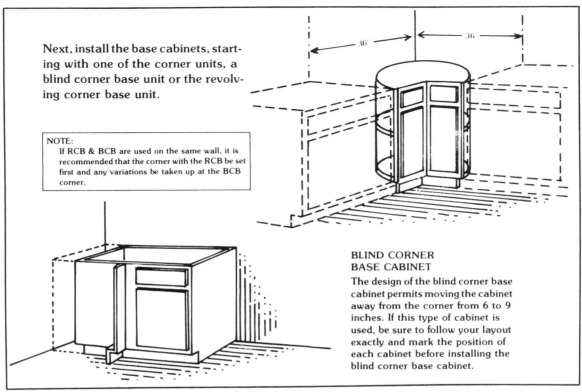

Next, install the base cabinets, starting with one of the corner units, a blind corner base unit or the revolving corner base unit.

NOTE:
If RCB & BCB are used on the same wall, it is recommended that the corner with the RCB be set first and any variations be taken up at the BCB corner.

BLIND CORNER BASE CABINET

The design of the blind corner base cabinet permits moving the cabinet away from the corner from 6 to 9 inches. If this type of cabinet is used, be sure to follow your layout exactly and mark the position of each cabinet before installing the blind corner base cabinet.

Fig. 8-30. Start in corners (courtesy Yorktowne Cabinets).

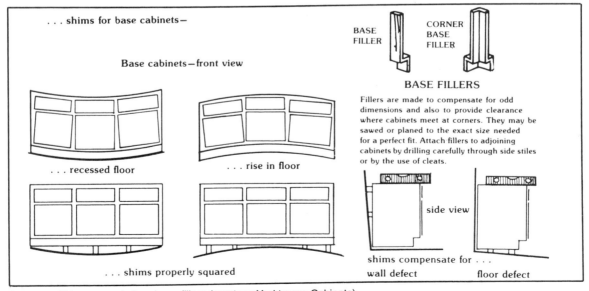

. . . shims for base cabinets—

Base cabinets—front view

. . . recessed floor

. . . rise in floor

. . . shims properly squared

BASE FILLER

CORNER BASE FILLER

BASE FILLERS

Fillers are made to compensate for odd dimensions and also to provide clearance where cabinets meet at corners. They may be sawed or planed to the exact size needed for a perfect fit. Attach fillers to adjoining cabinets by drilling carefully through side stiles or by the use of cleats.

side view

shims compensate for . . .

wall defect

floor defect

Fig. 8-31. Shim as needed and use fillers (courtesy Yorktowne Cabinets).

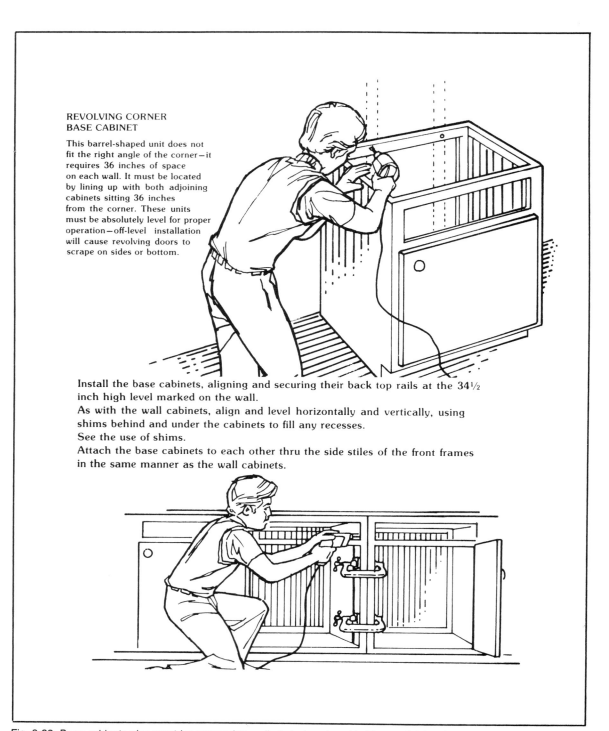

REVOLVING CORNER BASE CABINET

This barrel-shaped unit does not fit the right angle of the corner—it requires 36 inches of space on each wall. It must be located by lining up with both adjoining cabinets sitting 36 inches from the corner. These units must be absolutely level for proper operation—off-level installation will cause revolving doors to scrape on sides or bottom.

Install the base cabinets, aligning and securing their back top rails at the 34½ inch high level marked on the wall.

As with the wall cabinets, align and level horizontally and vertically, using shims behind and under the cabinets to fill any recesses.

See the use of shims.

Attach the base cabinets to each other thru the side stiles of the front frames in the same manner as the wall cabinets.

Fig. 8-32. Base cabinets also must be screwed to wall studs (courtesy Yorktowne Cabinets).

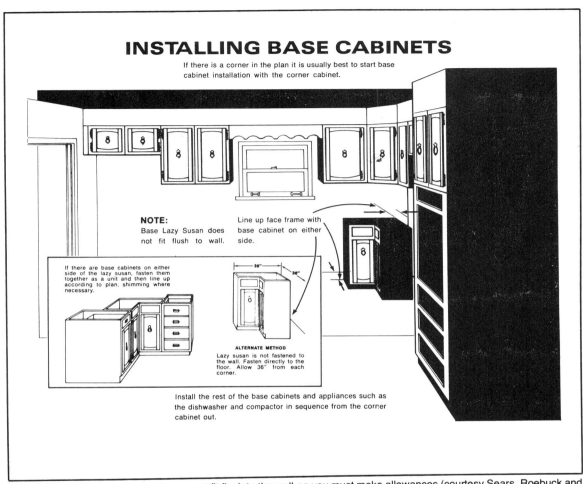

INSTALLING BASE CABINETS

If there is a corner in the plan it is usually best to start base cabinet installation with the corner cabinet.

NOTE:
Base Lazy Susan does not fit flush to wall.

Line up face frame with base cabinet on either side.

If there are base cabinets on either side of the lazy susan, fasten them together as a unit and then line up according to plan, shimming where necessary.

ALTERNATE METHOD
Lazy susan is not fastened to the wall. Fasten directly to the floor. Allow 36" from each corner.

36"

36"

Install the rest of the base cabinets and appliances such as the dishwasher and compactor in sequence from the corner cabinet out.

Fig. 8-33. Lazy Susan corner units may not fit flush to the wall, so you must make allowances (courtesy Sears, Roebuck and Company).

Surfaces

Adhesives are the secret to a good tiling job. Check the surface. It needs to be dry and clear of flaking paint, grease, and dirt (Fig. 8-44). If the surface is plywood, it should be in good condition. Countertops and floors should be of exterior plywood grades. Remove all loose and damaged plaster. Pull out protruding nails and screws. Wallpaper and loose paint must also be removed. If the wall to be done is of new gypsum wallboard, it should be sealed. Alcohol base shellac makes a good sealer. Glossy paint needs to be sanded lightly to give it a tooth for the adhesive to grip.

Lay out the work. Make sure you have the right kinds of moldings and edges for the job (Fig. 8-45).

Always select an epoxy or acrylic latex, or rubberized silicone grout, and a thin-set adhesive.

Tools

You will need a good 2-foot level, a notched trowel, chalk line, scraper, sponge, tape rule or folding rule, straightedge, square, and cleaning rags. A tile nipper and a tile cutter can be rented or bought. You will also want a rubber trowel or squeegee for applying the grout (Figs. 8-46 and 8-47).

Setting

The subsurface for the countertop needs to be smooth and solid. If the base is plywood, sand off any

Countertops are made 1½ inches thick to bring the countertop level with conventional 36 inch appliance height.

Counter blanks, in standard 6, 8 and 12-ft. lengths, or custom made tops, can be purchased through your cabinet supplier.

Place the countertop on the cabinets and insure alignment with the cabinets and the wall. The countertop should have 1 inch overhang in the front of the cabinets. It is also recommended that the top overhang the ends of the cabinets by 1 inch, except where adjacent to appliances.

Attach countertops to cabinets with screws through cabinet corner blocks into the bottom frame of countertops. Screw length as recommended by top maker.

Drop-in ranges and sinks may be cut in before or after top is secured, at the installer's option.

Be careful, in using your drill, that you do not drill through the countertop. (Once damaged, countertops are very difficult to repair.) If necessary, install metal cove molding behind backsplash of top to compensate for any imperfections in the fit between the wall and the countertop.

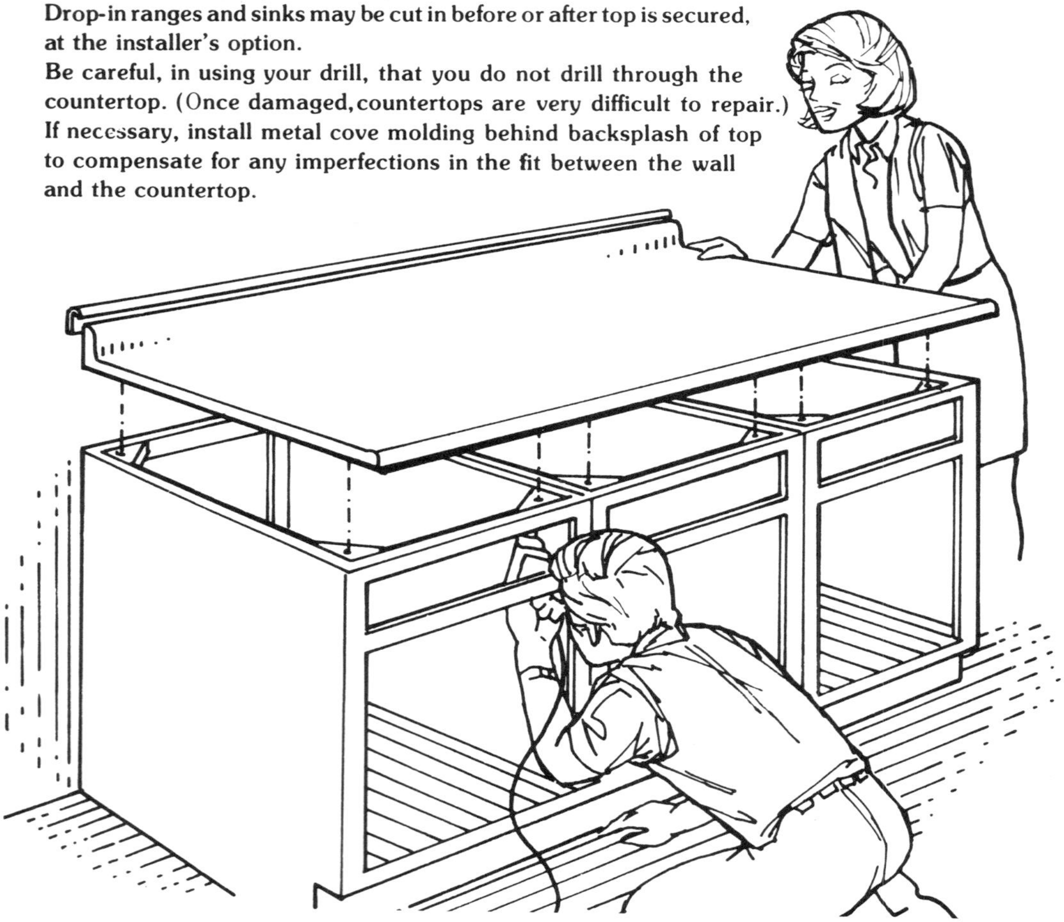

Fig. 8-34. Start the countertops (courtesy Yorktowne Cabinets).

Shown are a few examples of soffit treatments. Soffits should be 84-1/8 inches from floor. Generally, tall cabinets are 84 inches high. The extra 1/8 inch will give clearance area so that tall cabinets can be slid into place without binding.

The 1/8 inch space between cabinet and soffit is usually covered with the M-1 trim molding which is used to trim off the tops of wall cabinets at the soffit. When building soffits, remember wall cabinets are 12 inches deep. An extra 1-inch soffit overhang will give you ample space to trim with molding.

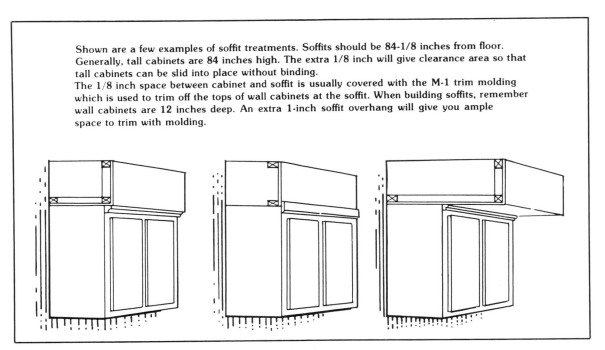

Fig. 8-35. Check soffit treatment (courtesy Yorktowne Cabinets).

After your cabinetry is completely installed, you may find that a few of your door and drawer fronts are not parallel with each other. If this occurs, these doors and drawers can be realigned. For doors, remove the set of hinge screws from the door or cabinet frame, depending which way you want to move the door. Visually determine how much you wish to tilt the door at top or bottom. Fill the old screw holes with a wood match stick or 1/8 inch dowel, and redrill a new pilot hole at the new determined location. Place old screw in the new hole. Drawers with removable drawer fronts can be aligned in much the same manner, by removing the drawer front from the drawer box. Fill holes with a wood dowel and redrill a new pilot hole and replace screws.

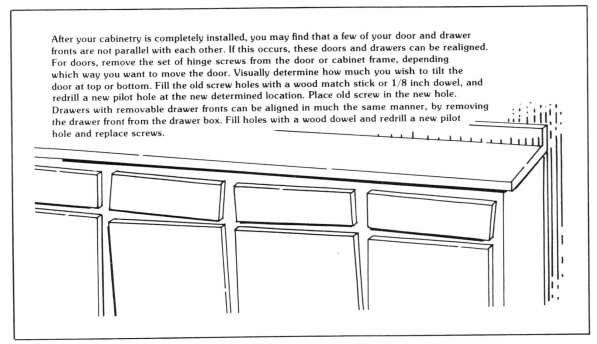

Fig. 8-36. Check door-drawer alignment (courtesy Yorktowne Cabinets).

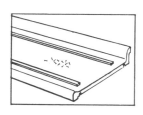

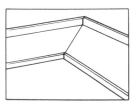

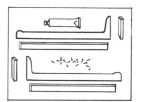

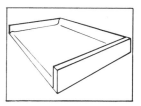

STRAIGHT SECTIONS Available in a variety of lengths with support blocks included.

MITERED SECTIONS Right and Left sections with support blocks, 4 joint fasteners and adhesive included.

END CAPS. One right end and one left end cap, support blocks with nails and adhesive are included. Refer to instructions with materials.

END SPLASH. Reversible for right or left side. One end support block with nails is included. Refer to instructions packed with materials.

Fig. 8-37. Get all countertop parts and assemble them in one area (courtesy Sears, Roebuck and Company).

Fig. 8-38. Summitville's Lombardic tile series (courtesy Tile Council of America).

Fig. 8-39. Maltese tile from Wenczel Tile Company (courtesy Tile Council of America).

Fig. 8-40. Potter's Touch tile from Florida Tile (courtesy Tile Council of America).

Fig. 8-41. More tiles from Wenczel (courtesy Tile Council of America).

Fig. 8-42. Leather tile from Wenczel (courtesy Tile Council of America).

bumps and splinters. Brush on a latex primer to give a smooth surface and good bite for the tile adhesive. If the surface is a laminate, you will probably need a top grade of sandpaper to provide a tooth. One of the manmade papers will cut the laminate's surface to give bite. If the laminate has a curved front and backsplash, cut those off and install replacements. Simply remove the countertop, saw off the offending portions, and replace—using nails and glue—with straight material forming a 90-degree angle.

Trim pieces along the front edge are installed first. You can then put in sink edge tiles, corners, and any other special pieces using a carpenter's (framing) square to make sure that all courses are straight and true (Fig. 8-48). After the tile pattern has been laid out, you should cut the tile to fit. Apply the adhesive with the notched trowel. Hold the trowel at a 45-degree angle for top coverage (Fig. 8-49). Follow the adhesive manufacturer's directions as to the amount of adhesive to spread at any one time. When the tile is to be placed on walls, with or without tile on the countertop below, start the bottom row with no less than half a tile. Use a level to set the horizontal line properly (Fig. 8-50).

Set each tile with a slight twisting motion. Press the tile firmly into place. Tiles must be aligned so that all joints are uniform and straight. Most modern tiles

240

Fig. 8-43. Teardrops tile from Florida Tile (courtesy Tile Council of America).

Fig. 8-44. Make sure the surface is clean and smooth (courtesy Tile Council of America).

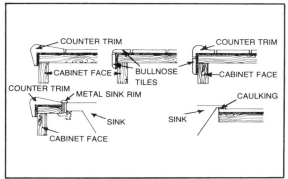

Fig. 8-45. Trim tile shapes available (courtesy Tile Council of America).

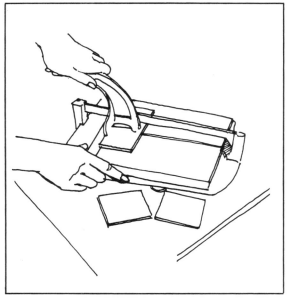

Fig. 8-46. Tile cutter (courtesy Tile Council of America).

have built-in spacers, so getting the proper tile joint is not difficult. Check any fancy tile, such as that in Fig. 8-51, to make sure it is easily spaced without special tools or care. You can then install the sink and other items that were removed for tiling (Fig. 8-52). Self-rimming sinks (with a rim extending over the tile) have clamps underneath that hold them in place.

After the tile is in place, wait at least 24 hours before grouting the surfaces. If the grout is not pre-mixed, mix it according to the manufacturer's directions. Smear it over the tile and into the joints, using a

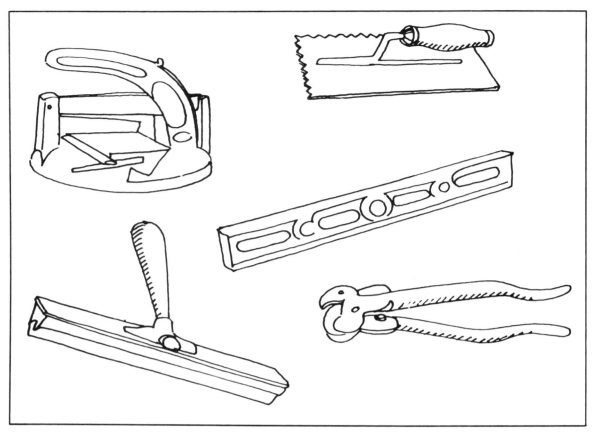

Fig. 8-47. Tiling tools (courtesy Tile Council of America).

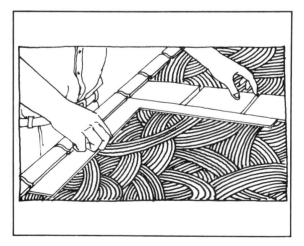

Fig. 8-48. Use a carpenter's square to keep tiles aligned (courtesy Tile Council of America).

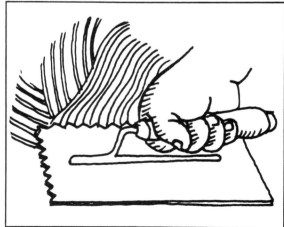

Fig. 8-49. Spread the adhesive with a notched trowel (courtesy Tile Council of America).

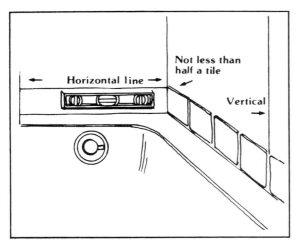

Fig. 8-50. Set a starting line for walls (courtesy Tile Council of America).

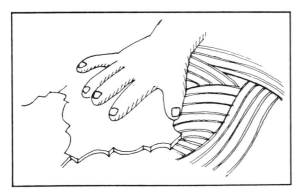

Fig. 8-51. Set each tile with a slight twisting motion (courtesy Tile Council of America).

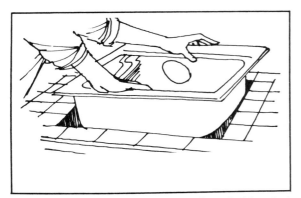

Fig. 8-52. Place the sink (courtesy Tile Council of America).

Fig. 8-53. Start grouting (courtesy Tile Council of America).

Fig. 8-54. Squeegee the grout hard to make sure it fills the joints (courtesy Tile Council of America).

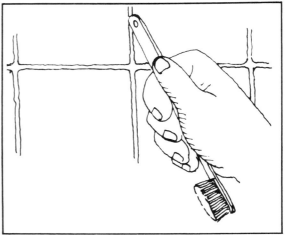

Fig. 8-55. Use a toothbrush handle to smooth and shape the joints (courtesy Tile Council of America).

243

Fig. 8-56. The completed job will make a large difference in appearance and ease of cleanup (courtesy Tile Council of America).

Use a toothbrush handle to strike the joints ventilation and no open flames around the area. rubber trowel or squeegee (Figs. 8-53 and 8-54). Do a final squeegeeing to make sure the grout is well down into the joints. Wipe the surface of the tiles with a damp rag. The rag should be dampened with whatever substance the grout manufacturer says is a solvent. If the solvent is not water, make sure you have adequate around each tile. Do this just as the grout sets or becomes hard (Fig. 8-55). If the material will just take a print when you press hard with your thumb, then it's ready for final tooling. The result is quite striking (Figs. 8-56 and 8-57).

Tiling is not as difficult as it once was, mostly because of thin-set adhesives. Also, the American tile companies have decided to make ceramic tiles to a more rigorous thickness standard. Deep-set adhesives are needed when tiles are set over uneven surfaces and when uneven tile thicknesses are involved. Today, surfaces are readily evened up using plywood, Masonite, gypsum wallboard, or even joint-filling cement (compound).

Fig. 8-57. American Olean's light ceramic mosaics with dark grout lines have a dramatic appearance (courtesy Tile Council of America).

244

Chapter 9

Appliances

YOU SHOULD OBTAIN THE LEAST EXPENSIVE appliances that have the greatest energy efficiency. Appearance is a less important consideration.

RANGES

The *range* is used for cooking and is one of the hardest appliances to clean (Fig. 9-1). Gas and electric ranges are available.

Possibly 1 range in 10 is the type with a high oven. Many larger families opt for a second oven, usually of the drop-in, countertop style or a built-in wall model. Ranges can be bought with two ovens, usually with a smaller upper oven and a larger lower one. You will find many expensive models with *microwave ovens* built in on top. Always check oven size to make certain it will fit your needs.

Make sure the burners and inserts are easily taken apart and removed for cleaning. The oven doors and any oven liners should also be easily removed for cleaning (Fig. 9-2).

Self-cleaning ovens use very high temperatures to turn all residue to a light ash that is easily wiped away. Continuous-cleaning ovens have a special coating for easier removal of grease and baked-on

materials. The self-cleaning ovens cost more to operate, but they are popular with people who do a lot of baking.

Some ranges offer programmed cooking and delayed cooking ovens, with slightly different features on gas ovens than on electric ovens. Most gas ovens do the cooking first and then cool to about 170 degrees Fahrenheit to keep things warm, while electric ovens start at a particular time.

Smooth-top ranges usually require special flat-bottom pots and pans for greatest efficiency in cooking. Special cleaning products are required for the ceramic glass tops. Heating and cooling times are longer than with standard electric ranges (Fig. 9-3).

Look for quality in the sheet metal work and in the attachment of oven doors. Check the sealing strips around the window for neatness. Inspect knobs to make sure the numbers are embossed or engraved. Painted numbers are easily worn off during washing, especially if you soak them in a strong cleaner. Controls should be easy to operate and sensibly spaced and located. Controls should not be easily blocked by utensils set on burners. Oven racks should be easily removable and designed with a support bar on the back, so items do not fall off the back easily when you

Fig. 9-1. The range is often combined with a microwave oven in many kitchens, either in the wall or as a freestanding unit (courtesy General Electric).

pull the rack forward to check oven contents. Four spacers for oven racks are ideal.

Microwave ovens are easy to clean. Only plastic, glass, and ceramic utensils can be used around the oven, because metals block the flow of the microwaves.

It takes time to learn to use a microwave oven. The price may be as low as 250 dollars and as high as 800 dollars. All kinds of timers and cooking cycles are available. A small microwave oven may have a capacity of as little as ½ cubic foot (with a usable oven space measuring 12-½ by 11-½ by 6-½ inches). Larger ovens can have up to about a 1.4-cubic-foot capacity (14-½ by 16-½-by 9-½ inches).

For my part, a microwave with a simple defrost cycle added to baking and roasting functions would do the job. Ovens have up to six automatic cooking programs, defrost, pause control, delayed start, warming and hold cycles, and others. Microwave ovens are energy-savers. Some models use less than 600 watts on full power (while others will have ranges from 90 to 625 watts). Conventional ovens will usually use more than 4,000 watts.

REFRIGERATORS

Refrigerators keep foods cold and fresh. Shelf and compartment design affect the usefulness of a refrigerator. Crispers must have tight covers, as their only purpose is to keep fresh fruits and vegetables from drying out. Adjustable, pull-out shelves are far

246

handier than fixed shelves. Even an inexpensive refrigerator must have removable shelves for cleaning purposes (Figs 9-4 and 9-5).

Possibly 20 percent of the refrigerators marketed today are side-by-side models. A smaller freezer is set to one side of the refrigerator, with widths ranging from about 30 inches to 5 feet. The narrow doors open in less space, and the arrangement is sometimes more convenient than top-and-bottom refrigerator/freezers.

Flush-mount refrigerators are made with the condenser coils under the cold food compartment. A fan blows across the coils from the condenser to cool them. These refrigerators may be pushed right up against a wall. With less expensive standard back-mounted coils, the refrigerator must have some clearance for air flow.

Frost-free refrigerators have cooling aids behind the refrigerator/freezer compartments and a defrost cycle. Frost-free refrigerators cost more than manual defrost models and are more expensive to operate.

Check the latch, usually magnetic, to make sure it grabs and holds well. The door must seal well. A refrigerator needs to be level for best operation, and most have leveling units built into the legs for this purpose. Any level refrigerator should allow the door to slowly close if it is not held open

FREEZERS

People are more interested in *freezers* due to the increase in home gardening. Home gardeners must have some place to store their food. Canning and freezing are two food preservation methods. Freezing is generally easier and safer with low-acid foods. The

Fig. 9-2. A microwave range (courtesy General Electric).

Fig. 9-3. Glass ceramic cooktops look great and have no crevices for grease collection (courtesy General Electric).

cost of operating a freezer is usually more than equaled by the cost of energy used during canning.

Two types of freezers are available. The chest type and the upright style can offer equal storage space, but the chest type is generally a bit less convenient to work with when items must be stored on the bottom of the freezer. The upright freezers seem more apt to dump items in your lap if you don't load them carefully. Upright models generally cost more for similar capacities, but there is little difference in operating costs among the new energy-efficient (more heavily insulated) models. Cost for running a freezer will run from about 50 to 60 dollars a year, depending on its efficiency and the cost of electricity in your area. The freezer itself may run anywhere from 285 dollars for a very small model (5 or 6 cubic feet of storage capacity) to more than 700 dollars for a huge model (30 or more cubic feet of storage capacity).

Upright freezers are more likely to be available with the frost-free (nondefrost) cycling. The constant cooling and heating cycling to keep the unit frost-free actually reduces safe storage time and increases your electricity bill. Some chest freezers also offer this option. When selecting a freezer, check to see that the interior is coated with epoxy or porcelain enamel for longest life, and that the freezing coils are in touch with the liner (many are welded right to the liners). For chest freezers, a counterbalanced lid is essential. A keylock is a good idea on all models, especially if you plan to keep the freezer on a porch or in an outbuilding.

Interior lights, sliding baskets, full-width and adjustable shelves, adjustable temperature controls, a power-interruption warning light, and other features are nice. Check for a bottom drain, and look for models with a flash defrost feature.

DISHWASHERS

Until a few years ago, *dishwashers* were considered luxury appliances. About 40 percent of homes have dishwashers today. Dishwashers do save time in cleanup chores. Space is also saved. Dirty dishes can be stacked inside. The machine is run through a rinse or prewash cycle, with the actual washing done only once a day (Fig. 9-6).

Cycle choices on newer models are numerous. Select the one that uses the least amount of energy to accomplish its work. New models offer a cool air blower for drying instead of heated air or, often, in addition to heated air so that you have a choice. Loading for one wash a day and using rinse-and-hold cycles can also reduce energy use with dishwashers (Fig. 9-7).

GARBAGE DISPOSAL UNITS AND TRASH COMPACTORS

Garbage disposal units are particularly popular with apartment dwellers. You should grind all garbage right away because food decays rapidly. Acids can eat into disposal parts. Use cold water when grinding to help solidify fats, so they won't clog drains.

Although *compactors* reduce the volume of your trash, with little or no effort on your part, odors may develop in them. The bags used are not cheap, Operating costs are not very high—at less than 50 cents a year in most cases. Most compactors cost more than 300 dollars.

Make sure the compactor has a floor pedal and a locking system. Most units stop when the drawer is opened, but a removable start/stop switch and a keylock are essential in a house with toddlers.

SMALL APPLIANCES

Toaster ovens have a wide range of uses. They

Fig. 9-4. Storage space is laid out well in this 15.6-cubic-foot model (courtesy General Electric).

Fig. 9-5. Half-shelves provide the greatest storage flexibility (courtesy General Electric).

Fig. 9-7. Under-sink dishwashers need special sinks—with one shallow bowl—but save space (courtesy General Electric).

are not full-sized ovens, but neither are they tiny toasters suitable only for browning two slices of bread. Today's toaster ovens may bake, roast, toast, and broil. Most use two coils, one at the top of the oven and one at the bottom. The bottom coil does the baking and roasting. The top coil browns and broils.

Some Toaster ovens may heat up to 500 degrees Fahrenheit. Price can range from 35 dollars to more than 80 dollars. All ovens reduce the amount of electricity needed to make small meals.

Electric *percolators, can openers,* and *coffee makers* are useful. Mixers, blenders, and food processors make food preparation easier.

Fig. 9-6. Full-sized dishwashers are for spacious kitchens (courtesy General Electric).

Chapter 10

Laundry Rooms

THE LAUNDRY ROOM CAN BE USED FOR OTHER activities. Sewing or other hobbies can be done there. Figure 10-1 shows two layouts for laundry rooms.

According to General Electric, the average family does eight wash loads a week. *Family Circle* magazine and General Electric's kitchen/laundry design manager W.J. Ketcham checked with the Women's Auxiliary of the National Association of Home Builders to see what was wanted in a laundry center.

Two rooms were designed to fit the ideas presented by this women's group. One is a workroom of good size that offers space for sewing, potting, and other tasks, along with a complete laundry area (Fig. 10-2). The second is a tiny mini-laundry that might even fit in a decent-sized closet.

All laundry appliances are available in white, and white is usually the cheapest color for any appliance. Use white cabinets, a white sink, white shelves, etc. Use bright colors as accents, if you wish, or try a combination of muted colors.

Leave plenty of counter, shelf, or table space to fold clothing after washing and drying and to sort-

clothing before laundering. Have a rolling table that allows you to unload the washer without having to put the washed clothes in a chair or directly in the dryer. An overhead shelf at the appliance area provides storage for detergents and bleaches.

Tiny laundry rooms are best served with compact appliances. The tight space makes for tighter working areas, too, but shelving is a help.

Resilient tile or sheet flooring is your best bet for the laundry room floor. Appliances tend to be harder to move on ceramic tile with its joints; otherwise, ceramic tile makes an excellent floor. Hot and cold water supplies should be properly spaced for the washer. There should be a vent for any gas dryer, a good outlet for an electric dryer, and a standpipe at least 32 inches high for drainage from the washing machine.

Sinks or lavatories today don't just come in one color or material. Fiberglass, porcelain over cast iron, stainless steel, and ceramic are readily available. You can obtain anything from deep washing tubs to a simpler bar sink with fixtures. Fixtures may come in chrome finish (either shiny or satin), solid brass, or 24-karat gold plated.

251

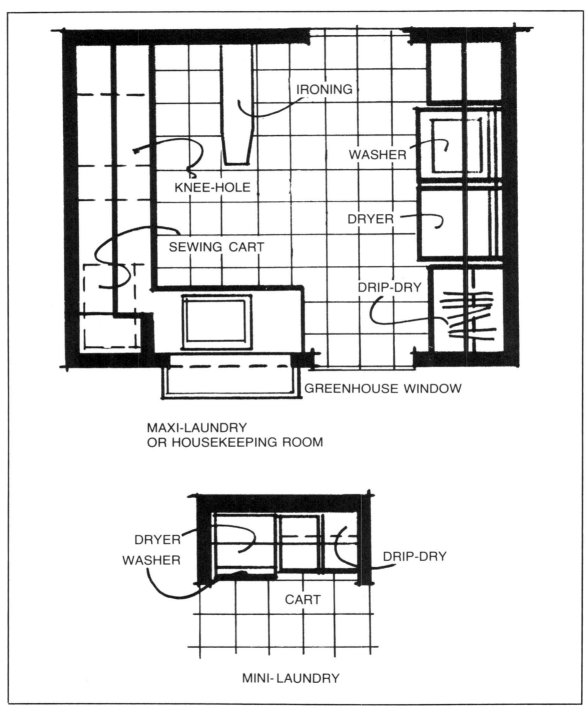

IRONING

WASHER

KNEE-HOLE

DRYER

SEWING CART

DRIP-DRY

GREENHOUSE WINDOW

MAXI-LAUNDRY
OR HOUSEKEEPING ROOM

DRYER
WASHER

DRIP-DRY

CART

MINI-LAUNDRY

Fig. 10-1. Floor layouts illustrate how to best use the space you have for laundry areas (courtesy General Electric).

Fig. 10-2. The General Electric/Family Circle laundry room.

Fig. 10-3. Compact, stackable washer and dryer sets are very handy in small homes (courtesy General Electric).

Consider the uses you want and design your laundry room to fit some of them. It can be a bookkeeping room, a hobby room, or a reading room. Do not design it for hobbies that produce lots of dirt or dust. Otherwise, the sky really is the limit if you have the space, time, and money to build a laundry room as an addition to your kitchen.

Index

Index

Edited by Bob Ostrander